Vocabulary for Champions

Over 2,000 Words and Activities to Improve Your Reading, Writing, Speaking, Test-taking, and Resume-building Skills

Joe Oswald
Threshold Publishing, LLC

Vocabulary for Champions

Copyright © 2019 by Joe Oswald
ISBN-13: 978-0-9709734-3-6

Threshold Publishing, LLC
Chicago, Illinois
www.joeoswald.com

For additional information please contact the author at joe@joeoswald.com

Word puzzles made using puzzle-maker.com

Contents

This book is dedicated to my beautiful daughter, Katie, whose youthful exuberance and love of learning has given new meaning to my life.

About the Author

Joe Oswald was born and raised in Chicago's historic Beverly Hills neighborhood where he continues to live and raise his own family. He has a bachelor's degree in Secondary Education and a master's degree in history from De Paul University as well as a master's degree in Educational Administration from Governors State University. Joe has worked as a Chicago public high school history teacher for over twenty years, including the last fifteen years at Thomas Kelly High School. He served as a member of his school's Literacy Team, served as departmental coordinator for the Chicago Reading Initiative, and has been a member of the North Central writing improvement committee, the school grant writing committee, and supervised numerous student teachers. While at Kelly, he served as chairman of the history department and on the School Leadership Team for nine years and continues to teach Chicago history. Additionally, Joe has endorsements in special education, English as a Second Language, and is a certified International Baccalaureate teacher. Joe currently teaches Chicago history, an AP research course, and a Dual Credit (college credit) Chicago history course.

While serving as department chair he oversaw the implementation of standardized test prep reading programs for his department that focused on preparing students for the ACT,® and later the SAT.® He also coordinated the marketing committee for his school, wrote numerous newspaper articles about the school that appeared in local newspapers, and created a mentoring program for new teachers. His previous work includes a book about the historic Beverly Hills/Morgan Park neighborhood in Chicago published by Arcadia Publishing as part of their Images of America series, and he has been interviewed on television and radio. When he was twenty-one years old he passed the Illinois Real Estate exam and began selling real estate with a local Century-21 office. He also worked as a new home consultant for a real estate developer and served on the board of directors for the Beverly Ridge Homeowners' Association, a civic association that represented and promoted the civic affairs for over 1,000 households in the association's boundaries.

As a professional educator for over twenty years, Joe Oswald has experience working with adults and students from various educational backgrounds, including special needs students and English Language Learners. He has seen first-hand students struggle with their reading and writing assignments, tests, and on important college entrance exams because they lack a strong vocabulary.

Outside of education, many of his accomplishments would not have been possible without strong academic skills and a command of the English language, both of which are based on having an extensive vocabulary. The words in this book were chosen based on over twenty years of teaching and other professional experiences that witnessed the types of words adults and students struggle with in a variety of settings. The first-hand knowledge of the importance of a strong vocabulary and the proven correlation between an extensive vocabulary and higher socioeconomic status inspired him to write this book and to help others unlock their academic, personal, and professional potential.

For more information please visit www.joeoswald.com or email Joe at joe@joeoswald.com.

Introduction

Being an only child I was always surrounded more by adults when I was growing up than other children. Listening to the adults speak and carry on with one another about a wide-range of topics would have a profound effect on my development in ways I would not appreciate until later in life. All that adult interaction influenced the way I acted, thought, and talked as a grew older. The acquisition from a young age of adult vocabulary and an interest in many topics and types of knowledge improved my ability to speak, write, and interact successfully with a wide-range of people, even those many years beyond my age. When I was in school people always said I talked like an adult. In my early twenties people always said I spoke like a professional and was very mature for my age. The vocabulary I used affected people's perception of me in extremely positive ways that opened many doors for me and allowed me to be successful in a variety of endeavors.

From the time I was in my early twenties a strong vocabulary allowed me to write resumes and fill out job applications that sounded like they were written by people older and more experienced. On job interviews, my vocabulary and speaking ability gave me a distinct edge over other candidates. This was perhaps most noticeable when I received my Illinois real estate license at the age of twenty-one. I had not even graduated college yet, but I was creating my own marketing materials and going into people's homes trying to get them to list their homes with me while also working with buyers to find them their dream home. I looked young, but I came off as energetic, trustworthy, and knowledge about a variety of topics, from the real estate market, to mortgages, to home inspections. The way I presented myself gave me an advantage over other people, even those more experienced but who could not communicate their knowledge and experience very effectively. The words I used and the confidence in which I used them would play a big role in my life, from success in school to success in adult life. A strong vocabulary also improved my reading ability and allowed me to access knowledge I was able put to use to use in a variety of endeavors I have pursed throughout my adult life. This book reflects the importance I place on learning vocabulary and its impact on our academic, professional, and social lives.

Lastly, this book is an updated, expanded, and improved edition of a book I wrote in 2002 called *Vocabulary for an Educated Society* (ISBN: 0-9709734-1-1). The new title, *Vocabulary for Champions*, is not meant to be gimmicky but inspirational in the sense I know having a strong vocabulary will give people an edge over others with whom they will compete against in life. It also reflects changes in the SAT®, which was completely updated in 2016. This edition of the book also includes expanded academic vocabulary from the core subject areas of math, science, English Language Arts, and social science, making it a great tool to help students master important content-area vocabulary in school while also helping students prepare for college entrance exams. The inclusion of a chapter devoted to the vocabulary of economics is meant to help students and adults better understand the factors that affect the economic health of the country while the terms related to personal finance are meant to increase the financial literacy and independence of all people. Additionally, the chapter on resume and interviewing vocabulary targets key words crucial to the job search and conducting successful interviews. Whether it's getting into a good college, landing that dream job, getting a promotion, or just being a more-informed person, it is my hope you will use a strong vocabulary to unlock all of your potential, give yourself an edge over the competition, and be a champion in whatever you set your sights upon.

Why is Vocabulary Important?

A March 11, 2010 article by Ammon Shea titled "Vocabulary Size" appeared in New York Times Magazine. In the article, Shea cited a 2009 study by the Educational Testing Service called "Parsing the Achievement Gap II." According to the article, The Educational Testing Service has been concerned with improving vocabulary since 1947, and their report explained some of the benefits of having an extensive vocabulary, including stating that numerous studies over the last one hundred years has linked higher vocabularies to higher incomes and socioeconomic status. This is true because vocabulary is linked to reading and academic achievement, and academic achievement is directly linked to career opportunities and therefore income and socioeconomic status. In fact, high levels of reading comprehension are not possible without a strong vocabulary, and reading comprehension is the key to accessing knowledge by all people, young or old, student or adult. Whether studying for a college entrance exam, a professional licensing test, or teaching oneself to prepare for a new career or job position, the ability to access information for personal and professional advancement is not possible without strong comprehension and vocabulary skills.

According to the New York Times Magazine article, by the age of three, children raised in a professional household know twice as many words as children raised on welfare. Furthermore, according to an online article in Psychology Today from February 16, 2014, "It is believed that by age three children from lower-income families may hear up to 30 million fewer words than their more privileged counterparts." In a lecture by Dr. Anne Fernald at the annual American Association for the Advancement of Science conference held at the University of Chicago on February 14, 2014, Dr. Fernald stated "five-year-old children of lower socioeconomic status score two years behind on standardized language development tests by the time they enter school." Dr. Fernald contends signs of vocabulary deficiencies are evident before a child is even two-years-old. The good news, even as researchers state, the lack of an extensive vocabulary and the long-term consequences in achievement gaps and income status statistically linked to lower vocabularies can be overcome once people realize the importance of a good vocabulary and a person's ability to improve their own vocabulary and their children's. One of the best ways to improve one's vocabulary is reading a lot and to read more complex texts. Unfortunately, studies also show that people of all ages are reading less and less, and the over-reliance of texting and other forms of social media continue to butcher the English language and diminish the use of proper grammar, sentence structure, and advanced vocabulary.

In fact, an article that appeared in the Washington Post on June 29, 2018 by Christopher Ingram stated that leisure reading in the United States is at an all-time low according to the "American Time Use Survey" compiled by the Bureau of Labor Statistics. The number of people who read for pleasure on a given day has declined by more than 30 percent since 2004. The study also shows the amount of time spent reading has declined from 23 minutes per day in 2004 to 17 minutes per day in 2017. The article also states, that according to survey data from the Pew Research Center and Gallup, the number of people not reading any book in a given year almost tripled between 1978 and 2014. This tragedy has been exacerbated in urban school districts, such as the Chicago Public Schools, where budgetary decisions resulted in the closing of hundreds of school libraries leaving the most vulnerable children without any access to books. Furthermore, vocabulary simply is not emphasized in school like it used to be, especially after elementary school, and students are expected to figure out the meaning of words from "context clues." The problem with this is that many words simply cannot be figured out from context clues, especially for people who are already struggling readers or are not native English speakers.

Why Buy This Book?

This book was written to help people of various ages and backgrounds improve their reading, writing, and communication skills by improving their vocabulary. People will find this book useful when filling out job applications, preparing for job interviews, giving presentations, and interacting with people in various social and professional settings. Since a strong vocabulary is a key component of reading comprehension and proficiency, and therefore general academic ability, this book can help students perform better in school, on advanced placement tests, and prepare for high school and college entrance exams such as the ACT,® SAT,® and GRE.® These types of exams require proficiency in reading and word knowledge. In fact, without a solid foundation in vocabulary, many students find it hard just to understand many of the questions on standardized tests let alone understand the complex reading passages. A strong vocabulary is also a must for English language learners of all ages. With quizzes and challenging word puzzles, this book reinforces the meaning as well as the spelling of words in a fun and interactive way.

With words related to science, business, government, society, economics, politics, world religions, history, and world affairs, this book can also help people become more informed citizens. The words in this book represent words that a well-informed person should know, regardless of their education level, and will encounter every day in the news. The words were chosen because of their significance to all levels of academic and professional communication that a person will likely encounter during school age years, adult life, and life in the employment world. This book contains words that many people can benefit from regardless of their present vocabulary level. Dozens of self-quizzes, twenty challenging crossword puzzles, and fifteen word search puzzles are included to help the reader practice and reinforce newly learned words. The word puzzles are particularly useful for reinforcing the spelling of words, and the word search puzzles can be solved by looking for words in the puzzles forward, backward, up, down, and diagonally.

The better a person's vocabulary, the better that person will be able to read, write, and communicate his or her ideas clearly and effectively in a variety of situations. Communication skills are especially important in jobs that require a person to deal directly with the public or relate important information to co-workers or clients. A person who has a good vocabulary will almost certainly have an advantage on a job interview over other candidates who do not have proper speaking skills. A strong, professional vocabulary is a guaranteed way to impress people on a job interview or presentation.

This book also includes simple reference information that people will find useful, such as measurement conversions, a list of states with their capitals and postal abbreviations, common prefixes, common Latin expressions, and words many people commonly use improperly. The list of commonly misused words should be studied carefully to make sure these words are used correctly when writing and speaking. This book will give people the skills they need to be more knowledgeable, to better communicate that knowledge, to have more self-confidence, and give people access to more of life's opportunities.

How This Book is Organized

Some other vocabulary-improvement books assume the reader already has a strong vocabulary to start with, and therefore those books often include only higher-level vocabulary words that most people do not use on a regular basis. This book starts off with the assumption the reader has an average vocabulary and would like to make it stronger for more everyday use, as well as learn many advanced words for more sophisticated communication. This makes the book helpful to younger people as well as adults.

The first part of the book contains vocabulary common to the core academic subjects of science, math, English Language Arts, economics, and history/social science. These sections are ideal for students who will encounter these words in their core subjects throughout high school and college and crucial for studying for college entrance exams. There are also chapters on economics and personal finance and resume building and job interviewing vocabulary. These sections are ideal for anyone, especially adults, looking for a job or promotion and contain action words and tips employers look for when going through resumes and conducting interviews. The economics and personal finance section are meant to educate people on important words they will encounter when applying for mortgages and other types of loans, staying informed about the economy and job market, interest rates, maintaining good credit scores, investment options, and general economic and personal finance words and concepts covered in books, on the news, and in newspapers.

Finally, the main chapter in this book is devoted to general vocabulary building to improve a person's reading, writing, comprehension, and communication skills. The words in the General Vocabulary section are arranged in alphabetical order with a common form of a word being listed, followed by an easy to use pronunciation guide. Since many words have different usages, depending on how they are used, each entry states whether the word is a noun (n.), verb (v.), adjective (adj.), adverb (adv.), etc. If a word has more than one meaning, other significant meanings are also given. A sample usage sentence is also provided as well as other forms of the words that might be common. The definitions are meant to be simple and easy for a variety of people to understand. See the examples below.

Example One:
effervescent (e-fer-ve-sent) adj. 1. cheerful, spirited, very outgoing. 2. literally to produce bubbles of gas. The effervescent attitude of the fellow made him very popular. / **effervescence** n.

In this example, *effervescent* is an adjective (adj.) that has two definitions given for it (1. and 2.). Since the word also has another common form, the word *effervescence* is listed as a noun (n).

Example Two:
fundamental adj. basic; essential; very important; formative; Proper hygiene is fundamental to good health.

In this example, *formative* is underlined telling the reader that this word is also defined in this book and can be referred to for its own meaning.

Pronunciation Guide

Thanks to modern technology, typing any word into an online dictionary App (application) or website, or using a simple internet search engine, such as Google, will give you the ability to hear the word pronounced correctly if your computer or smart phone has a speaker. This will work for any word you come across in any reading, not just the words in this book. For example, take the word "acumen...," simply type "pronounce acumen" into the internet search bar, and it will give you the ability to hear the word. Additionally, rather than using a pronunciation guide similar to the ones used in many dictionaries (with their many confusing symbols and characters such ä, ē, ã), a simple phonetic pronunciation and syllabication guide has been included after many potentially hard-to-pronounce words. The pronunciation and syllabication guides have been included after words that might be difficult to pronounce or that have pronunciations different from their spellings. The pronunciation and syllabication guides were designed to help the reader learn how to say the words quickly and easily without having to constantly refer back to a pronunciation key.

There are only a few sounds to keep in mind as you study the pronunciation guides in this book. The "a" sound, as in "father," is represented in the pronunciation guides as **"ah."** The first "a" sound in "abash" is represented as **"uh"** because this "a" sound is pronounced like the "u" in "under." The long "i" sound, as in "prize," is represented as a **"y."** The regular **"y"** sound as in "yes" is unchanged when not being used in place of **"i."** The long "o" sound as in "load" is represented as **"oe."** In some instances familiar combinations of letters have been used for certain sounds, as in exacerbate (eg-zas-er-bate). Here, the long "a" sound at the end is represented in the familiar combination of letters in **"ate."** In a few words **"oo"** has been used in place of the "u" sound in "you" or "too" to distinguish it from other "u" sounds in the word. Other combinations of letters include **"chew"** also for "u" as in conceptual, **"yu"** for "u" as in "universal," and **"ay"** for the long "a" sound as in "bake." Other sounds are said as they appear spelled out in the pronunciation guides.

Tips for Learning New Words

Learning new words is not hard, but it is a matter of practice and should be a steady process that you do over time. Do not try to learn too many words at once. Depending on your skill and time frame, try learning five words per day or twenty words per week. Say the words, study the words, use the words, and associate them to things you already know. Make up your own sentences with newly learned words and write them out. Use the practice quizzes and puzzles to test yourself and reinforce what you have learned. It does no good to remember new words only for a short period of time then forget them. The best way to make new words a permanent part of your vocabulary is to use them as often as you can whenever you speak or write. Reading, especially higher level books and texts, is the best way to increase your vocabulary. Always be on the lookout for words you do not know and look them up in a dictionary. Many people consider this an old-fashioned way to learn words, but it works.

A Note about the New SAT®

The SAT® exam was redesigned in 2016. There is no longer an emphasis on obscure vocabulary but on reading, understanding, comparing, and evaluating information in complex reading passages. Therefore, the old power lists of hundreds of words students were supposed to learn specifically for the SAT® are no longer as useful. The emphasis now is on evidenced-based reading, writing, and math; multiple-meaning words; and understanding the meaning of words as used within the context of a given passage. Figuring out the meaning of words from context clues in a passage is a crucial skill needed for the new SAT®, especially for multiple-meaning words that can have different meanings based on the context in which they are used. However, many struggling readers, especially special needs students and English language learners lack this skill and have probably never been exposed to many complex reading passages of the type that appear on exams such as the SAT® or ACT®. Furthermore, many students with lower reading and vocabulary levels are blown out of the water on standardized tests simply because they do not even understand many of the words in the questions. In fact, many of the math questions on the SAT® and ACT® are actually word problems that require a basic level of reading and vocabulary just to understand the questions and attack the answer.

I have taught numerous high school students over the years who did not understand such basic words as "agriculture," "boundary," and "peak," so if on a reading, math, or science test they are asked a question such as "In what year did unemployment peak?," they could not answer the question whether the question was based on reading a textual passage or a graph because they did not know what the word "peak" meant. I have seen countless students struggle just to understand the questions on standardized tests because they were unfamiliar with so many words. When reading complex passages with students I often have to stop several times in the same paragraph to go over the meaning of many of the words. Without doing this the paragraph, and the passage as a whole, would make no sense and leave students with huge gaps in information.

The complex reading passages and questions on college entrance exams are filled with words many students simply do not know that make it hard for them to read a passage let alone try to figure out context clues for targeted vocabulary words tested on the exam. Therefore, a solid foundation in vocabulary is still needed to score well on these tests just to read the questions and understand the reading passages even if obscure lists of vocabulary words are no longer tested. Additionally, many words simply cannot be figured out by context clues alone, especially in non-standardized test reading. This book is not meant to replace content and skills-based test preparation for the SAT® or ACT®; however, this book contains many general use and more complex words that many students just do not know or are exposed to often enough that are still necessary to perform well on standardized tests and improve one's reading, writing, and communication skills. In fact, there are countless students that have the skills and intelligence to perform on tests like the SAT® and ACT® but have language barriers or a weak English vocabulary that prevents them from doing their best on these types of tests.

Lastly, this book is meant to fill the void created by the fact people across many segments of our society just do not read as much as people used to and are not exposed to the amount of reading that contains complex vocabulary or reading levels. Our fast-paced, digital, on-demand, instant messaging, and social media world has many benefits, but it has produced many unintended consequences, especially in education and general literacy. Just ask any teacher. The implication for society is that many students leave elementary and high school and enter college and the professional world lacking the skills and knowledge that a highly competitive and ever-changing society demands.

Tone Words Important for the SAT®

The Evidenced-based Reading and Writing portion of the SAT® and other standardized tests such as the ACT® contain questions that ask the reader to identity the author's tone, the author's point of view, and the author's purpose. Sometimes these are expressly stated by the author. Other times the reader has to infer the meaning using clues from the text. The author's choice of words often shape the tone and point of view expressed in a passage. Understanding what tone is and being able to identify tone words in a textual passage will be very helpful in answering these types of questions correctly and in identifying bias in certain writings.

Tone is the author or narrator's attitude about something, such as the characters in a story or the person or topic an author is writing about in an informational or persuasive text. Tone plays an important role in how the author wants the audience or the reader to feel about something. Tone is the mood the author is trying to express about something. There are countless words authors can use to express tone so the words below are meant to be examples only, not a complete list. It is these types of words (categories of words) that help convey tone. Many of these words and others are contained in the vocabulary-building sections of this book.

There are several categories of tone words. Just a few of the common ones are listed below. Categories of tone words include ones that convey seriousness, humor, optimism, pessimism, or sarcasm. Try typing any of the words in this section into an online dictionary App (application) or website search engine to hear the words pronounced properly.

Words with a positive connotation

amiable- friendly, likeable
amused- finding something entertaining
appreciative- showing gratitude or appreciation
benevolent-good, well-meaning
brave-showing courage or bravery
calm-not worried or upset
cheerful-happy
compassionate-caring, showing compassion
complimentary-expressing praise
confident-showing confidence
consoling-to comfort someone
content-to be okay with, satisfied
ecstatic-very happy, excited
elated-happy
elevated-increased, raised up
encouraging-to express support or confidence
energetic-displaying energy in movement, vitality
enthusiastic-showing enthusiasm or excitement
exuberant-very happy, excited
fanciful-unrealistic, too imaginative

friendly-kind, pleasant
happy-showing pleasure
hopeful-feelings of hope and optimism
impassioned-full of passion or emotion
jovial-cheerful, friendly, kind
jubilant-excited, happy, cheerful
lighthearted-amusing
loving-showing love, concern, or kindness
optimistic-hopeful
peaceful-quite, calm, no disturbances
playful-fun, amusing
pleasant-nice, calm, tranquil
romantic-expressing feelings of love
reverent-expressing deep respect
soothing-calming, relieving pain or discomfort
sweet-pleasant
sympathetic-expressing sympathy or concern
vibrant-full of energy or enthusiasm or colorful
whimsical-playful, lighthearted

Words with a negative connotation

accusing/accusatory-suggesting a wrongdoing
aggravated-made worse
agitated-bothered
angry-upset, mad
apathetic-showing no interest or concern
arrogant-conceited, having too much self-confidence
artificial-not real, man-made
audacious-taking risks or showing no respect
belligerent-rude, aggressive
bitter-angry, not pleasant
boring-not fun, not interesting
brash-overbearing
callous-cold, not caring or sympathetic
childish-immature, child-like
choleric-having a bad temper
coarse-rough, abrasive
cold-callous, not caring
condescending-patronizing, acting superior
contemptuous-showing contempt or scorn
contradictory- disagreeing, showing an opposing point of view
critical-disapproving, judgmental or important
desperate-hopeless, invoking despair, seriously bad situation
disappointed-sad because something did not turn on the way one wanted
disgruntled-unhappy, upset over something
disgusted-expressing strong disapproval
disinterested-displaying a lack of concern or interest
disdain-contempt or strong dislike
facetious- displaying inappropriate humor
furious-very mad or upset
harsh-tough, severe
haughty-arrogant, acting superior
hurtful-causing pain or suffering
indignant-very mad or very upset over a perceived wrongdoing
inflammatory-something that make things worse or causing bad feelings
insulting-putting down or to cast an insult
irritated-bothersome, annoyed
manipulative-controlling a person or situation for personal benefit
obnoxious-rude, annoying
outraged-very mad or upset
pessimistic-not hopeful
quarrelsome-willing to always argue
scornful-showing dislike or looking down upon someone
shameful-causing disgrace or shame
snooty-arrogant, conceited
superficial-on the surface, not real or genuine, not deep
surly-unfriendly

threatening-scary, hostile, causing fright
tired-worn out
uninterested-showing no emotion or interest

Words with a gloomy, sad, or fearful connotation

anxious-nervous, worried
apologetic-regretful
apprehensive-unsure, fearful
bleak-not bright, not hopeful or optimistic
concerned-worried, anxious
confused-unsure, not thinking clearly or understanding
dark-gloomy, serious
dejected-feeling down or hopeless
depressed-sad, feeling badly about something
despair-feeling of hopelessness
disturbed-bothered, disrupted, moved around
embarrassed-feeling shame
fearful-scared or worried
foreboding-worried something bad is going to happen
gloomy-dark, not optimistic
grave-very serious
hollow-empty, not solid or strong, weak
hopeless-having no hope or optimism
horrific-very bad
irreverent-showing lack of respect or seriousness
melancholy-sad, gloomy
morose-in a bad mood
mournful-feelings of sadness or regret
nervous-worried, anxious
numb-having no feeling or sensation
ominous-worried that something bad is going to happen
paranoid-always feeling worried for no apparent reason
poignant-evoking emotions such as sadness
regretful-full of sorrow and regret
remorseful-full of sorrow and regret, showing remorse
resigned-determined or dedicated to doing or accepting something that is unpleasant
sad-gloomy, expressing sadness
sober-serious, solemn sensible
solemn-dignified, serious or formal
somber-gloomy, dark, serious

Words expressing sarcasm or irony

amused- finding something entertaining
comical-funny, not taken seriously
cynical-not believing, distrusting in people's intentions or sincerity
droll-boring, not outwardly funny, provoking a dry sense of humor
facetious-displaying inappropriate humor
flippant-lacking respect
ironic-things not turning out as expected or displaying irony, twist of fate
mock-to make fun of something in a negative way
patronizing-condescending, acting superior to another
ridicule-to put someone down, make fun of them, or show contempt
sarcastic-mocking or showing contempt by using irony
sardonic-cynical, showing contempt
satirical-using sarcasm to make fun of someone's weakness
taunting-provoking in an insulting or hurtful manner, instigating
teasing-making fun of someone in a playful or sometimes hurtful way

Neutral Tone Words

baffled-confused
candid-honest in a direct manner
ceremonial-expressing importance
clinical-related to treatment based on observation or acting unemotional and detached
contemplative-using much thought
conventional-normal, accepted, standard
didactic-related to teaching with a moral or ulterior purpose
earnest-sincere, expressing sincerity
factual-based on fact rather than opinion
formal-according to accepted practices or etiquette
forthright-direct or straightforward when speaking
humble-modest, showing humility, opposite of boastful
informative-displaying or relaying information
inquisitive-curious, full of questions
lyrical-able to express beautiful emotions in writing related to art, music, literature, or poetry
meditative-displaying careful thought and reflection, using meditation to think and concentrate
nostalgic-fondness for a time or event that has long passed
objective-unbiased, not influenced by emotional or personal feelings
obsequious-showing too much obedience or attentiveness
persuasive-able to convince, convincing
reflective-giving something much thought especially to find new meaning or understanding
reminiscent-reminding one of something
restrained-holding back or keeping from doing something, keep under control
sincere-honest, truthful, altruistic
vexed-confused in an annoying way, frustrated

Question Stems for the SAT® and ACT®

Solid reading and comprehension skills grounded in a strong vocabulary is a must for doing well on tests such as the SAT® and ACT® ; however, understanding the types of questions asked on these tests can also can be very helpful. In general, students should be able to identity main ideas and significant details; make generalizations and draw conclusions; answer inference-type questions where the reader must draw a logical conclusion based on the information given; understand the author's purpose; define the meaning words in context; and understand sequential, comparative, and cause & effect relationships. Furthermore, the SAT® has evidence-based questions and analysis questions that require the reader to evaluate the author's tone, point of view, text structure, and writing style. A great way to tackle these tested skills is to be able to identify the types of questions that target those skills. By becoming familiar with these question stems students will have a much better chance of answering them correctly. There are many questions stems and various test prep strategies that are beyond the scope of this book, but below are a few types of question stems. Research more of them and identify what skills they target.

The main purpose of this passage is to:

Which of the following titles best describes the content of the passage?

The author is primarily concerned with discussing the:

According to the passage, _____ have all of the following in common EXCEPT:

In the final paragraph, the author discusses:

The author makes all of the following points about _____ EXCEPT:

According to the passage, all of the following are true of _____ EXCEPT

The passage most strongly supports which of the following conclusions _____?

It can be inferred from the passage that:

Which choice best describes the developmental pattern of the passage?

As used in lines 4 and 25, "_____" most nearly means:

Which choice provides the best evidence for the answer to the previous question?

The authors would likely attribute the difference in _____ and _____ to:

Which statement best describes the relationship between the passages?

The central claim of the passage is that:

Which statement best summarizes the information presented in the graph?

Common Prefixes, Roots, and Suffixes

A prefix comes at the beginning of a word and helps change the meaning of the word. A root is the basic part of a word that determines its meaning and can be surrounded by a prefix and suffix. Many words in the English language are derived from Greek and Latin words and contain Greek and Latin roots. A suffix comes at the end of word. It can also change the meaning of a word or make the word grammatically correct. Knowing common prefixes, roots, and suffixes can help you figure out the meaning of a word and how to use it properly.

Common Prefixes

ab	to move away, as in abdicate or abstain
ante	before, as in antediluvian
anti	against, as in antiestablishment
arch	first, the first, as in archetype
auto	self, by itself, as in automatic pilot
ben	good, not bad, good to other people, as in beneficiary or benign
bi	two, as in biped or bicameral
cogn	to learn, as in cognitive
contra	against, as in contrary
contro	against, as in controvert
de	the opposite of or to remove, as in deforest, meaning to remove the forest (trees)
demi	half or something like, as in demigod
di	two, as dissect or cut in two
dia	across, as in diameter
dys	abnormal, poor, bad, not working, as in dysfunctional
epi	meaning on, over, or upon, as in epidermis, epicenter
equi	equal or balanced, as in equilibrium
eu	good, well, or better, as in euphemism eulogy, euthanasia
ex	from outside or elsewhere, as in exterior
extra	beyond, as in extraordinary
fore	in the front, as in foreground
geo	related to the earth, as in geopolitics, geothermal, and geography
homo	same, of the same kind, as in homogenous
hyper	above or beyond, or too much, as in hyperactive
hypo	under, beneath, or too little, as in a hypodermic needle, meaning under the skin
im/in/ir	not, as in impossible, inappropriate, and irregular
inter	between, such as interstate trade, meaning trade between states
intra	within, such as intrastate trade, which means trade within a state
mal	bad, badly, or poor, as in maladjusted, meaning poorly adjusted
mis	wrongly, as in misinformed or mistreat
mono	one, as in monochromatic
neo	new, as in neophyte
non	not, as in nonentity
omni	all, as in omniscient
pac/pax	refers to period of peace or peaceful, as in pacify, Pax Americana or Pax Romana
pan	all of, as in Pan-American, meaning everything in the Americas
para	beside or next to, as in paragraph or paradox

peri		around, on the side, as in peripheral
poly		many, as in polytheism
pre		before, first, as in prequel
pro		good or in favor of something, as in pros and cons, professional, proponent
post		after, as in postdate
proto		the first, coming first in importance, as in prototype
re		again, as in repeat and replay
retro		back or backward, as in retroactive
semi		half, about, partly, as in semiannually
sub		lower, under, nearly, related to, or almost, as in subordinate, subterranean, subarctic
super		more, extra, above, as in superlative
supra		more, extra, above, as in supraorbital
sym		at the same time, as in sympathy
sys		at the same time, as in systemic
tele		from a distance, as in telephone and teleport
trans		meaning across, beyond, through, or changing, as in transatlantic
un		not, as in unchanged, meaning not changed
uni		one, as in universal
vice		in place of, next in line to, as in vice-president

Common Roots

alter	**English**	other, as in alternative
anthro	**Greek**	man, related to man, as in anthropology
aqua	**Latin**	water, as in aquatic and aqueduct
astr	**Greek**	star, as in astronomy or asterisk
aud/audit	**Latin**	hear, as in auditory
auto	**Greek**	self, as in autograph, autobiography, automobile
bell	**Latin**	war, as in antebellum and belligerent
biblio	**Greek**	book, as in bibliophile
bio	**Greek**	life, as in biology
cata	**Greek**	down, as in catastrophe
chrom	**Greek**	color, as in chromatic
chron	**Greek**	time, as in chronology
circum	**Latin**	around, as in circumference,
creed	**Latin**	belief, as in credentials or credible
crypt	**Latin**	secret or hidden, as in cryptography
cycl	**Greek**	circle, wheel, as in cyclical and bicycle
dem	**Greek**	people, as in democracy and demographics
dic	**Latin**	to speak, as in dictation or dictionary
domin	**Latin**	rule or have authority, as in dominate
gen	**Latin**	to be born or of birth, as in genetics or genesis
graph	**Greek**	to write, as in autograph or cartography
hydr	**Greek**	water, as in dehydrated
iso	**Greek**	same as, equal, as in isometric
jur	**Latin**	related to law, as in jury, judiciary, or jurisprudence
lith	**Greek**	stones or rocks, as in megalith
log	**Greek**	think or thought, as in logic, logistics, analogy
logos	**Greek**	study, words, as in astronomy, zoology
macro	**Greek**	large, as in macrocosm

man	Latin	hand, as in manual, manufacture, manicure
mega	Greek	large, as in megalith
meso	Greek	middle, as in Mesoamerica, meaning the middle part of the Americas
meter	Greek	to measure, as in thermometer, millimeter
micro	Greek	small, as in microcosm
min	Latin	small, as in miniature
morph	Greek	shape, as in metamorphosis
multi	Latin	many, as in multiple
onym	Greek	name, as in synonym, pseudonym
path	Greek	feeling or disease such pathos, pathological, or psychopath
ped	Greek	child, as in pediatrician
ped	Latin	foot or walk, as in pedestal, pedestrian, and pedometer
phil	Greek	love, as in philanthropist
phob	Greek	fear, as in phobia and xenophobia
pho/photo	Greek	light, as in photograph
phon	Greek	sound, as in telephone, phonics and phonograph
port	Latin	to carry, as in transport, teleport, import, export
psych	Greek	mind, as in psychology
pyr	Greek	fire, as in pyromania
sci/scio	Latin	know, aware of, as in conscious
scribe	Latin	to write, as in prescribe or transcribe
script	Latin	to write, as in prescription or subscription
sens	Latin	to feel, as in sentiment, sensitive
sequ	Latin	in an order, following, as in sequential
struct	Latin	build, as in construct
tele	Greek	far away, as in telescope, telephone, television
terr	Latin	earth, as in territory, terrain, terrestrial, extraterrestrial
uni	Latin	one, as in unilateral
vid/vis	Latin	to see, as in visualize, vision, video, visible
zo	Greek	animal, as in zoology

Common Suffixes

cracy	to rule, as in democracy, theocracy, aristocracy, or bureaucracy
cy	state of, as in truancy, which is the state of being truant
er, or	referring to someone, as in winner and benefactor
fy	to make, as in beautify
gress	away, to move away, as in digress
ic/ac	similar, related to, of a kind, as in nostalgic
il/ile	having to do with, as in bibliophile
ious	characterized by, as in glorious
ist	refers to someone, as in psychologist
ness	having the quality of, as in weakness
ology	branch of knowledge as in anthropology or archeology
ory	having the quality of, as in sensory
ous	having or full of, as in magnanimous
ship	state of, skill in something, as in marksmanship
y	having or full of, as in messy

Common Latin Expressions

ad hoc Latin phrase meaning on a case by case basis; under special circumstances. The zoning requests will be reviewed ad hoc.

carpe diem (karpee dee-em) Latin term meaning seize the day. Refers to taking advantage of one's opportunities now rather than later; live for the moment.

de facto Latin term meaning from the fact itself, the way it really is, or as a result of (the result of something not planned or by design). Because of poverty, urban schools are often examples of de facto segregation.

de jure Latin term meaning by law or by deliberate act (differs from de facto in that de jure situations are created with intent). The Jim Crow laws that made racial segregation legal in the South were examples of de jure segregation.

e pluribus unum (ee pluribis oo-num) Latin meaning, out of many, one.

fait accompli Latin term referring to what is already done or will be done and cannot be changed. When the man realized the police car was pulling him over for speeding he knew that getting a ticket was a fait accompli.

habeas corpus (hay-bee-es kor-pus) Latin term which literally means "Bring forth the body" but refers to a law which states that an arrested person must be brought before a judge and told what he has been arrested for. Lincoln suspended the writ of habeas corpus during the Civil War.

ipso facto Latin term meaning by the fact itself. Murder is an ipso facto evil. Supply and demand is an ipso facto aspect of capitalism.

mea cupla Latin term meaning my fault. I was late for work but mea cupla, I over slept.

per diem (dee-em) Latin term meaning per day. She was paid $75 per diem.

per se (per say) Latin term meaning by itself or in and of itself. Bad weather, per se, is guaranteed to ruin the picnic.

persona non grata Latin term referring to a person who is not considered acceptable by others in certain situations. The boy wanted to play ball with the adults, but persona non grata, he was not welcomed.

pro bono short for pro bono publico, which is a Latin term meaning for the public good or welfare; refers to a service that is performed free of charge. The lawyer took the case pro bono.

quid pro quo Latin term for getting one thing in return for another. A quid pro quo agreement was worked out.

status quo (sta-tus kwoe) Latin for the way things are now. The manager tried to maintain the status quo in the company rather than looking for new ideas and methods.

Commonly Misused Words

accept/except. "Accept" means to get something, but "except" means to exclude something or something unusual, as in exceptional.

adverse/averse. "Adverse" means a negative effect on something. "Averse" means to not like something.

affect/effect. "Affect" is a verb meaning to influence or act on something. The rain affected our picnic. "Effect" is a noun meaning the result or outcome of something. The effect of more rain was a canceled picnic.

adapt/adopt/adept. "Adapt" means to get used to, change, or improve over time. "Adopt" means to take in or take over. "Adept" means to be good at something.

aid/aide. "Aid" means to offer help. "Aide" is an assistant.

all together/altogether. "All together" refers to a group. "Altogether" refers to something in its complete form.

allusion/illusion. "Allusion" is more of a literary term that makes an indirect reference to something. An "illusion" is something that appears real but is not, such as tricks by a magician.

amiable/amicable. "Amiable" refers to a person's good-natured disposition or friendliness. "Amicable" refers to the friendly relationship between people.

among/between. "Among" is used to refer to more than two people. "Between" is used to refer to two people.

anymore/any more. "Anymore" refers to the present or current situation, as in "There aren't many good television shows anymore." "Any more" refers to something more or additional, as in, I don't want any more food.

appraise/apprise. "Appraise" means to estimate the value of something. "Apprise" means to keep someone informed, as in "Keep me apprised of the situation."

ascent/assent. "Ascend" means to move up, as in ascending the hill. "Assent" means to agree.

assure/ensure. "Assure" means to reinforce or guarantee that something is true or okay. "Ensure" means to make sure something gets done.

bare/bear. "Bare" means having no clothes on, as in bare naked. "Bear" means to carry something, like the right to bear arms (guns) as in the 2nd Amendment to the Constitution or the old proverb "Beware of Greeks bearing gifts."

breach/breech. "Breach" means to break a contract. "Breech" means to forcibly gain entrance to something, as in "The soldiers breeched the castle walls."

28

capital/capitol. "Capital" means money but can also refer to the city where a state government is located, as in "The capital of Illinois is Springfield. "Capitol" is the actual building where a state or national government is located, as in the U.S. Capitol Building.

censor/censure. "Censor" means to evaluate and remove material considered inappropriate. "Censure" means to admonish or rebuke someone.

cite/site. "Cite" refers to listing a source of information. "Site" refers to a place or location.

complementary/complimentary. "Complementary" refers to something that adds to or completes something else. "Complimentary" refers to giving praise or something given for free, such as in "The winner was given two complimentary tickets."

connote/denote. "Connote" as in a connotation, means to imply a meaning. "Denote" means to explain something specifically and literally.

council/counsel. "Council" is a group of people who meet to discuss things, as in the city council or the council of elders. "Counsel" means to give advice or one who gives advice such as to seek counsel with your lawyer.

decent/descent. "Decent" mains good or okay, as in a decent price. "Descent" refers the act of moving downhill, as in the descending the hill.

desert/dessert. "Desert" is a hot sandy place. "Dessert" is a type of meal.

disburse/disperse. "Disburse" means to give out, allocate, or pay something, usually money, as in "Money was disbursed to the neediest families first." "Disperse" means to break up or scatter, as in "The crowd dispersed after the concert."

dual/duel. "Dual" refers to the number two such as serving dual purposes. "Duel" is a challenge between two people, such as a gun duel.

elicit/illicit. "Elicit" is a verb that means to bring forth or draw out. "Illicit" is an adjective that refers to something that is improper or immoral.

elusive/illusive. "Elusive" is something that is hard to catch or obtain, like the elusive bank robber. "Illusive" is something that never really existed, like the search for the illusive unicorn.

emigrate/immigrate. "Emigrate" means to move out of a country. "Immigrate" means to move into a country.

eminent/imminent. "Eminent" means very well-known and important on a wide scale, as in throughout the world. "Imminent" means about to happen.

eminent/prominent. "Eminent" means very well-known and important on a wide scale, as in throughout the world. "Prominent" means well-known and important on a smaller scale, such as in a town or community.

empathy/sympathy. "Empathy" is feeling or understanding someone's pain or suffering or situation. "Sympathy" is to feel sorry for someone.

epidemic/pandemic. An "epidemic" refers to a disease that is widespread in a certain area or country. A "pandemic" is a disease that spreads around the world or across continents.

epistemology/etymology/ ontology. "Epistemology" is the branch of philosophy that studies the nature of human knowledge along with the origins and limits of knowledge and reality. "Etymology" is the study of the origin, meaning, and history of words. "Ontology" is the philosophy concerned with the study of reality and the nature of being.

epitaph/epithet. An "epitaph" is something written on the headstone of a grave. An "epithet" is a description of someone, often negative or abusive in nature, as in a racial epithet.

exacerbate/exasperate. "Exacerbate" means to make worse. "Exasperate" means to bother or annoy.

farther/further. "Farther" refers to distance. "Further" refers to more of something or a quantity.

faint/feint. "Faint" refers to something weak, as in a faint sound in the distance. "Feint" refers to something deceptive, distracting, fake, or a trick. Boxers are known for their feints.

hoard/horde. "Hoard" means to keep holding on to things or take more than your fair share. A "horde" refers to a large group of people or things, like a horde of people or a horde of warriors.

imply/infer. "Imply" means to hint at something. "Infer" means to take an educated guess based on the information available, as in to make an inference from the reading passage.

it's/its. "It's" is a contraction of "it is," as in, "It's cold outside." "Its" shows possession as in, "The watch stopped because its battery was dead."

latitude/longitude. "Latitude" is the distance north or south of the equator signified by horizontal lines on a map and measured in degrees. "Longitude" is the distance east or west on the earth and measure in degrees along vertical lines.

mercenary/missionary. "Mercenary" is a paid soldier who fights for whichever country pays him. "Missionary" is a person who goes to another country to spread religion.

metal/medal. "Metal" means something made out of steel. A "medal" is an award for a great accomplishment, like a Gold Medal or the Congressional Medal of Honor.

meddle/mettle. "Meddle" means to interfere with something or get in the middle of something. "Mettle" refers to a person's characteristics or qualities that help them through difficult situations, as in "The final round of the match tested the boxer's mettle."

moral/morale. "Moral" refers to right and wrong. "Morale" refers to enthusiasm or state of mind, such as in "Morale was low after the defeat."

objective/subjective. "Objective" means a clear unbiased fact or standard on something. "Subjective" means interpretation is open to personal opinion or personal evaluation.

parody/parity. A "parody" is a spoof or something that makes fun of something else. "Parity" means to be equal, as in to achieve parity with the other team.

peak/peek/pique. "Peak" means the top of something, as in the peak of the mountain or to be in peak physical shape. "Peek" means to take a quick look. "Pique" means to excite someone, as in pique their interest.

pray/prey. "Pray" means to speak to God as in a prayer. "Prey" is an animal(s) that is hunted by another animal.

precede/proceed. "Precede" means to come before. "Proceed" means to move forward or continue.

principal/principle. "Principal" refers to the most important thing or person, as with the person in charge of a school. "Principle" refers to a belief, rule, or idea as in the guiding or principle.

rain/reign/rein. "Rain" is water from the sky. "Reign" is a verb meaning to rule or have control over people like a king reigns over his country. "Reins" refer to straps that control animals, such as on a horse.

raise/raze. "Raise" means to bring up. "Raze" means to tear down, such as when a building is razed.

reek/wreak. "Reek" means to smell bad. "Wreak" means to cause damage or chaos, as in wreak havoc.

regardless/ irregardless. "Irregardless" is not a proper word. Use regardless instead, as in "We are going to drive to Florida regardless of how long it takes," rather than "We are going to drive to Florida irregardless of how long it takes."

slight/sleight. "Slight" means a little, as in a slight rain. "Sleight" means something sneaky as in the magician's sleight of hand.

than/then. "Than" is used when comparing items, such as in " Brian is taller than Sue." Use "then" when referring to time, such as in "It was then necessary to walk to school" or "Then we all went home."

that/which. Use "that" to complete a thought in a sentence as in, "The shirt that I left outside got wet." Use "which" to add additional information as in, "The shirt that I left outside, which I had gotten for my birthday, got wet." "Which" should be preceded by a comma.

veracious/voracious. "Veracious" means truthful, as in the ability to verify. "Voracious" means really hungry, as in a voracious appetite.

weather/whether. "Weather" refers to the conditions outside as related to rain, temperature, etc. "Whether" refers to a choice as in "Whether or not you decide to go."

who/that. Use "who" when referring to a person and use "that" when referring to a thing. " The boy who was at my party won the spelling bee," instead of "The boy that was at my party won the spelling bee." "The toy that I left outside got wet."

who/whom. "Who" is used to refer to the subject one is talking about, as in "Who was at the dance?" "Whom" refers to the object of an action or the object of the verb in the sentence. "Whom are you referring to?"

wear/ware. "Wear" means to put something on your body or to be worn out from over use, as in "Wear your clothes" or "Don't wear out the tires." "Ware" or "wares" refers to items that are made to sell or be used, as in housewares … "Many food vendors offered a variety of wares."

who's/whose. "Who's" is a contraction of "who is," as in, "Who is the girl who won the race?" "Whose" shows possession, as in " Whose shirt is this?"

Idioms

An idiom is a phrase or figure of speech that has a meaning that does not make sense according to the literal reading of the words in the phrase. Idioms usually only make sense to people familiar with them and can be very hard for non-native language speakers to understand. They are particularly troublesome to English language learners. Below are some common idioms.

Add fuel to the fire-make things worse
Raining cats and dogs-raining really hard
You can say that again-to be very right about something (usually said for emphasis)
Think outside the box-to think creatively to solve a problem
Playing the devil's advocate-to offer a counterargument or another point of view
Cost an arm and a leg-something that is very expensive
Cool as a cucumber-very calm and confident; not nervous or worried at all
Zip your lip-to be quiet
Call it a day-time to stop or quit working for the day
Down to the wire-something that came or was decided upon at the last minute
Apple of his eye- to be someone's favorite person
See eye to eye-to agree with someone
Eat like a horse- to be very hungry or have a big appetite
Cross your fingers-hope for luck
To bite off more than you can chew- to take on more than one can handle
Hold your horses-slow down and be patient
Pass with flying colors-passed with high marks
Straight from the horse's mouth-to get information directly from the person who said it
Best thing since sliced bread-something that is really good
Sitting on the fence-to be in the middle of an issue and not able to make a decision
Get off your high horse-quit acting like you are better than someone else
Read between the lines-look for the real or hidden meaning
The ball is in your court-up to the other person to act now
When pigs fly-something that will never happen
Jump on the bandwagon-to go along with what others are doing; to follow the trend
Icing on the cake- something extra that is really good; that one thing that takes something from being good to being great
Wolf in sheep's clothing-a person pretending to be something they are not
Taste of your own medicine-someone gets treated in the same bad way that they treated others
Cake walk-something that is very easy
At a snail's pace-to move very slowly
Break a leg-wishing someone good luck
A little birdie told me-to learn a secret from someone
Fish out of water-to feel out of place or out one's comfort zone
Feeling under the weather-feeling sick or ill
Miss the boat-to miss an opportunity
Give someone the cold shoulder-to ignore someone on purpose
Play it by ear-see how it goes and proceed as things develop
That ship already sailed- to miss an opportunity because the chance already passed
Speak your mind-say what you really think

Spill the beans-tell a secret

It's in the bag-to think something is a sure thing or guaranteed

Hit the sack-go to bed

Once in a blue moon-not very often

Let the cat out of the bag-to tell a secret

It's a piece of cake- to be very easy

It's a blessing in disguise-to find something good in something bad that happened

In the same boat-to be in the same situation

I'm all ears-to give someone your full attention

Go down in flames-to fail really badly at something

Pull someone's leg-to fool someone

By the skin of your teeth- to just barely succeed, barely or by a narrow margin

Come rain or shine- do something no matter what the obstacles might be or even if raining outside

Too hot to handle- something that is too hard to do

Through thick and thin-to stay with or be loyal to someone through good times and bad times

Always by your side-to always be available to help or comfort someone

Cut corners-to do things quickly and cheaply to save time and money; to sacrifice quality

Beat around the bush-to waste time in order to keep from doing or saying something

Take it with a grain of salt-not believe something so easily because you know it might not be completely true

Fit as a fiddle-healthy and in good shape

What goes around comes around-what one does to others will eventually be the way others treat that person

In hot water-to be in trouble

Cat got your tongue- to be too quiet and unwilling to speak

Get cold feet- to be nervous and want to back out of doing something

The world is your oyster-to be able to achieve great things

Science Terms

Science is an all-encompassing term, but the sciences can be broken down into different disciplines, branches, and fields within branches. Generally speaking, science can be broken down into what are known as the **Natural Sciences**, the **Social Sciences**, and the **Formal Sciences**. Formal Sciences refer specifically to the study of formal systems that create knowledge, such as mathematics, logic systems, statistics, and even theoretical computer science. However, most science and scientific vocabulary fall within the Natural and Social Sciences.

The **Natural Sciences** are related to the study of things that occur in nature as well as biological processes within living beings. Natural Science is often broken down into two branches, **life science (sometimes called biological science) and physical science**. Life sciences include **biology, zoology, anatomy, neuroscience, botany, evolution, genetics, ecology, microbiology, molecular biology, biomechanics,** and many other fields.

Physical science deals with non-living systems and includes **chemistry; physics; earth science; geology; meteorology; astronomy; and oceanography**, which is sometimes classified as a life science because it involves the study of ocean organisms and sea life. **Paleontology** is another field that overlaps life, earth, and the social sciences because so many different disciplines are involved in studying fossils and the history of life on the earth, including, biology, geology, and chemistry.

The **Social Sciences** deal with people and the interactions of people among each other and within their environments. Branches of Social Science include, **history; anthropology; archeology; psychology; economics; sociology; linguistics** (the study of language and speech)**; human geography; political science; and jurisprudence**, which is the study of law.

There are hundreds and hundreds of vocabulary words related to science. Below are words people will encounter most in their every-day lives as well as in school and that are used outside the realm of science classes.

Again, try typing any of the words in this section into an online dictionary App (application) or website, or using a simple internet search engine, such as Google, and it will give you the ability to hear the word pronounced correctly if your computer or smart phone has a speaker. Try it!

anatomy n. the study of the human body and other living organisms. One has to have a strong stomach for anatomy with the all dissection involved.

acceleration n./ **accelerate** v. the rate at which an object gains speed. A sports car has greater acceleration than a minivan.

amphibian n. an animal that can live on land and in water. Frogs are amphibians. / **amphibious** adj. having water-like characteristics.

anthropology n. the study of man and his development. Anthropology often goes hand in hand with archeology. / **anthropologist** n. / **anthropological** adj.

aquatic adj. of the water, having water-like characteristics. Plants found in the ocean are aquatic in nature.

archeology (ar-kee-o-lo-jee) n. the study of ancient people and artifacts. Archeology is an important aspect of historical knowledge.

botany n. the study of plants and flowers. Botany is useful for knowing which plants are poisonous.

carcinogen n. something that causes cancer. Tobacco is a known carcinogen. / **carcinogenic** adj.

carnivorous n. an animal that eats meat

catalyst n. something that causes a change or reaction in something else. Sunlight is a catalyst for photosynthesis in plants. The person's unhappiness with his work was a catalyst for a new career.

celestial adj. related to space or the starts. Only some celestial objects can be seen without a telescope.

centrifugal adj. the force that pushes an object away from the center, outward force. Astronauts and pilots train to see how much centrifugal force their bodies can tolerate. The force that keeps a string straight when it is swung around like a lasso is centrifugal force.

centripetal adj. force that pulls an object inward, toward the center, or keeps an object in motion along a curved path. The centripetal force of gravity is the force that keeps planets in rotation around the sun and moons in orbit around planets.

chromosome n. part of an organism's DNA that contains most of the genetic information of the organism.

chronic adj. something that occurs on a regular basis. The man's chronic shoulder pain was a sign that something serious was wrong with his shoulder.

conservation n. the planning and action of saving or preserving something, particularly the earth's resources. Conservation efforts have increased as humans have become more aware of how pollution and others actions hurt the environment and affect other creatures.

conduction n. the act of passing heat or energy directly from one surface to another by touch. If you are boiling water in pot and it has a metal handle, the handle will also get hot through the process of conduction. Copper is a good conductor of electricity since electrons flow through it easily; that's why copper is used in electrical wiring.

convection n. the process of transferring heat by causing hotter material to rise and cooler material to be forced down. Convection ovens provide more even heating of foods.

data n. information. Computers can handle a lot of data at one time.

density n. the amount of something in a defined space. Cities have greater population densities than rural area because more people live within smaller, more confined spaces. /**dense** adj. thick,

dilute v. to make something less strong. Water was poured into the bucket to dilute the bleach.

dissolve v. to break apart or break down. The vinegar helped dissolve the mineral deposits and clean the shower head.

ecology n. the relationship between organisms and their environment. Ecology is a branch of science. /**ecological** adj. The ecological impact of insecticides, human encroachment, and global warming has been devastating on many species of plants and animals.

ecosystem n. the geographic area of a relationship between organisms and their environment. The oceans' ecosystems are much different that the ecosystems on dry land.

element n. the basic building blocks of something. The periodic table of elements lists the most basic elements known to man, which combine to make other substances. /**elemental** adj. of the elements or basic.

entropy n. 1. the breaking down of a substance or physical state over time, especially as the energy that maintains the balance is decreased. 2. To decay or fall apart. Ice melting is an example of the entropy that occurs when temperatures rise above freezing.

fauna n. animals of a particular area. The asteroid that is believed to have killed off the dinosaurs also killed off much of the other fauna on the planet.

fission n. nuclear process of splitting an atom. The energy released by today's nuclear power plants and the atomic bombs dropped during World War II used nuclear fission energy, which is less powerful than <u>fusion</u> energy.

flora n. plant-life of a particular area. The asteroid that is believed to have killed off the dinosaurs also killed of much of the flora on the planet.

fossil fuel n. fuel sources found in nature such as coal, petroleum, and natural gas. Fossil fuels pollute the environment when they burn, but they are still an abundant and cheap source of fuel.

friction n. resistance energy created by the contact of one material with another. The friction of the road against bicycle tires is what makes it hard to pedal. The friction of the car's brakes against the wheels is what stops a car. Friction slows things down and wear's things out over time.

forensic/ forensic science n. the application of science, scientific test, and medical knowledge to investigate crimes and used in courts of law. A forensic medical expert explained the evidence to the judge.

fusion n. nuclear process of smashing atoms together to create other atoms. The sun's energy comes from fusion reactions, which is more powerful than nuclear <u>fission</u>.

geothermal n. source of heat that comes from the ground or from within the earth. Some homes use geothermal systems to provide heat by running tubes with water in them far below the ground to capture heat where it is warmer in the winter.

germination n. the process of which something grows from a seed or when a plant or flower sprouts. Water and sunlight help the process of germination.

Greenhouse Effect/Greenhouse gas n. term that refers to the warming of the planet by certain gases that trap heat within the atmosphere and break down the ozone layer.

habitat n. the natural environment in which animals live. Zoos try to recreate the natural habitats of where the animals came from in the wild.

Fill in the blank quiz #1

1. The rate at which objects gain speeds is _____.
2. An _____ is an animal that can live on land or in the water.
3. Something that is known to cause cancer is called a _____.
4. Something that causes a change or reaction in something else is known as a _____.
5. _____ is the type of force that pushes outward on something.
6. _____ is the type of force that pushes something inward.
7. The man had a _____ illness because he was sick all the time.
8. Cities have a greater population _____ because people live close together.
9. In chemistry class you might have to _____ one solution with something else such as water.
10. Coal, natural gas, and petroleum (oil) are examples of _____.
11. _____ is the application of science and medical knowledge to solve crimes.
12. _____ is the process of which something grows from a seed.
13. A _____ gas contributes to the warming of the earth.
14. _____ is the study of man and his development.
15. The resistance of the road against a car's tires is an example of _____.

---

hemisphere n. equal halves of the earth. The earth is divided into four hemispheres, the Northern, Southern, Western, and Eastern hemispheres. The equator is the dividing line between the northern and southern hemispheres. The brain is has two hemispheres.

herbivore n. eating only plants. Some dinosaurs were herbivores.

heredity n. mental and physical traits that are genetically passed down from one generation to the next, also known as biological inheritance. Heredity plays an important role in how a person looks and in their intelligence. Heredity is at the center of the nature versus nurture argument. / **hereditary** adj.

hypothesis n. an unproven or assumed idea or theory. For a hypothesis to be accepted as truth it must be proven and verified.

indigenous adj. people or animals naturally or originally inhabiting a certain area. Native Americans are the indigenous people of the Americas. Polar bears are indigenous to arctic areas.

inertia n. the tendency of an object to stay in motion or at rest unless acted upon by an opposing force. Tendency to stay unchanged. A car's breaks provide the inertia to slow it down when it is moving.

inherit v. 1. to take on the genetic traits that are passed down from parents to offspring. The boy inherited his blue eyes from this father. 2. To have property passed down. The child inherited his parent's home.

insoluble adj. something that cannot be dissolved or separated from the liquid solution. Sugar and salt dissolve in water, but oil is an insoluble substance because it does not dissolve.

invertebrate n. a creature that has no backbone. Insects are invertebrates.

luminous adj. something that gives off light. Stars are luminous in the night sky.

marine adj. related to the ocean or water. Marine biologists study the animal and plant life of marine ecosystems.

mass n. 1. the total number of electrons, protons, and neutrons in an object. 2. an object's resistance to inertia or movement. An object's mass is not the same as its weight.

matter n. any physical substance. Matter can be in the form, or state, of a solid, liquid, gas, or plasma.

metamorphosis n. the process of changing from one thing into something completely different. A metamorphosis occurs when a caterpillar changes into a butterfly.

mutation n. a structural change in something, particularly genes. Radiation can cause genes to undergo mutations. / **mutate** v. Carcinogens can cause normal cells to mutate into cancer cells.

molecule n. the smallest compound made up of atoms bonded together. Water molecules are made from hydrogen and oxygen atoms.

osmosis n. the process by which molecules or substances pass through other substances or permeable membranes. Plants take on water through their leaves by the process of osmosis.

omnivorous adj. eating plants and animals. Some dinosaurs were omnivorous.

opaque adj. does not allow light to come through. The glass was covered in an opaque material.

paleontology n. the study of life on earth particularly through fossil records. Paleontology is not limited to the study of dinosaurs.

phenomenon (phenomena plural) n. an occurrence that is interesting because it is hard to explain or understand. UFO sittings are an example of a phenomenon.

physiology n. the study of the mechanics and functions of living organisms. Anatomy and physiology go hand in hand and are important in understanding how the human body works.

permeable adj. substance that allows liquid, gases, or other smaller substances to pass through. The permeable membranes on plant leaves allow water to pass through.

permutation n. a set of possible outcomes or ways of arranging things, either in nature or mathematically. Having a list of things to do but doing them in a different order throughout the day can produce different permutations. Combining different genes or compounds can produce many different chemical or biological permutations.

Fill in the blank quiz # 2

1. The earth and the human brain both have two _____.

2. _____ is the process by which mental and physical traits are genetically passed along.

3. _____ people are native to an area, meaning they originated from there.

4. To _____ something means to have it passed down from parents to children.

5. If something is _____ that means it gives off light.

6. Caterpillars undergo a _____ when they change into a butterfly.

7. A _____ is a structural change to the cellular makeup of something.

8. _____ glass does not allow light through.

9. If something is _____ that means something small can pass through it.

10. A _____ is a set of possible outcomes or possible ways of arranging things.

---

pollination n. the process of transferring pollen grains from a male part of a flower called an anther to the female part of flower called a stigma. Bees play an important role in the pollination of many types of flowers.

propagation n. the act of breeding, multiplying, increasing, or spreading out for the purpose of reproduction. Creatures survive by propagating their species, and the ones that do not propagate go extinct.

qualitative adj. refers to the quality of something rather than the amount of something. Qualitative data is useful information even if there is not a lot of it.

quantitative adj. refers to the amount of something rather than the quality of something. The data is quantitative in amount but not very useful because a lot of it is inaccurate.

quantum adj. something very small. Quantum mechanics is the study of matter and energy at a very small, quantum, or sub-atomic scale.

seismic adj. large in nature, derived from seismic energy vibrations created from earthquakes. Scientists detected a lot of seismic activity before the earthquake. The fallout from the politician's scandal was seismic in nature.

sphere 1.something round in shape, or spherical, like a planet and its orbiting bodies. The earth is a sphere. 2. sphere of influence are things affected by something close, such as a group of people whom someone has contact with. He can use his sphere of influence to find a new job.

spectrum n. range of something. Light is made from different wavelengths of electromagnetic radiation on the visible spectrum. The ball player's talents covered the spectrum of athletic ability.

subterranean adj. below ground. Caves can reveal the presence of an entire subterranean world.

symbiosis n. a relationship in which different groups benefit the other in some way. There is a great deal of symbiosis in nature between plant and animal life. / **symbiotic** adj. Flowers and bees have a symbiotic relationship.

synthesis n. the putting together of smaller elements to form a whole substance. The synthesis of different compounds was necessary to complete the experiment. /**synthesize** v. The detective had to synthesize all the information to solved the case.

Fill in the bank quiz # 3

1. The act of breeding or multiplying is known as _____.

2. _____ refers to how good something is, or its quality.

3. _____ refers to a number, or how many of something.

4. _____ mechanics is the study of very small particles of matter and energy.

5. If something is _____ then it is very large or important.

6. Something round in shape, such as a ball or planet, is known as a _____.

7. The electromagnetic _____ contains a range of wavelengths.

8. The _____ cave was deep underground.

9. Bees and flowers have a _____ relationship.

10. To put different parts together to make a whole substance or idea is known as
_____.

---

terrestrial adj. of the earth. The planet contains countless examples of terrestrial life. Anything not from earth would be extra-terrestrial.

trait n. genetic information that is passed down form parent to offspring. Traits are inherited but not characteristics.

translucent adj. letting light through but not able to clearly see through. The frosted glass on the shower door is translucent to protect the privacy of the person in the shower.

velocity n. the speed and direction of an object. Knowing a car's speed is not the same as its velocity unless you also include the car's direction.

vertebrate n. a creature that has a backbone. Humans and many animals are vertebrates.

volume n. the amount of three-dimensional space in an object or that an object occupies. The amount of liquid a container will hold always refers to its volume. Area is measured in two dimensions, such as length and width, but volume is measured in three dimensions of length, width, and height.

zoology n. the study of animals and their scientific classifications, <u>physiology</u>, <u>habitats</u>, and behavior. Zoology covers many aspects of animal life.

Fill in the blank quiz # 4

1. If something is _____ then it is from the earth.

2. A human is a _____ because humans have a backbone.

3. In physics _____ is the speed and direction of an object.

4. The amount of liquid or gas a container can hold is known as its _____.

5. If something lets light through but you still cannot see through it clearly then it is _____.

6. Eye color is an example of a _____.

Literary Devices and Terms

Again, try typing any of the words in this section into an online dictionary App (application) or website, or using a simple internet search engine, such as Google, and it will give you the ability to hear the word pronounced correctly if your computer or smart phone has a speaker. Try it!

active voice in writing, active voice is where the subject in a sentence performs the action, as opposed to passive voice, where the subject receives some type of action in a sentence. Active voice sentences are easier to read, are often short, make more sense, and are preferred for academic writing.

allegory story that is used to symbolize a message about real-life events. Some people believe the Wizard of Oz was an allegory symbolizing the plight of farmers, the Populist Movement, and the Gold Standard.

alliteration a series of words or phrases that start with the same sound. Alliteration is common in poetry.

allusion when an author makes an indirect reference to something or to an idea originating from beyond the text. If someone calls you a "Benedict Arnold" they are saying you are acting like a traitor by alluding to the soldier who betrayed the United States in the Revolutionary War.

anachronism this is when something is out of place in time or there is a mistake in the chronology of events. A story set in Middles Ages where a character has a cell phone would be an anachronism. / **anachronistic** adj.

antagonist this is usually the bad guy in the story, or someone who opposes someone else. In Harry Potter, Voldemort was the antagonist.

anthropomorphism this is when something nonhuman such as an animal, place, or object actually behaves as if it were human. Mickey Mouse acting like an actual person is an example of anthropomorphism.

characterization this is how something is characterized, or represented, or described. The characterization of the town made it sound like an awful place to live.

colloquialism this is the use of informal language and slang, or speech common to a particular area and is used to create a of sense of realism. Mark Twain used a lot of colloquialisms in the books Tom Sawyer and Huckleberry Finn.

climax this is the high point of a story or when a story reaches its most exciting part. The climax in Return of the Jedi is when Luke Skywalker battled Darth Vader.

conflict this is the struggle or problem in a story or when people or ideas opposes one another. The conflict in Lord of the Flies could be considered man versus man.

connotation the implied meaning of words, not their literal meaning. The Soup Nazi in the Seinfeld show was not really a Nazi, but it was a connotation referencing the Nazi's strict adherence to rules.

denouement this is a French word that literally means the untying of something, and it refers to the resolution of a story when all problems are solved and questions are answered.

diction refers to word choice. Academic writing requires higher levels of diction.

didactic this is an adjective that negatively describes someone when they are acting too much like a teacher.

dramatic irony: literary tool to create drama when the audience or reader is aware of the true intentions or outcomes in a story but the characters are unaware. This allows the reader or audience to have a different understanding of what is going on than the characters.

genre refers to a category of literature or artistic composition, such as poetry, prose, fiction, non-fiction, and media

euphemism this is a tool to use a more subtle, gentler, or more indirect word or expression instead of a word that would be considered more harsh. Telling someone they like to be in control is a euphemism for acting bossy.

falling action events in a story after the climax and resolution

fate one's destiny or events that happen to someone beyond their control. The story of Oedipus Rex contains cruel twists of fate and much irony.

foreshadowing is when an author indirectly hints at things to come later in the story.

Fill in the blank quiz # 5

1. The Wizard of Oz is believed by some to be an _____.
2. Calling someone a "Daddy Warbucks" is an example of an _____.
3. If something occurs out of sequence in time then it is an _____.
4. In Harry Potter, Voldemort is the _____.
5. Mickey Mouse is an example of _____.
6. A _____ is a word or phrase, such as slang, that is common to a particular location.
7. When something is implied but not a directly stated then it is a _____.
8. French word for the resolution of a plot _____.
9. _____ creates drama when the audience knows something the characters do not.
10. Poetry, music, prose, and fiction are examples of _____.
11. The high point of a plot is the _____.
12. Destiny or events beyond one's control are known as _____.

hubris excessive self-confidence or pride. A person's hubris can often lead to their downfall.

hyperbole this is an exaggerated statement not meant to be taken literally. It is often used for effect or emphasis.

iambic pentameter a line of prose or poetry that consists of iambs, or five metrical feet consisting of one short/unstressed syllable, and followed by one long/stressed syllable. From the Greek "penta" for "five." Shakespeare was known for his use of iambic pentameter.

idiom figure of speech whose meaning cannot be understood from the literal meaning of the words used in the phrase. Examples include: beat around the bush, cold feet, dime a dozen, back to the drawing board, etc.

imagery this is a tool an author uses to describes a scene or to help the reader visualize something.

irony is when a statement or event is used to express the opposite meaning of the one literally expressed. There is **verbal irony**, often used to he sarcastic; **situational irony** is where the outcome of something is the opposite of what might be expected, and **dramatic irony**. Captain Ahab's fate contained a cruel bit of irony.

juxtaposition this is the comparing and contrasting of two or more different, often opposing, ideas or characters, sometimes to highlight the differences. The juxtaposition of Yoda and the Emperor shows they could not have more been unlike.

metaphor a device to describe or compare objects, people, ideas, or places in non-literal terms. Calling the man's backyard The Garden of Eden is a metaphor for describing how beautiful it is.

mood this is the feeling the writer wants the audience to have.

onomatopoeia this is a word or phrase that represents a sound or imitates the sound it stands for. "Baa" is the sounds a sheep makes.

oxymoron this is a combination of two words that express a contradictory meaning, like a short skyscraper.

palindrome a word or phrases that is spelled the same backwards as it is forwards, such as madam, kayak, and rotor.

passive voice in writing creates a sentence where the subject receives some type of action, as opposed to active voice where the subject performs an action. **Passive voice** often produces unclear, wordy, and ambiguous sentences and is not preferred for academic or formal writing.

paradox a statement that contains a contradiction or something that appears to be not possible, but might actually be possible. A self-admitted liar saying he is telling the truth would be a paradox. Going back in time to prevent your birth would be a paradox.

personification when a object, place, or something other non-human is described as having human-like qualities or characteristics to create imagery. From the verb "personify," as in embody or exemplify. Carl Sandburg used personification when he described Chicago as the city of big shoulders.

protagonist the central character in a story, the good guy.

quatrain I n poetry this is a stanza, or paragraph, of exactly four lines

repetition this is a device when a word or phrase is written multiple times, usually for emphasis.

resolution the final part of a story where problems are resolved. Also known as the denouement.

rising action series of events in a story that creates suspense leading to a climax.

setting this is where the story takes place.

Fill in the blank quiz # 6

1. Exaggerated statements not meant to be taken literally are known as _____.

2. _____ is when the outcome of something is the opposite of what was expected.

3. Comparing the beliefs of Yoda and Darth Vader is an example of _____.

4. Calling someone's beautiful backyard the Garden of Eden is an example of a _____.

5. A word that represents a sound is called _____.

6. Two words together that contradict each other is an _____.

7. Going back in time to prevent your birth is an example of a _____.

8. Giving non-human objects a human-like characteristic is known as _____.

9. The central character of a story is the _____.

10. The part of a story where all problems are resolved is the _____.

11. _____ leads to the climax.

12. Excessive pride is known as _____.

---

simile a simile is a type of metaphor in which something is compared to something else using the words "like" or "as." Saying the pool water is like bath water is an example of a simile.

soliloquy a monologue used in dramas. Aa soliloquy is when a character speaks aloud to himself and in doing so reveals his inner thoughts and feelings. Shakespeare's characters were known for their long soliloquies.

sonnet a poem of 14 rhyming lines. Sonnets are often about love.

style the method and techniques in which an author writes, including the use of literary devices, text structure, word choice, tone, etc. There are four basic types of literary writing...persuasive, narrative, descriptive, and expository writing, which includes informative writing.

symbolism the use of an object, event, person, or other idea that represents, or symbolizes something else of deeper meaning. The image of the torn of picture of her friend contained a great deal of symbolism.

theme an underlying meaning or idea that runs throughout the story. The challenges of being a teenager is a common theme in many coming-of-age stories.

tone this is the writer's attitude toward something.

tragedy/Greek tragedy something dramatic that causes suffering, unhappiness, and loss; a story that has a great deal of dramatic irony and twists of fate. The ancient Greeks were known for their tragedies that often taught some type of moral lesson.

transcendentalism (tran-sen-den-tuh-liz-um) n. philosophical movement of the 1820s and 1830s that emphasized the importance of thought and reason over experience and stressed individualism, idealism, and nature. Transcendentalism worked its way into American literature in the early 19th century. / **transcendentalist** n. Henry David Thoreau and Ralf Waldo Emerson were famous transcendentalist writers.

vernacular the common, everyday language of people in a particular area. Mark Twain, Chaucer, and Dante were known for writing in the vernacular.

voice this refers to the author's voice, which can include the author's writing style and point of view and is important in expository and informative writing. Author's voice is something personal and unique to that author. Examples include academic-style writing, which is very formal and has many declaratory statements as opposed to a conversational or vernacular style. There is also character's voice, which refers to the way a character views the world.

Fill in the blank quiz # 7

1. "Her eyes are as blue as the ocean" is an example of a _____.

2. A long speech given by a character to himself or herself is called a _____.

3. _____ is the use of an object or idea to represent something else of deeper meaning.

4. The author's _____ is his or hers attitude toward something.

5. The ancient Greeks were known for their _____, which were stories filled with much suffering but often meant to teach a moral lesson.

6. Mark Twain and Chaucer were known for writing in the _____.

Math Terms

absolute value the distance from zero a number is on a number line and is always a positive number

acute angle an angle that is less than 90°

adjacent angles two angles with a common side and <u>vertex</u>, which is the point where two lines (rays) meet to form an angle

algebra a branch of mathematics that uses symbols or letters to represent numbers, values, or <u>variables</u> in an operation or formula to solve equations

algorithm a step-by-step procedure, especially in computer programs, that spells out how directions or operations should be carried out. Mapping software uses advanced algorithms to map out directions for people from one point to another.

array an arrangement of numbers or objects into columns and rows. A multiplication table is an example of an array.

area The space within a shape and expressed in square units of measure. The room needs 20 square feet of carpeting.

axiom an idea or hypothesis that has not been proved or demonstrated but is generally accepted, often as a basis for deducing or inferring other truths.

bell curve named for the shape of a graphed line that shows a normal distribution of results in probability and statistics. Some teachers use a bell curve to calculate grades for their classes based on how the entire of the class performed.

binomial an algebraic expression that has two terms

Fill in the blank quiz # 8

1. An _____ angle is less than 90°.

2. An _____ is a set of step-by-step procedures a computer program follows.

3. _____ angles have a common side and vertex.

4. Multiplication tables are an example of an _____.

5. _____ is the distance a number is on a number line.

6. Teachers often use a _____ to grade students.

7. A mathematical expression with two terms is called a _____.

8. The space within a two-dimensional shape is known as its _____.

---

bisect to divide into two equal sections or where one line crosses another

48

calculus a branch of advanced mathematics using <u>derivatives</u> and <u>integrals</u>, often used to study motion and changing values

Cartesian coordinates numbers that represent a point or location on a plane or graph derived from the point's distance from starting point and usually expressed as the X axis and Y axis

circumference the distance around a circle

coefficient the number in front of a <u>variable</u> in an equation or formula. For example, in 3x + 2y, "3" and "2" are the coefficients.

common denominator number that can be divided evenly by all denominators in a math problem

complementary angles two angles that when added together equal 90°

congruent /congruent angles angles that are exactly the same. Angles that have the same exact measurement.

constant a variable whose value does not change

denominator the bottom number of a fraction

Fill on the blank quiz # 9

1. The distance around a circle is known as its _____.
2. In 3x + 2y, "3" is known as the _____.
3. If two angles are added together and equal 90°, then they are called _____.
4. Angles that have exactly the same measurement are called _____.
5. A _____ is a variable whose value does not change.
6. To cut something in two is to _____ it.
7. The x and y numbers on a plane or graph are known as _____.
8. The bottom number of a fraction is called the _____.
9. _____ uses derivatives and integrals to study motion and changing values.
10. The _____ can be divided by all the denominators in a math problem.

---

derivative: used in calculus to show the rate of change or as a measure of how a function or curve changes as its input changes and expressed as a unit of differentiation.

diameter the distance across the center of a circle, the width of a circle.

exponent number that can be either positive or negative that expresses the power to which a number is raised or lowered and is positioned above and to the right of the number. Exponents are often used in science to show very large or very small numbers. / **exponential** adj. / **exponentially** adv. The company saw exponential growth. With compound interest, money can grow exponentially.

Fibonacci sequence set of numbers formed by adding the last two numbers together to get the next number in the series. Each number in a series is the sum of the two previous numbers…0, 1, 1, 2, 3, 5, 8, 13, 21, 34, 55, 89, etc. Also known as the Golden Ratio in nature because this pattern seems to occur in nature, such as the pattern of pedals on a flower, patterns on leaves, patterns on pine cones, etc.

function this is the relationship between input (x-values) and outputs (y-values), such as $y=f(x)$ or $f(x)=x+1$

geometry branch of mathematics dealing with the size, shape, and position of lines, shapes, angles, and other figures

hypotenuse the side opposite from the 90° angle in a right triangle

improper fraction fraction in which the numerator is larger than the denominator

inequality looks like an equation but uses inequality signs such as less than (<), greater than (>), less than or equal to (≤), or greater than or equal to (≥)

integer a whole number that can be positive, negative, or zero

integral mathematical component of calculus that represents the area or a generalization of an area

interval numbers within two specific boundaries, such as "all the numbers between 5 and 25" or the time between two values, such as the time between 10:00 am and 10:30am. The crime was committed between the interval of 10:00 am and 10:30am.

Fill in the blank quiz # 10

1. A type of equation that uses less than or more than symbols is called an _____.

2. The side of a right triangle that is opposite the 90° angle is called the _____.

3. A _____ defines the relationship between inputs and outputs in a mathematical problem.

4. If something grows _____ that means it grows very fast.

5. An _____ raises or lowers numbers to a power and shows very small or very large numbers.

6. The distance across a circle is called the _____.

7. An _____ is a fraction where the numerator is larger than the denominator.

8. An _____ is a whole number that can be positive, negative, or zero.

9. The time between midnight and 5:00am is called an _____.

10. A _____ is used in calculus to show a rate of change or how a function changes when the input changes.

---

irrational number number that is not rational, which means it cannot be written as a simple fraction

Isosceles triangle triangle with two equal sides

linear in a straight line or a function that produces a straight line when graphed

mean average number in a set of numbers

median middle number or item in a list

mode a number that occurs most often in a set. Out of 3,4,5,5,5,7, the mode is 5.

numerator top number of a fraction

multiple all the numbers that are products of the original number and any other integer, such as 2,4,6,8,10.

obtuse angle an angle that is larger than 90° but less than 180°

ordered pair the set of (x,y) coordinates on a plane

Fill in the blank quiz # 11

1. An _____ angle is larger than 90° but less than 180°.

2. An _____ triangle is a triangle with two equal sides.

3. The _____ is the same as the average of a set of numbers.

4. _____ means in a straight line.

5. The top number in a fraction is called the _____.

6. The set of x and y coordinates on a plane is called an _____.

7. The _____ is the number that occurs most often in a set.

8. _____ refers to the middle number in a list.

9. The numbers 5,10,15, and 20 are _____ of the number 5.

10. An _____ is a number that cannot be written as a simple fraction.

---

outlier a number or item that is most unlike others. Out of 15, 20, 25, 1500, 1500 would be the outlier.

parabola a symmetrical, u-shaped curve on a graph or plane where any two sets of points are equidistant from a fixed focus point

parallel lines two or more lines next to each other and running the same way that never meet or cross

perpendicular lines two lines that intersect at right angles

plane flat, two-dimensional surface that can be real or theoretical

polynomial expression in algebra that consists of two or more terms

polygon shape with many sides, usually more than 4 sides

prime number number that can only be divided by itself and 1

probability theory the branch of mathematics that deals with predicting random <u>variables</u> and events, such as the likelihood of something happening. Gambling contains a lot of mathematical probability.

product the answer in a multiplication problem. In 2x2=4, the product is 4.

proportion equation that represents the relationship between a sub group and the total group, like saying 4 out of 5 students passed the test.

Pythagorean theorem theorem from Greek mathematician Pythagoras dealing with right triangles where the sum of the squares of a right triangle's two sides is equal to the square of the hypotenuse, or $a^2 + b^2 = c^2$

quadratic equation is an equation to the second degree made of four terms with at least one the terms being squared. The standard form a quadratic equation is $ax^2+bx+c=0$

quotient the answer in a division problem. The quotient of 20 divided by 5 is 4.

radius   the length from the center of a circle to the outside of the circle

range the distance or difference between the largest and smallest number

Fill in the blank quiz # 12

1. Lines that run next to each other and never cross are called _____.

2. Lines that intersect at right angles are called _____.

3. Trying to predict future events mathematically is called _____.

4. A flat, two-dimensional surface that is real or imagined is called a _____.

5. A _____ is a shape with more than four sides.

6. A _____ is an algebraic expression that has two or more terms.

7. The answer in a multiplication problem is called the _____.

8. The answer in a division problem is call the _____.

9. A _____ is a number that can only be divided by itself and 1.

10. $a^2 + b^2 = c^2$ is the bases of the _____.

11. The distance from the center of a circle to the outside of the circle is called the
    _____.

12. The difference between the largest and smallest numbers in a set is called the
    _____.

13. A _____ is an equation that has four terms with at least one of them being
    squared.

14. An _____ is something that is most unlike the other numbers or items in a
    set.

15. A symmetrical, u-shaped curve where all the points are equidistant from the focus point is
    called a _____.

ratio comparison between two values that can be expressed in different ways, such as x:y, x/y, or x is to y. The ratio of red cars to blue cars is 2:1, meaning there are twice as many red cars as there are blue ones.

reciprocal the inverse of a number. For example, the reciprocal of 3/4 is 4/3. / **reciprocity** is the state of having a reciprocal ability or arrangement. Some states have reciprocity in licensing laws, which means if you are licensed in one state for something then your license is valid in the other state.

right angle angle which measures 90°

scalene triangle triangle where none of the sides or angles are equal

supplementary angles two angles that when added together equal 180°

symmetrical/symmetry looking the same or is the same size on both sides. A line of symmetry divides two sides that are the same in size or appearance. Many architectural designs are symmetrical because the symmetry creates a balance that is pleasing and simple in appearance.

tangent term used in geometry to refer to a straight line that touches a curve on a plane at some point but does not cross the curve. Not to be confused with the tangent function in trigonometry, which is derived from dividing the length of the opposite side in a right triangle over the length of the adjacent side of a right triangle.

trigonometry branch of mathematics that deals with relationships between the sides and the angles of right triangles and the accompanying trigonometric functions of sine, cosine, and tangent

variable 1. A symbol that represents a number in a formula, operation, or expression such 2x where "x" is the variable. 2. Something that can change the outcome of something. Too many variables affect the weather making it hard to predict.

vector object in math or physics that has magnitude (speed or force) and direction.

vertex the point where lines (rays) meet to form an angle

volume amount of something which can be held in a three-dimensional container or space and measured in cubic units. The volume of dirt that had to be removed to build the swimming pool was 400 cubic yards.

Fill in the blank quiz # 13

1. The _____ is the point where lines meet to form an angle.

2. _____ are two angles that when added equal 180°.

3. The comparison of two numbers is known as a _____.

4. If two ratios are equal it is called a _____.

5. A _____ equals 90°.

6. If something is _____ that means it is the same on both sides.

7. A _____ is an object that has both speed or direction.

8. A _____ is something that changes or is unknown.

9. The amount of cubic space within a three-dimensional container is known as _____.

10. The inverse of a number is called the _____.

11. A _____ is a triangle where none of the sides are equal.

Economics and Personal Finance Terms

Financial literacy is the key to becoming financially independent and to understanding the economic and financial forces that affect people's lives. The more a person understands the vocabulary associated with personal finance the less likely a person will be taken advantage of or make bad decisions regarding his or her personal finances, and the more likely they will be able to leverage their financial situation into a higher standard of living. There are countless books and articles that educate people on personal finance and general economic activity, but having a working understanding of the vocabulary used in these fields is crucial to unlocking the information in these informative works and in documents and financial products people encounter in their adult lives. Having a fundamental understanding of economic terms helps people understand the world around them and the forces that shape economic health of one's city, state, and country. Again, try typing any word into an online dictionary App (application) or website, or using a simple internet search engine, such as Google, and it will give you the ability to hear the word pronounced correctly if your computer or smart phone has a speaker. Try it!

accrue to acquire, to add to, or build upon. Interest accrues every month the loan still has a balance.

aggregate the sum total of something whole formed by combining several other parts or materials. The aggregate of all the product sales yielded the company a profit. The aggregate of goods and services in the economy forms the basis for the Gross Domestic Product.

adjustable rate mortgage (ARM) type of loan where the interest rate can change over time when the federal interest rates change. Many people found themselves in trouble when the rate went up on their ARM, and they were no longer able to afford the higher payment on their mortgage.

amortization the calculation of loan payments based on the number of years or payments the loan is spread out over, with the amount owed deceasing with each payment. The interest rates are usually higher on loans where the amortization is based on a longer period of time. /**amortize** v. The loan was amortized over thirty years.

annual percentage rate (APR) the total cost of borrowing money on a yearly basis including interest and other fees. The APR on a loan is often higher than the listed interest rate because it also includes other costs and fees associated with the loan.

annuity a type of investment, usually a retirement investment, that pays out a fixed amount of money every year when the investment annuitizes, or reaches the annuitization phase (payout phase). Annuities are a great way to save and plan for retirement.

appraisal an estimation of the value of something, such as a home, business, or valuable item. An appraisal is always required before a bank will lend someone money to buy a house. / **appraised** v. The antique bed was appraised for a lot of money.

appreciation to increase in value over time. The appreciation on real estate is usually greater than on cars. /**appreciate** v.

asset property or items one has that have value or that are worth money. A person's home is usually their most important asset. A house, a car, a savings account, and a retirement account are all examples of assets. A bank might look at all your assets as collateral before giving you a loan.

balance/balance of payments the amount still owed on a bill or loan. After their last payment they only had a small balance left on their credit card.

balloon payment a payment that pays off the remaining balance of a loan. The loan was for five years with a balloon payment at the end. Be careful of loans with a balloon payment because you might wind up having to pay off the entire loan sooner than possible.

Fill in the blank quiz # 14

1. An estimation of value is an _____.

2. _____ occurs when something increases in value.

3. The interest on the loan will continue to _____ until the loan is paid off.

4. The loan payments were _____ over a 30 year period.

5. The loan has a large _____ where the rest of the loan has to be paid off all at one time.

6. _____, or all the things you own that are worth money, such cars, homes, and stocks.

7. The amount still owed on something is called the _____.

8. The total interest and other fees associated each year with a loan is called the _____.

9. The interest on an _____ can increase and cause the payments to increase too.

10. Something whole formed by combining other materials is called an _____.

11. An _____ is a great way to plan for retirement because it pays out a fixed sum of money every year.

---

bond a financial certificate sold by governments to raise money where the buyer of the bond is guaranteed to receive a specific amount of money or interest over a specific amount of time when the bond matures. When interest rates were high savings bonds were common investments. The city sold bonds to pay for the new park. Bonds were sold by the U.S. government to help pay for World War II.

capital money, money to start a business. They had to raise a lot of capital to start their business.

capitalism n. economic system organized around the private ownership of property and the means of the production and distribution of goods and services; characterized by competition, supply and demand, profit-making, and using market forces over government regulations to determine prices, wages, and goods to be produced; factories, land, resources, and distribution facilities all owned by individuals and not the government. The United States economy is based on free-market capitalism.

certificate of deposit (CD) type of savings account that usually yields a higher interest rate than a regular savings account but requires that a certain amount of money be left in the account for a certain amount of time. There are penalties associated with withdrawing money early from a CD.

56

collateral something of value, usually in the form of <u>assets</u>, that is promised to a lender if the borrower <u>defaults</u> on a loan. The bank wanted to use the man's house as collateral before giving him a business loan.

commerce another word for business or trade or the of buying and selling goods or services. The rate of commerce is an indication of the health of the economy.

commercial having to do with business or the buying and selling of goods and services. The commercial activity in the town dropped when the factory closed.

commercial loan a loan to buy a business. The lending terms are quite different for commercial property loans compared to a residential mortgage loan for a house.

commercial property an income-producing property such as an apartment building, strip mall, storefront, or office building. Commercial property is appraised much differently than a house.

commodity an economic good or item that has value and is used by people, usually a raw material, natural resource, or agricultural product and that's price is affected by its availability and the <u>supply and demand</u> of the product. Oil, soy beans, copper, natural gas, beef, hogs, corn, wheat, oranges, and gold are examples of commodities. The Chicago Board of Trade is the largest <u>commodities market</u> in the world and was established in 1848 to handle all the agriculture products coming through the city.

commodities market a <u>market</u>, or trading place where commodities are bought and sold. The Chicago Board of Trade is the largest commodities market in the world and was established in 1848 to handle all the agriculture products coming through the city.

consumer price index measurement of the cost of living determined by the Bureau of Labor Statistics.

cooperative (co-op) a union of people that offers mutual assistance in working toward a common goal, often owned and run by its members who share profits, benefits, and responsibilities. The apartment building is operated as a cooperative. Many small farmers have joined cooperatives to keep prices down and take advantage of the <u>economies of scale</u>.

cosigner a person who signs for the loan in addition to the primary borrower. The bank required the person to have a cosigner for the loan. A cosigner is still responsible for the loan even if the primary borrower defaults on the loan or cannot make the payments.

credit /credit rating/credit score a term to describe how credit-worthy a person is or how likely they are to repay their debts based a person's history of paying back loans and making payments in a complete and timely manner. Good credit is necessary to get a loan and a good interest rate. Missing payments, late payments, high credit card balances, too much debt, or failing to pay back money all negatively affect one's credit rating.

credit union financial union or <u>cooperative</u> organization whose members have something in common, such as where they work, where they live, or membership in a union, and uses the members' money they contribute to provide savings accounts and installment loans specifically for their members and pays interest on accounts in the form of <u>dividends</u>. Credit unions often have more competitive interest or fee rates than commercial banks.

Fill in the blank quiz # 15

1. The city sold _____ to finance the new library.

2. The man needed a _____ for the bank to give him the loan.

3. Any type of economic good that has value and is used by people is called a _____.

4. _____ is another word for business or trade or the buying and selling of goods.

5. Another word for money is _____.

6. The bank required the man put up something of value called _____, before giving him the loan.

7. Your _____ describes your history of paying back loans and debts in a timely manner.

8. A _____ is a union of similar people that offers each other mutual assistance.

9. _____ refers to something that makes money, such as an apartment or office building.

10. A _____ is type of long-term savings account that pays more interest than a regular savings account.

---

compound interest interest that is earned on top of the principal and interest that has already been earned, or <u>accrued</u>. Compound interest makes it possible to save large amounts of money over time as the compounding interest grows the investment at an exponential rate over time. Make sure your retirement account utilizes compound interest and start investing early in life to take advantage of the <u>time value of money</u>.

currency money. Currency from different countries have different values because of their <u>exchange rates</u>. Twenty dollars in United States currency is not the same as twenty <u>Eurodollars</u>.

debit n. or v. to withdraw money or have money withdrawn from an account, a payment. The payment showed up as a debit in her checking account. The payment was automatically debited from her account.

default to fall behind or be unable to pay back a loan or make payments on time

deficit the amount of money by which something is too small or shorted, a negative imbalance in the amount of money coming in versus going out. The business is running a deficit until sales pick up. The United States has a trade deficit with China.

depreciation a decrease in the value of something. The depreciation on cars is very high. / **depreciate** v. Cars depreciate faster than many other goods; they are a depreciating <u>assets</u>.

dividend money paid to <u>shareholders</u> or investors of a company based on the company's earnings and usually paid on a regular basis, usually every fiscal quarter. Stocks that pay dividends make it possible to earn money now or can sometimes be reinvested to buy more shares of stock.

disclosure the act of revealing all the important facts about a business, product, or transaction. The homeowner had to sign a disclosure revealing any possible defects with the house to the seller. /

disclose v. The attorney was forced to disclose his interest in the property before the sale.

economy the wealth and financial resources of a country including trade, employment, and business production. If a country's economy is healthy than employment rates are high. / **economics.** The study of the economy. The health of a country's economy is usually measured by the growth in the country's GDP (Gross Domestic Product) each fiscal quarter or year.

economies of scale the notion that the cost per unit of something is less when manufacturing, buying, or selling things in large quantities or in bulk instead of one at a time. It costs less per pencil to make 10,000 pencils at a time rather than making 100 pencils at a time. Large companies are able to take advantage of the economies of scale to sell their products for less money than smaller companies.

electronic funds transfer (EFT) having money sent electronically from one account to another. The health club uses an EFT billing program to debit payments directly from members' checking accounts.

employment/employment rate the number of people working in the job force. If a country's economy is healthy than employment rates are high.

equity the amount of value in something after debts or loan amounts are taken into consideration. The equity one has in their home is the value of the home minus the amount they still owe on their home.

Eurodollars (Euro) currency of the countries that belong to the European Union

exchange rate the value of one country's currency compared to another country's form of currency. One U.S. dollar is not the same as one Peso or one Euro because the exchange rates are different.

export(s) 1. v. to sell goods to other countries 2. n. goods that are sold to other countries. A country should strive to be independent or export more goods than it imports.

Fill in the blank quiz # 16

1. A form a money that differs from one country to another is called _____.

2. Revealing important facts or information about a business or a product is called _____.

3. The amount of value in something after all debts or loans are considered is called _____.

4. It is cheaper to produce things all at once in large quantities because of the _____.

5. To _____ on a loan means to not pay it back.

6. _____ occurs when something goes down in value.

7. When the amount needed for something is less than the money there is for something, it is called a _____.

8. A _____ is paid to shareholders of a company based on the company's earnings.

9. Interest that builds on previously earned interest is known as _____.

10. To withdraw money is known as a _____.

11. The value of one country's currency to another's is called the _____.

12. _____ refers to the wealth, resources, and business production of a country.

13. Goods sold to other countries are called _____.

Federal Deposit Insurance Corporation (FDIC) a federal government corporation that protects and insures people's banking deposits up to certain amount set by federal law. The FDIC was established in 1933 during the Great Depression. Make sure your bank accounts are FDIC insured.

federal funds rate is the interest rate banks charge other banks to borrow money so they can maintain the reserve funds required by federal law and is controlled by the Federal Reserve System of the United States, which acts as the central bank of the country. The federal funds rate affects the interest rates charged on auto loans, mortgages, bank deposits, credit cards, and a several other types of loans. The Fed raises or lowers rates to control the money supply in circulation, which affects economic growth and inflation, but also impacts the cost of borrowing money.

Federal Reserve System/Bank acts as the central bank of the United States and is composed of the twelve federal banks in districts throughout the country operating under the Federal Reserve System that manages the country's monetary supply through the federal funds rates, regulates the banking industry, protects consumers, and serves as the bank for the U.S. Treasury.

finance v. to pay for something or provide money (funds) for something . The house was financed with a home loan called a mortgage. / **finance** n. the management of large amounts of money. Many bankers and business people need a degree in finance for their jobs.

finance charge the fee charged for borrowing money often expressed as a percentage. The finance charges on credit cards are usually quite high and makes it hard to pay off the balance if only making minimum payments.

fiscal policy the ideas and actions a governments takes toward the city, state, or nation's economy. A candidate's fiscal policy should be considered when deciding whom to vote for in an election.

fixed rate an interest rate that is locked in and will not change over the life of the loan. A fixed interest rate loan is less risky than an adjustable rate loan.

funds/funding n. money to pay for something. The man did not have the funds to buy a new car. A new source of funding was needed to start the business. / **fund** v. to provide money for something. The man needed to find a new way to fund his business.

futures/futures market a type of commodities contract where the price of a good is specified for future delivery to protect buyers and sellers of commodities against unexpected changes in price and used by investment speculators to make a profit by betting the price of goods will increase over what they paid for them.

graduated payment type of payment that gradually (slowly) increases over time. School loans often have graduated repayment plans so that loan payments increase as the income of students is expected to increase over time once they find jobs and establish a career.

Fill in the blank quiz # 17

1. _____ means the interest rate is locked in and will not change.

2. A source of money to pay for something is known as _____.

3. A _____ is a loan payment that increases over time.

4. _____ determines what interest rate banks charge for loans.

5. The management of large amounts of money is known as _____.

6. The _____ is the fee charged for borrowing money.

7. The _____ protects people's bank deposits.

8. The _____ manages the country's money supply and regulates banks.

9. _____ refers to the government's ideas and actions toward the economy.

10. _____ is the type of market where the price of goods is specified for future delivery.

---

gross the total amount of something before taxes, expenses, and deductions. The worker's gross paycheck was $2,000, but after taxes she only netted $1,200. / **gross** v. The company grossed $12 million in sales but after all expenses were paid their net profit was only $5 million.

Gross Domestic Product (GDP) to total value of goods and services produced in the country and a strong measure of the country's economic health. The higher the GDP the better the economy is doing.

import(s) 1. v. to bring into a country. 2. n. Goods that are bought and brought into one country from another. Too many imports can lead to trade deficit for a country.

Individual retirement account (IRA) personal retirement savings accounts that have special guidelines and income tax rules different from regular savings accounts. Everyone should invest in some type of IRA as soon as possible because they help people save money for retirement and take advantage of <u>compounding interest</u> over a long period of time.

inflation the rate of increase of the price of goods and services in a country accompanied by the decreasing value of money since purchasing power is diminished due to the higher costs of goods. Countries cannot simply print more money for people because it would lead to massive inflation.

interest payment portion of the loan payment that is only paid toward the interest charged on the loan.

interest only loan type of loan, such as with a <u>Home Equity Line of Credit</u>, that only requires borrowers to make payments only based on the interest charge on the loan each month instead of interest and <u>principal</u>. Interest only loans are dangerous even though their payments are lower than conventional loans because you could make payments for years and still never pay down what is actually owned on the loan.

Home Equity Line of Credit (HELOC) type of loan where a bank lends money based on the amount of <u>equity</u> someone has in their home and is often referred to as a second mortgage. A HELOC is a great way to pay for major repairs to a house, but the HELOC often has to be paid off in a shorter amount of time than a regular mortgage and often has an <u>adjustable rate</u>.

levy n. a type of tax or fee, v. to place a tax or fee on something. The city imposed a new levy to pay for the new library. The city levied a new tax.

lien a judgment or legal right to a property until a debt is paid off. Mortgages and property taxes are examples of liens. If not paid the bank or the county that <u>levies</u> the property taxes can take your home.

margin 1. the different between what someone has and what someone needs. A large margin is desired between someone's monthly income and their bills if they want to have spending money and still be able to save money. The team won by a wide margin There can be no margin for error. 2. The amount of collateral someone puts up to buy something, such as stock. Too many stocks were bought on margin in the 1920s, which helped pave the way for Great Depression after the stock market crashed.

market/marketplace/market economy refers to the theoretical buying and selling of goods in the economy or the stock market where the price of goods and services is largely determined by supply and demand and competition rather than by government regulation. A business can only sell a product for as much as the market will bear, meaning, what people are willing to pay for it.

mature v. /**maturity** n. the date or length of time when a financial instrument is worth full value and can be redeemed without penalty. The CD matures in twelve months. The bond reaches maturity in three years.

Fill in the blank quiz # 18

1. The total amount of something before taxes or expenses is call the _____.

2. Goods brought into a country are called _____.

3. An increase in the cost of goods and services is called _____.

4. The total value of all goods and services produced in a country is called the _____.

5. A _____ is loan based on the amount of equity people have in their home.

6. When a financial instrument reaches full value it is said to _____.

7. The _____ is the theoretical buying and selling of goods in the economy.

8. Another word for a tax is a _____.

9. An _____ is a great way to save and build money for retirement.

10. The portion of a payment that only goes toward the interest owed on the loan is an _____.

11. The difference between what someone needs and what someone has for something is called the _____.

---

mortgage a loan on a home or building. Mortgage guidelines changed quite a bit after the Great Recession.

mutual fund an investment instrument that combines several different types of stocks into a fund rather than investing or buying only one type of stock. Mutual funds are often used for individual retirement accounts.

negative amortization when the principal balance on a loan increases over time instead of decreasing because the loan payments cannot keep up with the interest being charged because the interest keeps being added to the principal. HELOC loans can be a risk for negative amortization because of their adjustable interest rates and interest only payments.

net the amount left over after taxes and other expenses or deductions. The company grossed $12 million in sales but after all expenses were paid their net profit was only $5 million. / **net** v. The worker's gross paycheck was $2,000, but after taxes she only netted $1,200.

overdraft withdrawing more money than is in an account. The bank changed an overdraft fee for writing a check for more than the man had in his account.

pension form of retirement income provided by some private companies and many federal, state, and local governments for their employees, such as teachers, policemen, firemen, postal workers, and other government workers and known as a defined benefit plan because a person's retirement income is based on a specific formula related to the employee's and the employer's contributions over time rather than based on the stock market or other forces that can increase or decrease the amount in a retirement account. In general, pensions are safer than 401k-type retirement accounts because retirement income is not based on the stock market. Full pensions also typically pay much more than social security but maybe not as much as highly funded 401k-type accounts.

points prepaid interest on a loan where one point usually equals one percentage point of interest. Be careful of loans requiring you to pay points, however, points are a way of reducing the amount of interest you pay over the long term. Having a seller pay your points on a home loan might be a good negotiating strategy.

principal/ principal payments the original portion of a loan payment that goes directly to the balance owed on a loan and not the interest. Making extra payments directly toward the principal is a great way to save money over the long term and pay off a home loan faster.

profit margin margin needed by a business to turn a profit and make money.

prorated or pro rata Latin term meaning "according to the rate" that actually means in proportion to a total amount over a specific time of period. When you buy a house certain expenses such as taxes are billed or credited to either the buyer or seller on a prorated basis according to the number of days out of the month or year someone owns the home and will be responsible for the expenses.

recession a slowdown in the economy possibly accompanied by companies doing less business, making less money, and even laying off workers until business picks up again. There have been many recessions in our country's history, but the Great Recession of the early 2000s was the worst economic downturn since the Great Depression.

reserves the amount of money set aside for emergencies or to pay obligations. A bank might require a certain amount of reserves on hand to give someone a loan.

Fill in the blank quiz # 19

1. A _____ is a slowdown in the economy.

2. From Latin meaning "according to the rate" _____.

3. The original amount borrowed on a loan (the balance) is called the _____.

4. Money set aside for emergencies is known as _____.

5. Prepaid interest on loans are called _____.

6. The amount left over after taxes and other expenses is known as the _____.

7. Many people have defined-benefit retirement plans that are called a _____.

8. A loan for a house is called a _____.

9. The amount of money a business needs to make money after expenses is the _____.

10. A type of investment that combines many different types of stocks is called a _____.

---

revolving credit lines of credit such credit cards or store charge cards that can be used over and over again as the balance is paid down. These lines of credit usually have a limit to what can be charged on them.

securities financial instruments that have value such as shares of stock or debt liens such as mortgages. Securities can be bought and sold as a form of investment.

64

share/shareholder share of <u>stock</u>/ a person who owns shares of stock in a company. The major shareholders were not happy with the CEO (Chief Executive Officer) as the company was losing money.

simple interest interest on a loan that does not <u>compound</u> and is easy to calculate based on the daily interest rate, the principal, and the number of days between payments. Simple interest is most commonly used on car loans and other short-term loans.

socialism n. economic, social, and political system in which the government owns or tightly controls the major industries and means of production in an industrialized country, such as factories, transportation systems, health care, energy companies, etc., through regulations, price controls, and high taxes, with the proceeds being used to provide citizens with more social benefits and eliminate the historical criticisms associated with capitalism, such as worker exploitation, labor conflict, and the uneven distribution of wealth between rich and poor people. Socialism favors more government intervention in the economy and society than capitalism and has never worked where implemented.

speculate n. to bet, to wager, to make an educated guess on a financial risk or outcome in the hopes of making profit. People who invest in real estate speculate the property will rise in value. / **speculative** adj. The stock market is highly speculative. /**speculator** n. Real estate speculators can make a lot of money, but there can be a great deal of risk involved.

stock/stock market stock shares are a type of ownership in a company with the more stock someone owns the bigger share of the company they own. Stocks are sold by companies to raise money and bought by people as investments in the hope the price of the stock will increase if the company is successful. Stocks are bought and sold on the stock market.

supply and demand a main aspect of a capitalistic economy that says when the demand for something increases so does its value and therefor its price, but when supply is high because there is not enough demand then the value (the price of something) goes down. If a product sits on a store's shelves for months that means there is no demand for the product so the store has to lower the price to what people are willing to pay for it just to get the product sold.

tariff a tax a country places on <u>imports</u> or <u>exports</u>. Tariffs are often placed on cheaper imports coming into a country to protect the same kind of products that are made in the country that is <u>levying</u> the tariff.

tender to pay or give money. The customer tendered ten dollars to the cashier.

time value of money (TVM) 1. the ability of money to increase in value over time, which can be calculated with the interest rate and the length of time in which the money is invested. 2. The idea that a certain amount money or investment will be worth a lot more in the future based on its earnings potential. <u>Mutual funds</u> and other investments that utilize compound interest over a long period of time utilize the concept of the time value of money.

trade deficit the negative difference between what a country sells to other countries in the form of <u>exports</u> compared to what it buys as <u>imports</u>. The United States has a large trade deficit with China because China exports more products to the United States than in imports from the United States.

trust n. business or legal organization that takes control and manages the property or business of others. The parents put their house in a trust for their children.

unemployment rate the number of eligible workers in the county not actively employed in the workforce, expressed as a percentage, and used as a measure of the overall health of the <u>economy</u>.

U.S. Treasury Securities known as direct obligation securities issues by the United States government and the U.S. Treasury's Bureau of Public Debt, they are sold to investors as a way of raising money to finance the federal government. They include treasury bills, treasury bonds, and treasury notes.

variable rate interest rate on certain loans and adjustable rate mortgages that change or vary over time or with market forces, such as when general interest rates go up or down. Be care of loans with variable interest rates because your payments can increase dramatically if interest rates go up before you pay off the loan.

yield 1. n. the amount you make on something, such as an investment. The business venture did not yield as much money as we hoped. 2. v. to make or come away with, to produce. The business yielded a high profit.

Fill in the blank quiz # 20

1. A _____ takes a risk and makes an educated guess that something will increase in value.

2. A _____ is someone who owns shares of stock in a company.

3. Credit cards and store charge cards are examples of _____.

4. A type of ownership in a company expressed as shares of _____.

5. A legal organization that manages the property of others is called a _____.

6. The amount you make or walk away with from an investment is known as the _____.

7. A _____ loan means the interest rate can increase or decrease.

8. When supply goes up, _____ goes down.

9. When demand goes down, _____ go up.

10. Taxes on imports and exports are called _____.

11. The costumer _____ the money to the cashier.

12. Financial instruments that have value such as mortgages, debt liens, or stock shares are called _____.

13. A _____ occurs when a country imports more goods than it exports.

14. The _____ refers to the ability of money to increase over time based on its earning potential.

15. _____ is an economic system based on the private ownership of property.

16. _____ is an economic system based on government ownership of industry.

Resume Building and Interview Vocabulary

A person's vocabulary and speaking ability is a cumulative reflection of their knowledge, education, work or life experience, and general status in life. The words a person uses says a lot about who that person is, especially to a prospective employer or current boss. Unfortunately, many people no longer distinguish between personal and professional speaking and writing, a skill softened even more by the ubiquitous nature of social media that continues to skew the line between what is socially and professionally acceptable. A professional vocabulary can communicate your experience or expertise in a field and show an employer you are the right person for the job.

Online recruiting and networking sites that allow people to post resumes and search for jobs have changed the human resource industry, but setting one's self apart from others and convincing an employer you are the best candidate for the job is still the name of the game. Many online websites and job recruiters use computer programs to scan resumes for certain key words in an effort to save time and weed out less desirable applicants. According to an article titled "How to Make Your Resume Last More than 6 Seconds," by John Sanburn from April 13, 2012 in Time Magazines' business.time.com website, recruiters only spend about six seconds looking at a resume before going on the next one. If an applicant does not convey their expertise and sell themselves on why they are the best candidate for the job in a concise amount of space, they probably will not even get an interview. Resumes with poor grammar or punctuation or that use slang and other professionally unacceptable vocabulary most certainly will not be taken seriously.

Much of the vocabulary in this book can be used to convey a more professional image and combined with words common to a particular job will greatly enhance your chances of getting hired. With all this is mind, write your resume and cover letter and conduct your interview in a concise yet professional style. Use words that specifically highlight your skills, experience, and expertise. Research words and concepts related to the company or type of job you are applying for and provide concrete examples of your experience and success. Do not get hung up on empty buzzwords that everyone is using. Many buzzwords are overused and can actually hurt your chances of getting an interview even though they sound fancy. Do not simply use a buzz word like "skill set." Instead, explain what skills you have and give specific examples of how you have used those skills in a successful way. **And in an interview always find a way to turn a negative situation into a positive statement. Never speak negatively about previous jobs or employers!**

Also, change up your choice of words and avoid sounding repetitive in writing or in an interview. Use words and stories that inspire a manager to hire you. Use action words and specific examples that reflect your ability to set and achieve goals, meet deadlines, work with others, be creative, communicate with others of diverse backgrounds, and build consensus. Possible words to include are found in this section along with sample sentences. **Remember, you only have one chance to make a first impression!**

As an added bonus to help you, I have included a sample personal statement on the next page I have used. Several years ago I ran for teacher representative for my school's Local School Council and was elected. Only two candidates could be elected as representatives. Even though I was well-known and respected throughout the school, many people told me they really liked how I explained my experience and vision for the school in the personal statement all candidates submitted. For those who did not know me as well as others, the personal statement convinced many of them to vote for me. The personal statement on the next page can be used as an example for job or college applications, cover letters, or your own personal statement. It was the power of my vocabulary that supported and articulated my accomplishments in way that convinced others I was the right person for the job.

Personal Statement

"I began my career teaching 8th grade social studies in 1998. Since then I have worked in three public high schools in Chicago. Currently I am a teacher at Thomas Kelly High School where I have worked since 2005 and served as the chairman of the social studies department since 2007. While at Kelly I have taught United States history, world history, and I currently teach Urban Studies/Chicago history. Two years ago I published a guide for teaching United States history complete with lesson plans and reproducible activities and have written a Chicago neighborhood history book. I have a Bachelor of Arts degree in secondary education from DePaul University, a Master of Arts degree in history from DePaul University, and a second master's degree in educational administration from Governors State University. I have continued to further my education and expect an endorsement in special education in the summer of 2014.

I have taken an active role working with both students and staff while at Kelly High School. I have served on the school's Senior Leadership Team since 2007 (formally called the ILT), the AdvancED school accreditation team, supervised several student teachers, taught Saturday School and Evening School, interviewed and selected candidates for employment, created new elective classes for seniors, expanded advanced placement and dual college credit courses for the department, chaperoned numerous school functions, and planned various social events.

As department chair I have also coordinated the implementation of standardized test and reading preparation initiatives for the social studies department in conjunction with the literacy coordinator, grade level teachers, and TCT leads. The efforts of all the members of the social studies department to help students improve their reading skills and scores on the ACT has been a growth in standardized scores in which beginning-of-the year baseline data for juniors on an ACT practice exam has been compared to the end-of-the-year ACT exam, with a 1.9% growth in junior reading ACT scores from beginning-of-the-year to the end-of-the-year exam in 2012/2013 and a 1.6% growth for juniors from beginning-of-the-year to end-of- year in 2011/2012.

In addition to teaching, I have been deeply involved in my community and have had a variety of experience in other endeavors. I have served on the Board of Director's for the Beverly Ridge Homeowners' Association, a non-for-profit community organization serving over 1,200 households in the Beverly neighborhood where we worked to promote the civic interests of the community and sponsored many community events and public meetings. I have written a history of Chicago's historic Beverly community published by Arcadia Publishing as part of their *Images of America* series. As a result of this endeavor I was interviewed on Channel 11's *Chicago Tonight* television show and WBEZ radio and have given presentations to various community groups about the Beverly/Morgan Park neighborhood. I also held an Illinois real estate license for twenty years, passed the Illinois insurance exam, worked as a bank teller, worked in the family pizza business, and served as assistant manager for a national health and fitness corporation.

My accomplishments at Kelly High School and my other endeavors have given me experience in management, organization, communication, consensus-building, and fostering relationships with individuals of diverse backgrounds. I believe those attributes and my dedication to Kelly High School have provided me with the acumen needed to faithfully serve as LSC representative with the goal of keeping Kelly the best neighborhood school in the city and the number one school of choice for the community through expanding quality educational experiences for all students in the school. I hope to accomplish this by fostering a relationship of trust, fairness, and respect between the teachers, the administration, and the community while promoting shared-decision making, accountability, transparency, and integrity at all levels within the school."

accomplish to <u>achieve</u> something. I am sure I have the ability to accomplish any task assigned to me. / **accomplishment** n. Explain your accomplishments on a job interview.

accountability/accountable being responsible for something. This job requires a great deal of accountability. As project manager I understand I will be accountable for the success or failure of the project.

achieve v. to succeed at something or <u>accomplish</u> something. I strive hard to achieve whatever goals I set for myself. / **achievement** n. You have a lot of achievements for which you should be proud.

activate to start, begin, or <u>initiate</u> something. All the safety systems have to be activated before you start the machine. Make sure you activate the alarm system before you leave.

acumen set of skills, talents, awareness, knowledge, or insight that help someone. I am confident I have the acumen needed to be successful at whatever tasks I am asked to perform.

adapt to change as one's needs change, to learn new skills or ways of doing things, to keep up with advancements or new technology. I know I can adapt to whatever situation I might encounter on the job. People must learn to adapt to changes in the workplace. As a company we need to adapt to changes in the industry so we can stay competitive and profitable.

address to deal with something, to handle something. You must address the complaints of the customers. I will address the new rules with the employees.

advocate to support someone or something, to speak out on behalf of something. The job of the union representative is to advocate for better pay or working conditions for the employees. I promise to advocate for the needs of our company at the meeting.

allocate to set aside for use. We must allocate enough time and money in the <u>budget</u> to complete the project. Good planning involves allocating the appropriate amount of resources for the job.

analyze/analysis to go over, to examine and look for mistakes or ways of doing something better. We must analyze the results of election to see why we lost. After a careful analysis we determined if it would be better to use a more powerful motor. We must analyze our process to make sure mistakes like this do not happen again.

apply to make use of what you have or have learned. I am confident I can apply my skills and experience to this project.

articulate to explain something clearly and carefully in detail and sometimes in a step-by-step manner. Be sure to articulate your skills and previous accomplishments when you go on a job interview. Can you articulate how you would solve this problem?

broker v. to bring together, usually some type of financial interest. I brokered the deal that sold the business. / n. People often use a real estate broker when they sell their house or a stock broker for their other financial investments.

Fill in the blank quiz # 21

1. The real estate agent _____ the deal that sold the house in ten days.

2. _____ means to explain something in a clear and detailed way.

3. The company had to _____ enough money to finish the new project.

4. The company had _____ to changes in the marketplace or go out of business.

5. The teacher made sure to _____ on behalf of the good student.

6. A set of skills or talents needed to do a job successfully is known as _____.

7. The manager must be held _____ for his bad business decisions.

8. Be sure to explain your _____ on a job interview.

9. The manager had to _____ all the complaints against the worker.

10. A detailed _____ was needed to see where the mistake was made.

budget/budgeted to include in the cost of something. I know cost overruns and items not budgeted properly cut into profits so careful planning is needed. I will be sure to budget for the extra materials we will need. The overtime pay for the workers needs to be budgeted.

calculate to figure out mathematically or logistically. We must calculate the exact cost of producing the product before we set its price.

collaborate/collaboration to work together. I pride myself in being able to collaborate with different people. The contractor and the architect must collaborate on the project. The project requires a great deal of collaboration.

communicate/communication to explain things in writing or verbally. I have experience communicating with diverse groups of people. I am sure I can communicate the goals of the project to the stakeholders. The marketing campaign will communicate the benefits of the product to people. A manager must have good communication skills.

compile to put together. Compile a list of people who might benefit from this product. Compile a list of people who have used our service in the past.

conceptualize to visualize, to think of, to understand. We must conceptualize our plan before we try putting it into action.

consensus/consensus-building agreement, to bring people together in agreement and understanding. We must build consensus among the residents as to why they should support the project. I am confident I have the consensus-building skills needed to manage the department. I have experience in consensus-building.

conserve to save, to protect, to manage in way makes things last longer. We must conserve our natural resources or they will run out. We must find ways for the company to conserve its money.

consolidate to bring together, to combine things in a way that makes operation more efficient or stronger. The company consolidated all of its debts into one loan that was easier to pay off. The company consolidated all of the sales departments into one building. I am sure the company can become more efficient through a series of consolidations.

coordinate to manage, to be in charge of. I have a great deal of experience in coordinating events like this. I have all the skills needed to coordinate this project.

cultivate to develop, to help grow. The politician must cultivate a new group of voters or she will not be re-elected. The manager must cultivate positive relationships with the workers if he wants them to do a good job. The salesman must cultivate new customers for his product.

data information, sometimes mathematical information such as statistics. The data shows that sales slowed down in November but picked up again in December. We must change our plan according to the data.

data-driven using data, or hard facts to make decisions. I believe in a data-driven approach to decision making.

Fill in the blank quiz # 22

1. If you want the job you will be expected to _____ with other workers on projects.
2. Good salesmen and good bosses have excellent _____ skills.
3. The salesmen had to _____ a list of customers who might like his new service.
4. The marketing department had to _____ an advertising campaign for company's product.
5. _____ means using hard facts and data to make decisions.
6. The businessman worked hard to _____ new clients for this service.
7. If you are hired for the job you must be able to _____ several projects at one time.
8. To reach a _____ means to have everyone come to an agreement about something.
9. The company had to _____ all of its departments into the same building.
10. Rather than waste water and electricity, we must find better ways to _____ our resources.

---

delegate to assign, to put someone else in charge of something. A good manager knows how to delegate responsibility to the right people.

delineate to separate and explain or define something, to show exactly where something is. We must delineate the rules so everyone knows what is allowed and not allowed. We must delineate the exact boundaries of the property on the survey.

demonstrate to show, provide an example of. Can you demonstrate the use of the tool? Can you demonstrate how you would teach this lesson to a class? I have demonstrated this concept many times.

develop/development to grow, to create, to design. I have developed a new method of performing this task. I was on the team that developed this new method. I was responsible for the development of this product.

devise to think of a new way of doing something. We must devise a new plan. We must devise a new marketing strategy. I am sure I can devise a new method for doing this.

diagnose to figure out the problem. The mechanic diagnosed the problem with the car. The doctor diagnosed the illness. The engineer diagnosed the problem with the design.

efficient something that saves time and money. We need to find a more efficient way of doing the job. I am sure I can find efficient ways of running the company. / **efficiently** adv. The company is not run very efficiently.

efficiencies things that are efficient or designed to create efficiency. Many efficiencies were built into the manufacturing process.

entrepreneur someone who starts their own business or finds new ways to make money. Being an entrepreneur is not easy but can be very rewarding.

evaluate to observe and determine if something is good or not. We must evaluate our business plan and decide if we need to make changes. We must evaluate all of our options to see what makes the most sense.

execute to perform or carry out successfully. I am sure you will find me able to execute the most complicated tasks in a timely manner. The soldiers executed their mission perfectly.

expedite to speed up. We must find a way to expedite the shipping of our products to our customers. Expedited shipping usually costs more money.

Fill in the blank quiz #23

1. A good manager knows how to _____ authority to the right people.

2. We must _____ a new way to solve the problem.

3. _____ means to separate or define things.

4. The paperboy devised a new route to make his deliveries more _____.

5. The doctor used a new test to _____ the patient's illness.

6. The company had to _____ shipping so the product would get there on time.

7. The gymnast had to _____ all the moves perfectly to receive a good score.

8. The principal had to _____ his teachers twice a year to see if they were doing a good job.

9. The salesman had to _____ the product he was trying to sell.

10. The mayor had to explain how he would _____ a new plan for fighting crime.

---

expertise the experience and specialized knowledge needed to be an expert in something. I am sure you will find my expertise in this field very beneficial to your company. I have the expertise needed to perform this job.

facilitate to make happen, to bring together or oversee. We need someone to facilitate the meeting. I have a great deal of experience facilitating meetings and presentations.

fidelity 1. honestly, trustworthiness, faithfulness. Lawyers, stock brokers, and real estate agents owe their clients a great deal of fidelity. 2. Accuracy in which something is made or reproduced. The data was evaluated with much fidelity. The sound was reproduced with a great deal of fidelity.

focus n. the amount of attention paid to something. This project requires a great deal of focus. / v. When I start a project I do not focus on anything else. I am an extremely focused and motivated person.

foster to nurture or help grow and develop. A good manager needs to foster an atmosphere of respect and trust among his or her employees. We need you to foster this program along until it is successful.

galvanize to bring together in a supporting manner. We must galvanize the support of the local residents to get this project approved. I am sure I can galvanize the other employees to get this job finished.

generate to create. We must generate enough enthusiasm so the town gets behind the plan. We must generate enough sales to turn a profit. Explain to me how you will generate new sales.

illustrate to show in a clear way. You must illustrate to me that you can handle the job before I give you the promotion. My work history illustrates my ability and enthusiasm for the job.

implement to introduce or carry out. We must implement changes if we are to stay competitive. What changes will you implement to increase your sales? We must implement changes to the way we handle customer orders. I am sure you will find me able to implement whatever changes are needed.

increase to cause to go up. When I was at my last job I increased sales 50%. Test scores increases by 10% each year I was principal at my other school. We must increase our output if we are to meet the demand for our new product. How will you increase demand for this product if we hire you?

initiate to introduce, start, or implement something. I initiated a training program for new hires at my last job. Changes in the production line had to be initiated to make the process more efficient.   What changes would you initiate to increase sales in your department?

innovate to create, change, or improve something with new methods, ideas, materials, products, or ways of doing something. The car company had to innovate their assembly line techniques to improve production.

innovative adj. being able to innovate. He is a very innovative engineer.

innovation n. Innovation is the key to success. She is a master of innovation.

inspire to motivate. When you go on a job interview you must inspire the people to hire you. A coach must inspire his players to play hard, believe in themselves, and win. A manager must inspire his employees.

institute to <u>initiate,</u> to bring together. The school decided to institute a new dress code policy. If you are hired for the job what changes will you institute to increase sales?

integrate to bring together or combine something with another. The company had to integrate various methods to improve the product. Since there were not enough players for separate teams the boys and girls teams were integrated to make one team. / **integration** n.

Fill in the blank quiz # 24

1. On the job interview, the candidate had to explain her _____ in the field.

2. The manager had to _____ a new training program for the staff.

3. The union had to _____ the support of the workers for a possible strike.

4. The principal had to _____ a meeting for all new teachers.

5. The salesman had to explain how he would _____ sales the following month.

6. The school had to _____ changes to its attendance policy.

7. The engineer came up with an _____ new way to solve the problem.

8. The salesman worked hard to _____ new sales.

9. The business owner expected a great deal of _____ from his accountant.

10. The solution required the _____ of several ideas.

11. On a job interview, you must _____ the boss to hire you.

12. A good boss should _____ an atmosphere of mutual respect.

---

integrity having honestly and a sense of <u>morality</u> (knowing right from wrong). The company was run with integrity and a strong devotion to customer service.

launched started, initiated, to be the driving force behind something. The company launched a new product line. <u>Entrepreneurs</u> often launch their own businesses. When you go on a job interview be able to give examples of projects or products you have launched.

logistics a carefully planned set of steps for carrying out a task that often includes the management of the resources needed and accounts for potential problems so they can be avoided. Logistics is important in military combat if a mission is to be successful. / **logistical** adj. The fund raiser required a great deal of logistical planning. On a job interview give examples of your logistical abilities.

merge to combine or bring together. The companies merged their resources. The departments were merged to save money and make them more <u>efficient</u>.

mediate v. to bring parties together in an effort to help them <u>resolve</u> their differences. The principal had to mediate a dispute between two teachers. The teacher had to mediate the dispute between the students.

mediation n. A good manager needs great mediation skills so be sure to emphasize this when you go on a job interview for a management position.

organize v. to orange things in a clear and efficient way so they are manageable. A teacher must be able to organize all their duties, materials, and lessons effectively. Successful people are highly organized and know how to manage their time. /**organizational** adj. Be sure to stress your organizational skills on a job interview.

outpace to go faster than someone. The sales outpaced the company's expectations. If you are applying for a sales job explain why you expect your sales to outpace those of other salesmen.

personnel employees, workers. All the personnel had to be retrained.

persuade to convince others that your point of view is better. Salesmen must be able to persuade people to buy their products or do business with them. The power of persuasion can be very helpful.

procure v. to obtain or acquire often with careful effort. The teacher had to procure new books for the classroom. / **procurement** n. the act of procuring something. The Office of Procurement oversees new purchases.

project management the act of being in charge of a project. On a job interview be prepared to explain your project management skills and give examples of your project management accomplishments.

promote to highlight something or to make others aware of something. A company must promote its products. Advertising is a way for businesses to promote their goods and services. When you go on a job interview you must be able to promote yourself and your skills.

propose to suggest. How do you propose we increase sales?

proposal a detailed suggestion. The manager was required to submit a proposal for how to increase sales in his department. The store liked the man's proposal so they started working together.

prospect 1. the chance of something happening or being successful in the future. He liked the prospect of working with his new friends. The new company has a lot of prospects. 2. possible costumers. The salesman had a lot of prospects, or people who might buy his product.

Fill in the blank quiz# 25

1. _____ and honesty are good ways to keep your customers loyal to you.
2. The entrepreneur _____ her new business on the internet.
3. The owner offered to _____ the dispute between his employees.
4. _____ refers to carefully planning and carrying out tasks.
5. The company's sales _____ its competitors by a wide margin.
6. The man had to _____ a new source of funding for the loan.
7. Many business jobs require experience in _____.
8. To be successful, project management requires logistical and _____ skills.
9. The real estate sales agent always had to _____ himself.
10. The department head to submit a new _____ to her boss explaining her new idea.
11. The salesman was always looking for new_____.
12. What are the _____ of the company being successful?

pursue to go after something. The police had to pursue every possible lead to solve the crime. He is pursuing his dream of being an <u>entrepreneur</u>.

reduce to cut back or slow down. The company had to reduce its reliance on foreign materials. The company wanted to find ways to reduce its costs.

resolve 1. v. to find a solution to a problem or dispute. The friends resolved their differences. How will you resolve this problem? 2. v. To decide on something with great determination. The manager was resolved to finish the project on time. 3. n. The doctors set out to find a cure for the disease with much resolve.

restructure to reorganize things in a more efficient manner. The company restructured its debt. The department was restructured. How would you restructure the department to make it function better?

results-oriented to be focused on or driven by the end result of something when measuring success or to be concerned more with the outcome rather than the process of achieving something. The principal was a very results-oriented person who did not care how test scores went up as long as they went up. On a job interview emphasize how you are results-oriented in approaching your job.

revise v. to change or alter something in an effort to make it better. The teacher had to revise his lesson plans since the students were still struggling. / **revision** n. The man had to make revisions to his resume to better reflect his work experience.

revitalize to strengthen or improve. The department was revitalized with the new salesman's enthusiasm and success. The mayor had to explain his plan to revitalize blighted inner-city neighborhoods.

secure to acquire or make safe. The company secured the funding for the new project. Your job is to secure all the things we need for the fund raiser, such as food, beverages, and the entertainment.

self-starter motivated to do things, to start things on your own without waiting for anyone else or for any help. Most <u>entrepreneurs</u> are self-starters. On a job interview stress how you are a self-starter.

shared-decision making the ability to work with others and seek input from others to find solutions rather than being a top-down manager who thinks they are always right. Good principals include their teachers in a lot of shared-decision making. Team work requires the ability to work with others and <u>utilize</u> shared-decision making. If your potential new boss believes in collaboration and team work then emphasize your belief in shared-decision making.

Fill in the blank quiz # 26

1. The company had to _____ a new source of funding for the project.

2. The mayor planned to _____ blighted neighborhoods with new sources of revenue.

3. On a job interview make sure you give examples of how you are a _____ person.

4. The student had to _____ his essay according to the suggestions given by his teacher.

5. The friends had to _____ their problems.

6. The manager had to _____ the department so it would function better.

7. On a job interview make sure you stress how you are a _____ and do not need to wait for others to take action.

8. The company had to _____ its spending or lay off workers.

9. The man wanted to _____ his dreams of opening a restaurant.

10. Many company's now stress _____ as a way to involve more people in the decision-making process.

---

skills/skills set the set of skills and experiences you have that help you be successful at something. Being a good teacher requires a certain skill set. Emphasize your skill set on interviews and relate them to the job you are <u>pursuing.</u>

solution the answer to a problem. On a job interview stress how hiring you is the solution to the company's problems or how you are more focused on finding solutions rather than dwelling on problems.

solve to find a <u>solution</u> to a problem. On an interview stress how you are a problem-solver.

specialize to be an expert in something. They needed someone who specialized in internet security. **/specialization n.** Her specialization was working with autistic children. On an interview stress how your specialized training makes you the best person for the job.

stakeholder all the people who have an interest, or stake, in the success or failure of something. The school had a lot of stakeholders like the teachers, the students, the principal, the parents, and the community. The principal had to convince all the stakeholders that uniforms for students were a good idea for the school.

sustain to maintain something or continue to support it. The company was able to sustain losses during the recession because it was prepared for the economic slowdown and had plenty of cash reserves. Explain how you will sustain sales over the rest of the year.

timely to act or finish things in a reasonable or expected amount of time. On a job interview explain how you are able to start and complete tasks in a timely manner.

transact to carry out. They transact business on a regular basis. / transaction n. The transaction fell through at the last minute.

transform to change something. The school was transformed from a school no one wanted to attend to a highly successful school that became the envy of the city. On a job interview explain how you transformed things for the better on your previous jobs and how you can do the same in your new job.

transparency n. openness or the state of others to see and understand how and why things are done. The mayor believed in a great deal of transparency and was not trying to hide anything and did not have any ulterior motives for anything. Voters should demand a great deal of transparency from their elected officials. / **transparent.** He was not a very transparent boss.

upgrade to make better or to improve. The school was upgraded with new computers, new air conditioners, and a new security system. The computers were upgraded with the latest software.

utilize to make use of something or use whatever resources are available. The carpenter utilized all the materials he had to finish the job. On a job interview explain how you would utilize all the resources and personnel available to complete a project successfully.

validated to prove or support something. The results validated his methods. The data validated his statements. On a job interview be able to validate your claims of success with specific examples.

value the importance something has or what something is worth in money. The house is valued at $800,000. The employee has value beyond being good at his job because of all the other things he does. On a job interview explain the value you will add to the business if you are hired.

vision a belief in something or a belief in the way something could or should be. The principal had to explain her vision for the school when she applied for the job.

yield v. the results of something or money made from something, the return on an investment. The farmer's crops yielded the most corn in three years. The effort yielded no net gains. What results do you expect to yield from this project? / **yield** n. The yield on the investment was 3%.

78

Fill in the blank quiz # 27

1. On a job interview you must show your _____ to the company.

2. Be sure to explain your set of skills, or _____, on an job interview and resume.

3. The company was _____ from a small company to a giant in the industry.

4. A good salesman must _____ sales over a long period of time.

5. People who want to _____ in a certain field often get a master's degree or a doctorate.

6. The scientist had to _____ his claims before others would believe him.

7. The investment did not _____ the profits they expected.

8. Voters should demand honesty and _____ from their elected officials.

9. _____ are all the people who have an interest in the success or failure of something.

10. The carpenter had to_____ all of tools and materials he had to finish the job.

11. On the job be sure to complete all your tasks in a _____ manner.

12. On a job interview try to present yourself as the _____ to the company's problems.

History and Social Science Vocabulary

agriculture n. the growing and <u>cultivation</u> of crops and farm animals; farming. Many early settlers in this country relied on agriculture to support themselves. /**agricultural** adj. /**agrarian** adj. related to agriculture.

antebellum (an-tee-bel-um) adj. before the war; mainly in the U.S. before the Civil War (1861-1865). The antebellum South was quite different than it is today.

anthropology (an-throe-pol-oe-jee) n. the study of man and his development. Anthropology often goes hand in hand with archeology. / **anthropologist** n. / **anthropological** adj.

anti-Semitism n. discrimination, hatred or prejudice against Semitic people, mainly Jewish people. The <u>Nazis</u> displayed much anti-Semitism. / **anti-Semitic**-adj. / **anti-Semite** n. person who practices anti-Semitism.

archeology (ar-kee-o-lo-jee) n. the study of ancient people and artifacts. Archeology is an important aspect of historical knowledge.

aristocracy n. the elite, wealthy, or upper-class. Many European countries were once ruled by the aristocracy.

bicameral (by-kam-er-al) adj. made up of two legislative houses. The Founding Fathers created a bicameral legislature.

bipartisan adj. supported by two groups, usually political parties. The bipartisan agreement on tax reform was finally approved.

Bolshevik or bolshevik (boel-she-vik) n. adj. / n. 1. the political party led by Vladimir Lenin that seized control of Russia after the 1917 revolution and established a <u>communist</u> government. Lenin led the Bolsheviks to power in 1917. 2. a very radical person or idea. / adj. related to the Soviet Union's communist party.

bourgeois or bourgeoisie (boor-zhwah or boor-zhwah-zee) n. adj. /n. French word for the middle- class or business class. / adj. characteristic of the middle class. The bourgeois are above the lower classes but beneath the aristocracy.

bureaucracy (byu-rok-ra-see) n. organizational system in government or big business having many departments, managers, and workers and often characterized by strict adherence to procedure or paperwork, a chain of command, and delays in getting things done. The company's bureaucracy made it impossible to get a straight answer from anyone. / **bureaucratic** adj. / **bureaucrat** n. person working in a bureaucracy.

Matching   Quiz # 1

_____ 1.	agriculture		a.	large organizational system
_____ 2.	bipartisan		b.	study of man
_____ 3.	anti-Semitism		c.	raising of crops and farm animals
_____ 4.	anthropology		d.	supported by two groups
_____ 5.	aristocracy		e.	Russia's communist party
_____ 6.	antebellum		f.	the middle-class
_____ 7.	bicameral		g.	rule by the wealthy
_____ 8.	bureaucracy		h.	before the war
_____ 9.	bourgeoisie		i.	hatred of Jews
_____ 10.	Bolshevik		j.	two legislative houses

---

capitalism n. economic system organized around the private ownership of property and the means of the production and distribution of goods and services; characterized by competition, supply and demand, profit making, and using market forces over government policy to determine prices, wages, and goods to be produced; factories, land, resources, and distribution facilities all owned by individuals and not the government. The United States economy is based on capitalism.

civil disobedience n. peaceful way of protesting the government by not obeying some laws; refusal to follow some laws because of personal beliefs. Not paying taxes is a form of civil disobedience.

Cold War the intense diplomatic, economic, political, and weapons competition between the United States and the Soviet Union between 1945 and 1991. The Cold War does not refer to an actual military war between the these two countries.

colony n. a group of people who travel to another land to live but still remain loyal to the place they came from; a place where such people establish themselves. The English colonies thrived until the king started imposing many taxes upon them. / **colonist** n. person of a colony. / **colonial** adj. related to a colony. Colonial life was simple for some people but not for all the colonists.

commerce n. the buying and selling of goods; doing business. Laws regulating commerce and trade should be consistent from state to state.

common law n. laws based on the common practices of a region or by the previous decisions of judges. Common law is often based on the traditions that people in certain areas have practiced for a long time.

communism n. 1. social, political, and economic system conceived by Karl Marx in which there would be no private ownership of property; property was to be owned communally (together) by the people, in an effort to make everyone in society equal by eliminating social and economic class differences within society and by a more equal distribution of goods; achieved by a forceful revolution by the workers (proletariat) over capitalist rulers and major business owners with the workers going on to own the businesses and farms. The Bolshevik revolution in 1917 brought communism to Russia. /**communist** n. or adj. Russia became a communist country. 2. as practiced in some countries, an economic system where the government owns all the production and distribution components of the country's goods and services and controls all aspects of life within the country, especially manufacturing and labor; all property and businesses are owned by the government, not by private citizens, and individual rights are severely limited. Communism is the complete opposite of democratic <u>capitalism</u> and an extreme form of <u>socialism</u>. By the 1990s, it was clear that communism could not compete with capitalism.

conservative adj. n. / adj. 1. old fashioned or traditional in thought or action; resisting change; desire to keep things the way they were in the past. 2. favoring very little government intervention in the economy, business, and the lives of people; believing that people should do more to help themselves without government help. /n. a person having those qualities. He is very conservative in his thoughts about politics and economics.

constituency (kon-stich-yu-en-see) n. voters in a region; a politician's voters or supporters. The senator had to be careful not to upset his constituency. / **constituents** n.

coup d' état (koo-day-tah) n. French term for a rebellion or revolution (abbreviated- coup). Russia underwent a coup d' état in 1917. The coup left the czar dead.

Darwinism n. refers to Charles Darwin's theory of evolution and his idea of survival of the fittest (natural selection). Giraffes with short necks no longer existing is an example of Darwinism.

democracy n. government ruled by the will of the people who exercise their power by voting; rule of the majority; characterized by fairness and treating people equally. Democracy has proved to be the best form of government. / **democratic** adj. related to a democracy (not to be confused with the Democratic political party).

demographics n. <u>statistical</u> information about people in an area such as population counts and gender, race, income, and educational information. Demographic information is vital to meeting the needs of a community.

détente (day-tont) n. improved relations between people, groups, or countries usually hostile towards each other. Offering help in times of stress is always a move toward détente.

diplomacy n. ability to communicate or negotiate effectively between people or countries; ability to deal with others. /**diplomatic** adj./ **diplomat** n. one who exercises diplomacy or deals with other countries.

domestic policy n. the policies of a country related to affairs within that country. Lowering taxes and creating jobs was a major aspect of the President's domestic policy.

economy n. related to the production of goods and services, jobs, and the making of money. The economy experienced tremendous growth in the 1990s. /**economic** adj. related to the economy.

evangelism (e-van-je-liz-um) n. the spreading of religion; the preaching of religion. Evangelism is very strong in the South.

famine n. a lack of food. Many people in underdeveloped countries suffer from famine.

fascism (fash-iz-um) n. a strong centralized government with a single supreme leader who supports extreme <u>nationalism</u>, the use of military force, and limits personal freedoms. Fascism was a major cause of World War Two. / fascist n. a person who supports fascism. / Fascist: the governments of Nazi Germany and Italy during the 1930s and 1940s. Hitler and Mussolini were Fascists.

82

```
                          Matching Quiz #  2

____1.  capitalism            a.  a revolution
____2.  Darwinism             b.  voters
____3.  communism             c.  rule by the majority
____4.  constituency          d.  lack of food
____5.  demographics          e.  private ownership of business
____6.  fascism               f.  government ownership businesses
____7.  democracy             g.  information and statistics about people
____8.  domestic policy       h.  theory of evolution
____9.  coup d' état          i.  strong centralized government
___10.  famine                j.  government policy within a country
___11.  evangelism            k.  spreading of religion
```

finance n. related to money; the management of money or resources. The finance committee approved the purchase of more books. / **financial** adj. related to finance or money matters.

federalism n. system of government where power is divided between states and the national government. The United States Constitution is based on the theory of federalism.

feudalism n. the system in European society during the Middle Ages where small farmers pledged their loyalty and military support to a large land owner in exchange for the use of his land to farm and his protection. / **feudal** adj. related to the system of feudalism.

filibuster n. process of obstructing something such as a vote in a legislature by deliberately delaying action by giving a long speech. The senator made good use of a two-hour filibuster to keep Congress from voting on a law she did not like.

foreign policy n. the policies of a country related to affairs outside that country. Establishing greater economic trade with other countries was a major part of the President's foreign policy.

fundamentalism (fun-duh-men-tuh-liz-um) n. believing or interpreting something, such as the Bible, word for word (literally). Fundamentalism is strong in the South.

genocide n. the killing of an entire group or race. The Nazis embarked on a campaign of genocide during the Holocaust.

geology n. the study of the earth. Geology can tell us a lot about how the earth was formed.

geopolitics n. the interrelation of politics, government, and geography as related to boundaries between countries or cultures. Geopolitics has never been as important in Europe as it is now.

gerrymandering (jerry-man-der-ing) n. drawing or redrawing political boundaries or districts to give a certain group or party an advantage. Redrawing the town's political map was nothing short of ethnic gerrymandering. / **gerrymander** v.

Gestapo n. the secret police of Nazi Germany known for their brutal yet efficient methods of terror against enemies of Nazi Germany.

gold standard n. using gold to give value to a nation's currency. In theory, according to the gold standard, all the paper money in circulation should be backed up by its value in gold that is in the country's gold reserves.

habeas corpus (hay-bee-es kor-pus) Latin term which literally means "Bring forth the body" but refers to a law which states that an arrested person must be brought before a judge and told what he has been arrested for. Lincoln suspended the writ of habeas corpus during the Civil War.

Hebrew n. 1. a Jewish person. 2. the language of the Jews. Modern Hebrew differs from ancient Hebrew.

Himalayas n. mountain range in Asia forming a natural border between India and China. The highest mountain in the world, Mt. Everest, is located in the Himalayas.

Holocaust n. the systematic extermination of the Jews by the Nazis during WWII. We should never forget the lessons to be learned from the Holocaust.

imperialism (im-peer-ee-ah-liz-um) n. the extending of one country's control over another country; the economic, political, or military domination of one country over another. Great Britain has a long history of imperialism in Africa and India.

industrialization n. the process of a country becoming industrialized; developing large industries such as steel, oil, and manufacturing; characterized by a change from an agricultural society to a manufacturing society, from products being made by hand in small numbers to products being made by machines in large numbers (mass production), a shift from skilled craftsmen working for themselves to low-skilled workers working for someone else in a factory, and a shift from living in rural areas to people living in cities. Industrialization was made possible by new inventions and innovations such as the steam engine and electricity. / **industrialize** v. / **industrialized** adj.

Ivy League refers to a group of old and prominent universities in the Northeastern part of the United States, which include Brown, Yale, Harvard, Princeton, Cornell, Columbia, Dartmouth, and Pennsylvania.

Jim Crow (laws) n. laws passed in the Southern states after the Civil War that made it legal to segregate black and white people. Many Jim Crow laws were practiced until the 1960s.

Kamikaze (kah-mi-kah-zee) n. a Japanese fighter pilot during WWII that committed suicide by flying into ships. Literally means "Divine Wind." The Kamikaze pilots sank a number of ships.

Kremlin n. a palace in Russia where the government in housed. Not many people ever got to see the inside of the Kremlin during the communist period.

laissez faire (lay-zay fair) French term meaning "let people do as they chose" referring to a hands off style of management with minimum interference. The government took a laissez faire attitude toward big business in the late 1800s.

legislate (le-ji-slate) v. to make laws. There are some behaviors the government cannot legislate against. /**legislation** n. a law or set of laws. /**legislative** adj.

legislature (le-ji-slay-chur) n. law-making body of government. The state legislature just passed a new insurance law.

liberal adj. n. /adj. 1. having open minded or progressive ideas about things; not favoring many restrictions. The school is pretty liberal with its dress code. 2. favoring more government interaction in the economy for the well-being of people. / n. a person with those attributes.

liberty n. freedom; rights. Our nation was founded on the principles of liberty and equality.

libertarian n. a person who <u>advocates</u> liberty, freedom and minimum government interference.

lobby (lo-bee) v. n. /v. to work hard to influence a lawmaker's opinion or action. The gun control <u>advocates</u> lobbied very hard in Congress. /n. a group who lobbies. The gun control lobby is very strong in some states. /**lobbyist** n. person who tries to influence a lawmaker's opinion.

Marxism n. the social, political, and economic theories of Karl Marx, which became the basis of <u>communism</u>. / **Marxist** n. a supporter of Marxism.

medieval (mee-dee-ee-val) adj. refers to the uncivilized time period in Europe during the Middle Ages of world history between the fall of the Roman Empire (476 A.D.) and the Renaissance (1450 A.D.). Some forms of punishment are cruel and simply medieval.

mercantilism (mer-kan-ti-liz-um) n. economic system in which countries seek to export more goods than they import. European mercantilism relied on colonies to send the mother country raw materials, which would be turned into finished products then sold back to the colonies and elsewhere.

meritocracy (me-ri-tahk-ruh-see) n. a system that values the people of the highest skill or intelligence. Some government agencies operate under a meritocracy.

monarch (mo-nark) n. a king, queen, or similar ruler. The monarch of the country passed her power on to her daughter. **monarchy** (mo-nar-kee) n. a government ruled by a monarch. England's monarchy does not have much real power anymore since most decisions are made in <u>Parliament</u>.

monopoly (mo-no-poe-lee) n. the total and exclusive control over a product or industry; characterized by only having one company (or a few) being the major manufacturer or seller of a product; often resulted in price fixing and the elimination of competition. The huge oil, steel, and railroad companies of the 1890s were considered to be monopolies.

nationalism (nash-e-nah-liz-um) n. feelings of pride, loyalty, devotion, and patriotism towards one's country. The attack on the country resulted in a renewed spirit of nationalism.

nativism (na-ti-viz-um) n. belief or movement among native born citizens of a country that they are superior to and more important than foreigners. Nativism in the United States included trying to restrict immigration. /**nativist** n.

Matching Quiz # 3

____ 1. lobby	a. mass killing of the Jews
____ 2. gerrymandering	b. related to money
____ 3. genocide	c. interpret Bible word for word
____ 4. Jim Crow	d. a king
____ 5. Marxism	e. to make laws
____ 6. federalism	f. hands off policy
____ 7. foreign policy	g. control of an entire industry
____ 8. imperialism	h. redrawing political boundaries
____ 9. monarch	i. to influence law makers
____ 10. legislate	j. segregation laws
____ 11. finance	k. dominating another country
____ 12. fundamentalism	l. communist theory
____ 13. laissez faire	m. dealings with other countries
____ 14. Holocaust	n. division of government powers
____ 15. monopoly	o. killing of an entire race

Nazi (not-zee) n. a member of the National Socialist Workers Party of Germany led by Adolf Hitler in the 1920s, 1930s and 1940s. The Nazis were the political party that took control of Germany and started WWII.

Occident n. geographical term referring to the West as in Europe or America. The Occident still does not understand the Orient very well.

oligarchy n. government controlled by a few number of people. Many small towns could be compared to an oligarchy.

Orient n. the East as in Asia. The Orient contains many historical sites. /**Oriental** adj.

Palestine n. the Holy Land; homeland of Jesus Christ; the current land of the country of Israel.

Palestinian adj. n. /adj. related to Palestine. / n. a person from Palestine, particularly a person of Arab and Islamic background. The struggle between the Jews and the Palestinians still rages.

paleontology n. the study of life in prehistoric times, such as the study fossils and dinosaurs. Paleontology requires a broad knowledge of history, geology, and biology.

parliament n. the name of the law-making body in some countries. European parliaments often view foreign policy differently than the United States. /**Parliament** n. law-making body of Great Britain.

parochial (par-oe-kee-al) adj. related or having to do with a church. Many parents prefer to send their children to parochial schools.

philanthropy (fi-lan-throe-pee) n. love of mankind, often displayed through the donation of time or money to a good cause. One could argue that Andrew Carnegie was a firm believer in philanthropy.

86

philanthropist n. one who loves mankind and often donates money to help good causes. Others would argue that Carnegie was not the great philanthropist he has been made out to be in some circles. / **philanthropic** adj.

plagiarism (play-jer-iz-um) n. to use someone else's words, thoughts, ideas, or information as one's own without acknowledgment. The professor warned the students carefully about the penalty for plagiarism.

plurality n. the majority of votes in an election. The candidate only needed a plurality to be elected.

plutocracy n. government ruled by the rich. A plutocracy is not compatible with a true democracy. /**plutocratic** adj.

pork barrel (legislation) making laws or deals that benefit a specific area or group. The politician kept his loyal voters happy by constantly approving pork barrel projects that brought jobs and money to his home town.

pastoral adj. 1. pertaining to the raising of farm animals or livestock. 2. animal husbandry. Pastoralism is a branch of agriculture that deals with the raising of farm animals or livestock. **pastoralism** n.

pragmatism n. the belief that the right idea is the idea that works best or is the most practical. /**pragmatic** adj. /**pragmatist** n. Some people considered Theodore Roosevelt to be the quintessential pragmatist.

prohibition n. the law that made alcohol illegal in this country. The 18th Amendment resulted in prohibition in 1920 but was repealed in 1933 by the 21st Amendment.

proletariat (proe-le-tair-ee-et) n. the workers in an industrialized nation. According to Karl Marx, the proletariat would eventually rise up and overthrow all of their capitalistic rulers.

propaganda n. information designed to influence public opinion. The Nazis brainwashed the citizens of Germany with anti-Semitic propaganda and promises of a new German empire.

psychology (sy-ko-loe-jee) n. the study of the mind. Psychology students often study the theories of Sigmund Freud. /**psychological** adj.

Ptolemaic Universe (toe-le-may-ik) n. theory by Ptolemy that the earth was the center of the solar system and sun and other objects revolved around the earth. Galileo and Copernicus disproved the Ptolemaic Universe theory.

quorum (kwor-um) n. the smallest number of people needed to conduct business. A quorum of six justices is needed for the Supreme Court to make a decision.

recession n. a slowdown in the economy. Many businesses were hurt by the recession, and many people lost their jobs.

Reformation n. the European religious movement that tried to reform the Catholic Church in the 1500s and led to the establishment of various Protestant religions.

Renaissance (re-ne-sans) n. the period in time when Western Europe emerged from the Dark Ages, was rived, and rediscovered the knowledge of the past. Characterized by a renewed interest in classical learning and art from the ancient civilizations. The Renaissance began in Italy in the 1300s and spread to northern Europe about 1450 A.D.

republic n. a form of democracy in which citizens elect representatives to manage the government. A republic is more practical in today's world than a true democracy. /**republican** adj. referring to a government based on a republic (not to be confused with the Republican political party).

revolution n. 1. The overthrowing of a government or political system. The Russian revolution turned Russia into a communist country. 2. a rapid or complete change in something. The automobile was a revolution in transportation.

Semite n. refers to any group of people who speak one of the ancient Semitic languages. Jewish people are Semites because Hebrew is a Semitic language.

sheik (sheek or shake) n. the leader of an Arab tribe, family, or religious group. The sheik called upon his followers for a meeting.

Social Darwinism adaptation of Darwin's theory of evolution (which was based on the his idea of "survival of the fittest") by many people in society during the late 1800s that attempted to explain why some people were wealthy and successful while others were poor and unsuccessful. Social Darwinism stated that society progressed through natural competition and that some people were wealthy because they were hard working an intelligent while other people were poor because they were lazy and unintelligent.

socialism n. economic, social, and political system in which the government owns or tightly controls the major industries and means of production in an industrialized country, such as factories, transportation systems, health care, energy companies, etc., through regulations, price controls, and high taxes, with the proceeds being used to provide citizens with more social benefits and eliminate the problems associated with capitalism, such as worker exploitation, labor conflict, and the uneven distribution of wealth between rich and poor people. Many countries turned to socialism after WWII because many people blamed the inequalities and conflicts in the world on capitalism.

socialized medicine a system where health care is provided by or paid for by the government. Many European countries have some form of socialized medicine which guarantees that people will have access to health care. Also known as **single-payer health care** or **universal health care**.

sociology (so-see-o-loe-jee) n. the study of people, both individuals and groups, and their interaction with others in society. Sociology often deals with the study of crime, poverty, human relationships, and various institutions that make up a society, including the family and religion.

Socratic method method of reasoning or leading others to reason by asking a series of questions that probe for deeper understanding. The Socratic method was used by Socrates in ancient Greece.

Soviet Union the official name of communist Russia until 1991. The Bolshevik revolution in 1917 established Russia, which would later be called the Soviet Union, as a communist country. Another name for the Soviet Union was the U.S.S.R. (Union of the Soviet Socialist Republics).

statutory law a law made by a legislative body (law-making) such as Congress or a state government.

subsidize v. to assist with money. Many schools are subsidized by the government. / **subsidy** n. assistance in the form or money or payments.

suffrage n. the right to vote. The 19ᵗʰ Amendment granted women's suffrage.

supply and demand economic principle that has a major role in determining the price of goods in a <u>capitalistic</u> system. The price of a product usually goes up when there is a high demand for the product, and prices tend to go down when there is less demand and a high supply of a product.

swastika n. ancient symbol used by the <u>Nazi</u> Party in Germany. The swastika has become an offensive and hated symbol of terror and evil.

tariff n. a tax on imported or exported goods. Some people believe that <u>foreign</u> cars should carry heavy tariffs.

technocracy (tek-nah-kra-see) n. a government or system run by technical experts. Some businesses are so mechanized they seem to be run as a technocracy. /**technocrat** n.

theology n. the study of God and religion. A degree in theology requires a lot of reading of religious material. / **theologian** n.

Third Reich (rike) means Third Empire and refers to <u>Nazi</u> Germany during WWII. Adolf Hitler wanted to establish a third German empire he called the Third Reich.

Third World refers to the undeveloped and non-industrialized countries of the world, which are often characterized by poverty, reliance on agriculture, political instability, lack of technology, poor health care, low levels of education, and low standards of living. Many Third World countries are located in Africa, Asia, and Central America.

topography (to-pog-rah-fee) n. the surface of something, usually land and all its characteristics such as hills, mountains, flats, etc. The flat topography of the area makes for a perfect place to build a home. /**topographical** adj.

totalitarian (toe-tal-i-tair-ee-en) adj. form of government that brutally controls all aspects life, uses force and intimidation to control people, and will go to any means to retain power. <u>Nazi</u> Germany and the <u>Soviet Union</u>, especially under Stalin, were totalitarian countries. / **totalitarianism** n.

Trojan horse n. figurative for a gift that is not as it appears and causes great harm. The legend of the Trojan horse goes back to ancient Greece when the Greeks offered the Trojans a huge wooden horse as a gift, which secretly contained Greek soldiers who came out of the wooden structure and attacked the Trojans within the city walls of ancient Troy.

tyranny (teer-ah-nee) n. harsh, cruel, and unfair use of power or authority. The Founding Fathers spoke out against governmental tyranny. /**tyrannical** adj. /**tyrant** n. person who engages in tyranny.

utilitarianism (yu-til-uh-tair-ee-en-iz-um) n. the belief that thoughts and actions are good if they are useful. According to the doctrine of utilitarianism, building the Panama Canal was a good idea.

utopia (yu-toe-pee-ah) n. a perfect place; a place where no problems exist; an ideal existence. Finding or creating a utopia on earth would be quite difficult given all the differences of opinion and behavior that exist in the world. /**utopian** adj.

Victorian adj. related to the time period in which Victoria was queen of England (1837-1901); characterized by certain architectural and fashion styles, certain attitudes, certain beliefs, and certain behaviors that were popular during her reign. The home is decorated with Victorian furniture.

wholesale adv. adj. / adv. 1. refers to the buying or selling of items in large quantities or at discounted prices. The girl bought her car wholesale from the dealer. / adj. The wholesale price of a something is always cheaper than retail price. 2. the price from the manufacturer.

writ (rit) n. a law or written order from a court. Writs of assistance allowed British soldiers to look for smuggled goods in the American colonies.

Yankee n. adj. / n. refers to a person from the Northern states of the U.S. or to a person from the United States in general. The Southerners must have thought the Yankees had a strange accent. / adj. The Yankee soldiers sounded strange to the Confederates.

Zionism (zy-o-niz-um) n. the movement for a Jewish homeland or state of Israel in <u>Palestine</u>. The Zionists have met much hostility from Arab leaders. / **Zion** n. 1. the Jewish state of Israel or the people of Israel. / **Zionist** n. a supporter of Zionism.

Matching Quiz # 4

_____1. Third Reich	a. giving money to a good cause
_____2. socialism	b. to assist with money
_____3. suffrage	c. underdeveloped nations
_____4. recession	d. information that influences
_____5. plagiarism	e. industrialized workers
_____6. totalitarian	f. land surface
_____7. republic	g. a law-making body
_____8. statutory law	h. government control of industry
_____9. Third World	i. economic slowdown
_____10. proletariat	j. evil rule with absolute power
_____11. subsidize	k. elected representatives govern
_____12. topography	l. Nazi Germany of WWII
_____13. parliament	m. laws made by the government
_____14. philanthropy	n. to steal another's words
_____15. propaganda	o. right to vote

History and Social Science Crossword Puzzle

www.CrosswordWeaver.com

ACROSS	DOWN
3 the buying and selling of goods	1 the killing of an entire group or race
4 system that values people with the highest skills	2 long speech that delays an action
6 the study of man	5 person from the northern/northeastern part of the United States
7 the East as in China or other parts of Asia	8 laws or deals that benefit a specific area or group
10 system of government where power is divided between states and the federal government	9 idea that society progresses through a natural competition among people
11 having an open mind or favoring more government intervention	12 group of old and prominent universities
18 laws made by a law-making body	13 law-making body of government
21 communicating carefully between people or countries	14 symbol of the Nazi Party
22 associated with a church	15 movement for a Jewish homeland in Palestine
23 the spreading of religion	16 law-making body of government in many European countries
24 the smallest number of people needed to conduct business	17 the study of God and religion
25 resisting change or favoring little government intervention	19 a perfect place
	20 harsh or unfair use of power

Puzzle made at puzzle-maker.com

History and Social Science Word Search

```
D R Q X W R B P R L M W R Y B L B J M
X Y F M C B Q U A C N S G M A W J Y H
F B Z H W Y M D R R L O I V T X M T T
K H H D T N F L Z E L F E L C H Z F R
L L P Z V T F T G O A I R R A W B W R
D M A L T E R F E S D U A T N I M Y C
N T R Y Y B D H C E R J C M K V C W O
T Y O G J C C I M E Y L R R E M X O N
M G C O K R S Q C N L N X K A N K Z S
S O H L A M T E N O N K K T V C T D T
I L I O D H S A D R N Q N W W Y Y M I
L O A I N S R D K G F E M R X C X K T
A P L C I Y M N C Y K N G Y C F M F U
I O P O T T G A R I S T O C R A C Y E
R R N S T T O T A L I T A R I A N X N
E H M S I L A R E D E F L W K H R M C
P T X R J L P R O P A G A N D A T L Y
M N K E C N A S S I A N E R K R R Z F
I A I N D U S T R I A L I Z A T I O N
```

ANTHROPOLOGY	GENOCIDE	RECESSION
ARCHEOLOGY	IMPERIALISM	RENAISSANCE
ARISTOCRACY	INDUSTRIALIZATION	SOCIALISM
BUREAUCRACY	MEDIEVAL	SOCIOLOGY
CONSTITUENCY	PARLIAMENT	TOTALITARIAN
FASCISM	PAROCHIAL	TYRANNY
FEDERALISM	PROPAGANDA	

Puzzle made at puzzle-maker.com

Vocabulary of the World's Religions

Baptist n. a person who belongs to the Baptist denomination (branch) of the Protestant religion. Baptists and Methodists only make up some of the Protestant denominations.

Buddhism (bood-iz-um) n. a world religion prominent in parts of India and other parts of Asia. Buddhism is among the oldest religions in the world. / **Buddhist** n. believer in Buddhism.

Catholicism n. a Christian religion headquartered in Rome, Italy with the Pope as the head of the Church.

Christianity n. religion based on the teachings of Jesus Christ; based on the belief that Jesus Christ was the son of God and was put on the earth, and ultimately to death, to free mankind of its sins. Christianity is currently the most practiced religion in the world and has many different denominations (branches). / **Christian** n., adj.

Eastern Orthodox adj. related to the Eastern Orthodox Christian Church, such as the Greek and Russian Orthodox Churches. Eastern Europe has many Orthodox Christians.

Episcopalian n. a Protestant denomination (branch) in which the Church is organized around a hierarchy of bishops who decide church policy. / **Episcopalian** n. adj.

episcopal (e-pis-ke-pol) adj. having to do with a bishop or bishops; referring to the organizational structure of a church.

evangelism (e-van-je-liz-um) n. the spreading of the word of God; the preaching of religion. Evangelism is very strong in the South.

fundamentalism (fun-duh-men-tah-liz-um) n. believing or interpreting the Bible word for word (literally). Fundamentalism is strong in the South.

Hanukkah n. annual Jewish celebration lasting eight days, which celebrates the rededication of the temple in Jerusalem in 165 B.C. Candles are lit on each day of the Hanukkah celebration.

Hinduism n. religion of the Hindu people of India. Hinduism is one of the oldest religions known.

Islam n. religion of the Muslims delivered to people from God (Allah) by his prophet Mohammed. Islam is the second most practiced religion in the world.

Judaism (jew-day-iz-um) n. the religion of the Hebrews (Jews). Judaism predates Christianity.

Koran (kor-on) n. the holy book of the Islamic religion.

Lutheranism (loo-ther-an-iz-um) n. a Christian religion based on the teachings of Martin Luther and his attempts to reform the Roman Catholic Church in the 1500s. /**Lutheran** n. adj.

Methodism (me-thoe-diz-um) n. a denomination (branch) of the Protestant religion. Methodism is a Christian religion but has different origins than the Catholic Church. /**Methodist** n. adj.

Muslim (Moslem) (muz-lim) n. a believer in the religion of Islam. The Muslim community often centers around the mosque.

mosque (mosk) n. a church or place of worship for Muslims. Some of the most architecturally impressive mosques are in parts of Europe.

Passover n. the Jewish holiday celebrating the deliverance of the Jews out of captivity in Egypt during Biblical times.

Presbyterianism (pres-bi-teer-ee-an-iz-um) n. a denomination (branch) of the Protestant religion. Presbyterianism differs somewhat from the Episcopalian Church in how the Church is organized. / **Presbyterian** n. adj.

Protestantism n. a Christian religion and its denominations that split with the Roman Catholic Church; includes the Lutheran, Methodist, Baptist, Episcopalian, and Presbyterian denominations. Protestantism has its roots in the Reformation of the 1500s. /**Protestant** n. adj. The Pilgrims were members of a branch of the Protestant religion known as Puritans.

purgatory n. a place of temporary suffering where the soul stays until sins have been paid for. The child hated doing chores so much that she thought she was in purgatory.

rabbi (rab-y) n. a Jewish priest or religious teacher. The rabbi counseled the young members of the synagogue.

Ramadan n. Muslim religious holiday lasting one month. Strict fasting is observed during Ramadan.

Shinto n. the oldest Japanese religion, which literally means "way of the gods." Practitioners of Shinto believe in a close relationship with nature and nature's gods.

synagogue (syn-uh-gog) n. a Jewish church or place of worship. The marriage ceremony took place at the local synagogue.

Taoism (Daoism) (dow-iz-um) n. an old religion of China based on one's spirituality and harmony with nature. Taoism is based on the teachings of Lao Tzu and his book the *Tao Té Ching.*

theocracy (thee-ok-rah-see) n. a government ruled by priests or religious leaders. Some ancient civilizations were in many ways a theocracy.

theology n. the study of God and religion. A degree in theology requires a lot of reading of religious material. / **theologian** n.

Torah n. the Jewish name for the Old Testament and its teachings. The Torah is read in synagogues just as the Bible is read in Christian churches.

Trinity n. the holy union of the Father, Son, and Holy Spirit. The Trinity is a central aspect of the Christian religion.

94

Vatican n. the headquarters of the Roman Catholic Church in Rome. The Pope's palace is located in the Vatican.

Zen n. refers to Zen Buddhism, the Japanese form of Buddhism that stresses concentration, meditation, self-awareness, and sudden enlightenment. The art of Zen has taught many people how to relax and be more aware of their surroundings.

Zoroastrianism (zor-oe-as-tree-an-iz-um) n. religion popular in ancient Persia (Iran) founded by Zoroaster; characterized by a struggle between good and evil. Aspects of Zoroastrianism can be found in many popular movies and books. / **Zoroastrian** n. a believer in Zoroastrianism.

Religion Vocabulary Crossword

www.CrosswordWeaver.com

ACROSS	DOWN
1 the Hebrew name for the Old Testament 5 religion of the Hebrews 7 religion of many people in India 9 the holy book of Islam 10 Christian religion that split with the Catholic Church in the 1500s 11 teacher of Jewish religion 12 the oldest Japanese religion	2 Muslim religious holiday 3 Muslim church 4 interpreting the Bible word-for-word 6 Jewish religious holiday celebrating deliverance from captivity 7 Jewish holiday lasting eight days 8 believer in Islam

Puzzle made at puzzle-maker.com

General Vocabulary Building
AA

abash (uh-bash) v. to embarrass; make ashamed. The student was abashed because of his wrong answer.

abate v. to diminish; lessen; reduce in strength. He tried to abate the noise by closing the door.

abbey (a-bee) n. place where monks or nuns live in a religious manner; monastery or convent.

abdicate v. to surrender power; to give up authority. The king was forced to abdicate because of the scandal.

abduct (ab-dukt) v. to take without permission or by force. The boy was abducted from his home.

aberrant (ab-er-ant) adj. odd; irregular; not normal or correct; misguided or misdirected. The ship was on an aberrant course.

aberration (ab-er-ay-shun) n. something that is not as it should be; not usual or acceptable; something that goes wrong or is misguided. The answer was a complete aberration from what was expected.

abet v. to help or aid in doing something.   The man abetted the thief by helping him get away. / **abetting** n.

abhor v. to hate or despise something; to be scared or horrified of something. The child abhors the possibility of being left alone.

abhorrent adj. despised; hated, loathed; unacceptable. The student's unruly and abhorrent behavior outraged the teachers.

abide v. to obey; follow through with. Students must abide their teachers' directions. Children must abide their parents' wishes.

abiotic (ay-bee-a-tik) adj. not alive; devoid of or not having life; lifeless. The moon is cold, dark, and abiotic.

abject adj. detestable; horrible; hopeless. The abject living conditions of the tenement building leave much to be desired.

abjure v. to formally renounce or reject something. Before converting to the new religion, the man had to abjure his previous beliefs.

ablaze adj. to be on fire. The spark set the house ablaze.

abode (ah-bode) n. a home or a place to live. The man's abode was his castle.

abolish v. to end or do away with something. Slavery was abolished after the Civil War by the 13th Amendment.

abolition (a-boe-li-shun) n. the act of ending or stopping something. The abolition of slavery was one of Lincoln's goals. / **abolitionist** n. person who supports the abolition of something.

abominable (uh-bo-min-ah-bul) adj. hated; despised; loathed; horrible. The murder of the family was abominable. / **abomination** n. something that is abominable. Murder is an abomination.

aboriginal (a-be-ri-ji-nal) adj. earliest known; the first; the original. The aboriginal Indian tribes of Mexico were devastated by European diseases.

abort v. to stop or end something. The plane's takeoff was aborted because of engine trouble.

abound v. to be filled with; more than enough. The planet was abound with life. The air was abound with smoke.

abrasion (uh-bray-shun) n. area that is scraped or worn away. The abrasion on his arm required medical attention.

abreast (uh-brest) adj. 1. next to something. The athletes paraded abreast of each other. 2. to keep informed of or knowledgeable about. Doctors must keep abreast of the latest medical techniques.

abridge (uh-brij) v. to shorten or lessen. The long story was abridged every time it was told. / **abridged** adj. shorter. The abridged version was liked by more people.

abroad (uh-brawd) adj. 1. in another country or foreign region. 2. in many areas. The tourist is from abroad. The book is available here and abroad.

abrogate v. to cancel something; repeal or end. The new law abrogated the old law.

abrupt adj. sudden; without notice; unexpected. The abrupt change in the weather ruined their plans.

abscond (ab-skond) v. to leave in a hurry; leave without notice; leave secretly. The thief absconded with the diamonds.

absolve v. to forgive a wrongdoing or obligation. The priest absolved the man from his sins.

abstain v. to withhold or refrain from doing something; to keep from doing something. The girl abstained from drinking more soda.

abstinence (ab-sti-nens) n. the act of abstaining; the act of doing without something. Abstinence from heavy lifting is what the doctor ordered.

abstract adj. hard to comprehend; existing in the mind; general not specific. The artist's painting was abstract.

abysmal (uh-bis-mal) adj. not good; poor quality. The man has an abysmal driving record and has many moving violations.

abyss (uh-bis) n. place of vast openness, darkness, or depth. The astronaut gazed into the abyss of outer space.

academia (ak-a-dee-mee-ah) n. pertaining to academics; a college or scholarly lifestyle and its characteristics or surroundings. The professor prefers academia rather than corporate life.

academic adj. pertaining or characterized by schools, study, or research; educational practices. The student preferred academic life to the military.

accentuate (ak-sen-chu-ate) v. to emphasize or point out. The lawyer accentuated the previous violations of the criminal.

accessory (ak-ses-or-ee) n. something added or in addition to another; someone or something that helps or improves another. The outfit's accessories included a belt and hat.

acclaim (ak-lame) n. acceptance, approval, honor, applause, or fanfare. The writer received much acclaim for his latest book.

acclimate v. to become comfortable with; get to know; feel at ease with surroundings or situation. The tourist had to acclimate herself to the change in temperature.

accolade n. a notice or reward for something done well. The magazine was filled with accolades for the movie.

Matching Quiz # 5

___ 1. abode		a. vast openness
___ 2. aberration		b. to help in with something
___ 3. abyss		c. to get use to something
___ 4. acclimate		d. to give up power
___ 5. abject		e. to take off with something
___ 6. abet		f. home or place to live
___ 7. abdicate		g. to follow rules
___ 8. accolade		h. to keep from doing something
___ 9. absolve		i. to emphasize something
___ 10. abhorrent		j. horrible
___ 11. abstain		k. to lessen
___ 12. abate		l. notice for an accomplishment
___ 13. abide		m. hopeless
___ 14. abscond		n. something not as it should be
___ 15. accentuate		o. to forgive

---

accost v. to approach or bother someone. The actor was accosted by reporters who asked many questions.

accountable (uh-koun-tuh-bul) adj. to be held responsible for; made to explain. The driver was held accountable for the accident.

accouterments (uh-koo-ter-ments) n. personal belongings, equipment, or skills. The accouterments of successful business people include a good vocabulary, good communication skills, the ability to read and write well, determination, and good people skills.

accredited adj. accepted as legal, official, or having merit; meeting certain guidelines; widely accepted as legitimate. Students must be sure to attend only accredited colleges.

accrue v. to build up or increase over time; to come as a result of. Proper techniques will accrue with more practice. Your debt will accrue if the interest on the loan is not paid.

acculturate v. to embrace, accept, practice, or adopt the culture or lifestyle of others. Indians were expected to acculturate themselves according to European and American ways. /**acculturation** n. process of acculturating and adopting the culture of another group.

Achilles' heel (uh-kil-ees) n. figurative saying for a person's weakness; a shortcoming. His Achilles' heel was his lack of speed.

acidic (uh-si-dik) adj. containing acid; characteristic of acid; acid-like. The orange tasted acidic.

acme (ak-mee) n. point of greatest achievement; the pinnacle; the best. The improved test scores were the acme of the school's success.

acoustic (uh-koo-stik) adj. having to do with sound or hearing. The acoustics of the new theater were fabulous.

acumen n. intelligence, understanding, and strong skills. The man's scientific acumen led him to the top of his field.

acute adj. 1. sharp; severe; coming quickly. 2. smart; perceptive. The florist has an acute sense of smell. The acrobat has an acute sense of timing.

adept adj. good at something; having much skill. He was an adept quarterback.

adequate adj. just enough; satisfactory. The family had an adequate amount of time for the picnic.

ad hoc Latin phrase meaning on a case by case basis; under special circumstances. The zoning requests will be reviewed ad hoc.

admonish v. to scold; to discipline verbally for one's future benefit. The mother admonished her son for playing with matches.

adroit adj. skillful with the mind or body. The gymnast was very adroit.

adulterated adj. affected by something; not pure; contaminated. The good story line in the movie was adulterated by too much graphic violence. / **adulterate** v.

100

adversary (ad-ver-sair-ee) n. a foe; opponent; enemy. The baseball team was about to battle their toughest adversary.

advocate n. v. /n. (ad-voe-ket) a person who acts or speaks on behalf or in support of another. The teacher acted as the students' advocate in court. / v. (ad-voe-kate) To speak or act on behalf or support of another. The teacher advocated that the students were innocent.

aesthetic (es-the-tik) adj. n. / adj. having to do with appearance over function. / n. the appearance of something. The architect was concerned about the aesthetics of the building.

affiliate n. /n. (uh-fil-ee-et) something associated or connected to another. The pharmacy has affiliates in other states. / v. (uh-fil-ee-ate) to connect or associate with something. The grammar school is affiliated with the high school.

affinity (uh-fin-i-tee) n. a natural liking or interest in something. The boy has an affinity for chess.

agnostic (ag-no-stik) n. a person who does not believe or disbelieve in the existence of God. Agnostics want proof that God exists.

ajar adj. open a little; out of alignment. The man left the car door ajar.

albatross n. 1. a heavy burden one bares. Taken from a poem by Samuel Taylor called "The Rime of the Ancient Mariner" about a sailor who killed an albatross and was forced to wear its carcass around his neck as punishment. Never finishing college is his albatross. 2. a large sea bird and thought to bring good luck.

alchemy (al-ke-mee) n. science that combined the study of nature, chemistry, religion, and magic as practiced by wizards and sorcerers in the middle ages. The wizard's power lay in his knowledge of alchemy.

allegory n. a story that symbolizes or explains something else; a story with deeper meaning. Some people believe *The Wizard of Oz* was an allegory of American life in the late 1800s.

allocate v. to divide up and distribute. The charity money was allocated to the neediest families.

allude v. to make reference to or point out in a low-key manner. The teacher alluded to the student's past performance in class.

aloof adj. uninterested; without emotion. The man was aloof regarding the plight of his friends.

altruistic (all-true-is-tik) adj. genuine, often unselfish concern for others. The man displayed his altruistic side when his neighbors were in need.

amalgamate (uh-mal-ga-mate) v. to bring together; unite, combine to make whole. The school amalgamated all its resources to achieve its goal.

ambiance (am-bee-ons) n. the setting; atmosphere in a room. The restaurant had a pleasant ambiance conducive for fine dining.

ambidextrous (am-bi-dex-trus) adj. ability to be both right and left handed. The child must be ambidextrous to write with either hand.

ambiguous (am-bi-gyu-us) adj. not clear; having more than one meaning. The suspect's explanation was ambiguous at best.

ambivalent adj. contradicting attitude or meaning; opposite or conflicting. The doctor seemed ambivalent towards his patient.

amend v. to fix, change, or repair something. The man amended his relationship with his son./ **amendable** adv.

amiable (ay-mee-uh-bul) adj. pleasant; likeable; friendly. He has an amiable personality.

amnesty (am-nes-tee) n. forgiveness; freedom; pardon from wrongdoing. The prisoner sought amnesty from the government.

Matching Quiz # 6

_____1. altruistic	a. to build up over time
_____2. admonish	b. to scold
_____3. amend	c. not clear
_____4. affiliate	d. related to appearance
_____5. amnesty	e. an enemy or opponent
_____6. aloof	f. unselfish concern for others
_____7. ambiguous	g. to bother someone
_____8. aesthetic	h. skilled with the mind or body
_____9. adversary	i. a deep liking for something
_____10. accoutrements	j. showing no emotion
_____11. adroit	k. showing conflicting meanings
_____12. accost	l. to fix or change
_____13. affinity	m. forgiveness or freedom
_____14. accrue	n. to be associated with another
_____15. ambivalent	o. personal belongings or skills

---

amorous adj. lively or spirited towards someone; showing affection or love. The boy was quite amorous towards the new girl in class.

amphibious (am-fi-bee-us) adj. living or functioning in water or on land. The army unveiled its new amphibious vehicle yesterday.

anachronism (uh-na-kro-niz-um) n. something that is out of place in time. The picture is an anachronism because it shows people with cars during the Revolutionary War. / **anachronistic** adj.

antediluvian (an-tee-di-lu-vee-an) adj. 1. old; antiquated; outdated. Where did those antediluvian clothes come from? 2. before the flood (or before the Great Flood spoke about in the Bible). Geologists theorized about the antediluvian landscape.

antiquated (an-ti-kway-ted) adj. old; outdated. The carpenter's tools were antiquated but useful.

antiquity (an-ti-kwi-tee) n. of very old times; of ages gone past; very long ago. The archeologist found many rare treasures from antiquity.

antiestablishment (an-ty-es-tab-lish-ment) adj. a person, group, or thought process that opposes the accepted order or norms of society, governmental, and their social, political, or economic structure and policies. The antiestablishment movement was very strong in the 1960s with all the antiwar protests.

antithesis (an-ti-the-sis) n. the complete opposite of something. His generous personality makes him the antithesis of his greedy brother.

apathy (a-puh-thee) n. lack of feeling or emotion towards something; lack of importance placed on something. Young people seem to have much apathy toward our country these days.

aphasia (uh-fay-zhia) n. inability to communicate or use and understand words. Since aphasia has set in, the grandmother cannot talk to her children.

apocalypse (uh-po-ki-lips) n. the end of the world; a great worldly tragedy. Nuclear war would be an apocalypse. /**apocalyptic** adj. something tragic in the world; related to the end of the world.

apologetic (uh-po-le-je-tik) adj. expressing sorrow for something.

apologist (uh-po-li-jist) n. a person who defends or supports a point of view or person. The scientist had many apologists for his new theory.

appease (uh-peez) v. to give in to someone in order to avoid a larger conflict; to pacify someone. Hitler should not have been appeased by other European leaders. / **appeasement** n.

appraise (uh-praze) v. to estimate the value of something. The house was appraised for $150,000. / **appraisal** n. estimated value of something.

apprise (uh-prize) v. to keep informed about; to keep up to date about. The general was apprised of troop movements every hour.

aptitude n. skill or competence in something. The test measured the students' mathematical aptitude.

arbitrary adj. going by one's desires or personal opinions; not thought out carefully; not consistent; on a whim. People must not make arbitrary decisions concerning their jobs. / **arbitrarily** adv.

archetype (ar-ke-type) n. the first or original form of something. Thomas Edison created the archetype of the practical light bulb. / **archetypical** adj.

archipelago (ar-ki-pe-luh-goe) n. a group of islands; a sea with a group of islands in it. Many types of sea life can be studied in the South American archipelago.

array n. a wide range of something; a gamut; something in proper order. The new medicine makes an array of cures possible.

ascend (a-send) v. to move up; to climb; to advance upward in position or rank. The politician ascended the ranks of government all the way to the White House.

asphyxiate (as-fix-ee-ate) v. to suffocate; to cut off supply of oxygen. The astronauts almost asphyxiated in their spacecraft when the oxygen tank broke.

assail v. to attack with many weapons; to be bombarded by many things. The reporters assailed the politician with questions.

assimilate v. to make as one's own; to make or become a part of. Some Indians assimilated into American society. / **assimilation** n. process of assimilating.

astute adj. perceptive; intelligent; clever. The detective was very astute.

asymmetric (ay-si-me-trik) adj. not symmetric; not even or the same on both sides. The asymmetric desk would not fit through the door.

atheist (ay-thee-ist) n. person who does not believe in God. / **atheism** n. belief that there is no God.

atrophy (a-tro-fee) v. n. / v. to decay; become old and weak from lack of use. / n. the process of decaying or wasting away. Atrophy will set in as people get older if muscles are not used.

attrition (uh-tri-shun) n. process of decreasing in number or wearing down, especially over time. The Civil War became a war of attrition.

audacious (aw-day-shus) adj. bold; courageous; willing to take sometimes-unwise risks./ **audacity** n. The student had the audacity to insult the principal.

austerity n. strictness or sternness in one's manner or appearance; seriousness. Everyone knew by the austerity in the woman's voice that she was not joking. / **austere** adj.

authentic adj. real; genuine; reliable; original; what something claims to be. The painting was authentic. / **authenticate** v. to show that something is authentic. / **authenticity** n. the truth, reliability, or realness of something.

avant-garde (ah-vahnt gard) n. refers to a group of people, especially in the arts, who are the leaders in creating new methods, ideas, designs, and innovations in a field. Claude Monet and the rest of the avant-garde of the impressionist movement helped make art appeal to more people.

AA Crossword Puzzle AA

ACROSS	DOWN
2 to stop	1 to increase over time
3 to shorten	2 to emphasize or point out
4 skill or competence in something	3 to estimate value
5 to divide up and distribute	6 in another country
7 bold, courageous	8 likeable, friendly
9 unselfish concern for others	9 to give in to someone
10 a wide range of something	11 to move up or climb
12 atmosphere in a room	12 odd, irregular, not normal
15 story that symbolizes something else	13 going with one's personal feelings, not well thought out
16 good at something	14 process of decreasing in number of time
18 lack of feeling for something	17 on a case-by-case basis
19 original form of something	
20 to end or do away with something	

Puzzle made at puzzle-maker.com

AA Word Search Puzzle AA

```
C C M D T E T A C O L L A E M L M
K I Y R A R T I B R A Q C P X Y Q
A X T X V X D P M F V L J S C J E
K N Q S R W M T F T L J Z Y K D T
A L A W I V W I V T W R Z L T Z A
N K H C L U L B V T R E R A A L U
T W D L H I R K G S H C Q C D K T
I K Y N A R E T U N N N O E R N
Q R A T E T O O L E T A L P Q P E
U D E C U C U N D A P I T A U G C
A P H T C G S A I A T B T D A M C
T Z S L I R L A T S J M N T T P A
E A T B V O U H J W M A G D E N K
D B M X C Y Y E H R L M X X X R R
L A Q C W Q T B N A M I A B L E P
F R A A C C O U T E R M E N T S L
F R Z T C M A M P H I B I O U S K
```

ACCENTUATE	ALTRUISTIC	ANTIQUATED
ACCOLADE	AMBIANCE	APATHY
ACCOUTERMENTS	AMBIGUOUS	APOCALYSPE
ACCRUE	AMIABLE	ARBITRARY
ADEQUATE	AMPHIBIOUS	ASCEND
AFFILIATE	ANACHRONISM	ASTUTE
ALLOCATE		

Puzzle made at puzzle-maker.com

BB

baffle v. to confuse or make hard to understand; to <u>mystify</u>. The murder baffled the detective. / **baffling** adj. This is a baffling mystery.

balk v. to hesitate; to stop; to turn down. The student balked at the chance to go to Europe.

baneful adj. destructive; hurtful; causing harm. The storm had a baneful effect on the town.

barometer n. 1. a devise to measure air pressure. 2. figurative for something used as <u>benchmark</u> for comparison or change.

barrage n. an attack with many weapons; many things coming at once. The soldiers dodged a barrage of gunfire.

barrister (bair-i-ster) n. name for a lawyer in England. Barristers and attorneys perform similar work.

barter v. to trade goods rather than money to buy or obtain something; to <u>haggle</u> or negotiate over goods and services. In some countries bartering is preferable to the outright buying of goods.

bastion n. a safe haven or gathering point; place where something in great amounts exists. Wall Street is a bastion of capitalism.

bedlam n. much confusion; chaos; upheaval. Bedlam broke out during the earthquake.

befall v. to affect; happen to. The neighborhood was befallen by crime.

befuddle v. to confuse; <u>mystify</u>; <u>baffle</u>. The riddle befuddled the students.

begrudge (be-gruj) v. to be jealous of or not completely happy with; to agree or approve of unwillingly. The boy begrudged his brother's new car.

beguile (bee-gile)) v. to confuse, deceive, or trick; to misrepresent or mislead; to be dishonest or shady. The salesman beguiled the customer about the warranty.

behoove v. to be in one's best interest; to act to one's advantage or suffer some consequence. It behooves the child to be home on time.

belated adj. late; afterward. I must send him a belated birthday card.

bellicose (be-lee-koes) adj. quarrelsome; argumentative; confrontational. The bellicose coach was disliked by the parents.

belligerent (be-lij-er-ent) adj. rude; offensive; antagonistic; quarrelsome; aggressive. The parent was belligerent to the teacher.

benchmark n. something used to gauge a change in something; a reference point. Test scores are not the only benchmark of student success.

benefactor n. a person who helps another, usually in a monetary way. The millionaire was the school's benefactor.

beneficiary (ben-e-fish-ee-air-ee) n. someone or something that benefits from something. The student was the beneficiary of the teacher's understanding personality.

benevolence (be-ne-vo-lens) n. kindness; good will; desire to do good. The family's benevolence in the community was well-known. / **benevolent** adj.

benign (be-nine) adj. not harmful or life threatening. The accident only left benign injuries.

besiege (bee-seej) v. to overwhelm; to attack from all sides or all at once; to be attacked for a long period of time. The fort was besieged for six months.

bestow v. to place upon; to give to in good will; to entrust. The father bestowed the family business to his son.

bewilder v. to confuse; mystify; to baffle. The discovery bewildered scientists.

bias n. v. / n. a tendency for something; a prejudice; preconceived notion or attitude. Employers should not let a bias towards any group affect whom they hire. /v. The salesman was biased towards tourists. / **biased** adj.

bibliophile (bib-lee-oe-file) n. person who loves books. The librarian is a bibliophile.

bicentennial n. adj. a two hundred-year period or anniversary; occurring every two hundred years. The U.S. celebrated its bicentennial in 1976.

bidding n. following orders, commands, or another's desires; work. The private must do the general's bidding or be court-martialed.

bilateral adj. having two sides; having two opinions. The agreement between workers and management was bilateral.

bilingual adj. speaking two languages. Spanish teachers are bilingual.

billowed v. pouring forth; spewing; surging. Smoke billowed from the fire.

binary adj. containing two of something; a pair. Computer languages consist of binary numbers such as "ones" and "zeros."

bionics n. science of improving or replacing human anatomical or physiological systems with electronic motors and devices. Amputees will benefit from the improvements in bionic technology. /**bionic** adj.

biped n. having two legs. Humans are bipeds. / **bipedal** adj.

bipolar n. 1. having or occurring in two poles; having opposite elements or opinions. Batteries are bipolar devices. 2. Mental illness due to a chemical imbalance in the brain causing severe mood swings.

bisect v. to cut in two. The farm is bisected by a road.

blackball v. to conspire to exclude or reject someone or something. The worker was blackballed from being hired throughout the state.

bleak (bleek) adj. dismal; hopeless; depressing. Without an education one's future looks bleak.

bliss n. state of happiness or cheer. The newlyweds vacationed in bliss. / **blissful** adj.

blithe (blyth) adj. happy; blissful; in good spirits. He is a blithe young child.

Quiz # 7
Matching

_____ 1. benign
_____ 2. benefactor
_____ 3. benchmark
_____ 4. bestow
_____ 5. bias
_____ 6. begrudge
_____ 7. belligerent
_____ 8. bellicose
_____ 9. baffle
_____ 10. bionics
_____ 11. biped
_____ 12. beneficiary
_____ 13. barter
_____ 14. benevolence
_____ 15. behoove

a. having two legs
b. a prejudice toward something
c. one who benefits from something
d. one who helps another
e. to confuse
f. to trade goods
g. replace human parts with motors
h. good will
i. to be in one's best interest
j. to place upon or give to
k. rude
l. to be jealous of
m. something used to gauge change
n. argumentative
o. not harmful

---

bludgeon (blood-jen) v. to strike or hit with a heavy object. The poor victim was bludgeoned to death with a brick.

bluster n. v. / n. a loud violent noise; to act in a loud manner. The man's opinionated bluster caused people to ignore him. /v. The storm blustered from the west.

boisterous (boy-ster-us) adj. loud talking or merriment. The adults were more boisterous at the party than the children.

bona fide adj. real; genuine. The prospector produced the bona fide claim to the gold.

bonsai n. 1. Japanese skill of growing small trees and bushes. 2. a small tree or shrub.

botany n. the study of plants. The owners of the greenhouse studied botany. / **botanist** n. / **botanical** adj.

botulism (bo-chu-liz-um) n. a serious illness or poisoning caused by eating certain spoiled foods. The bad meat gave the whole family botulism.

Bowery or bowery n. 1. New York City street known for its lowlife appearance and destitute people. 2. any run down part of town that is slummy and has many poor people. The bowery has many homeless people.

brandish v. to take out or show in a hostile way. The boy brandished a club and scared the others away.

brazen (braze-en) adj. bold and sassy; without fear or concern of what someone might think. The child was very brazen in her response.

breach (breech) v. n. /v. to force an opening through. The soldiers breached the enemy's front lines. /n. a gap; a forced opening in something.

brinkmanship n. going to the limits of something before giving in; taking something as far as it can go without dire consequences. The U.S. and Soviet policy of brinkmanship almost led to nuclear war.

broach v. to bring up a subject. The parents broached the matter of their child's failing grades during dinner.

brunt n. the full force or effect of something. The rural town bore the brunt of the storm's destruction.

bulwark n. a protection against something; fortification or safeguard. The bulwark of the military was the air force. The bulwark of safety is proper planning.

buoyancy (boy-an-see) n. the ability to float. Ships must be designed for proper buoyancy. / **buoyant** adj.

burgeon (ber-jen) n. to grow out rapidly. New restaurants have burgeoned all over town.

bustle (bus-uhl) n. noise, confusion, and haste. The hustle and bustle of urban life is nerve-racking.

by-product n. the result of something; the effect or consequence. The by-product of war is more death.

BB Crossword Puzzle BB

www.CrosswordWeaver.com

ACROSS	DOWN
1 to work to exclude someone from something	1 the ability to float
5 to take out and show in a hostile way	2 kindness or good will
6 bold and sassy	3 person who benefits from something
7 to bring up a subject	4 to force an opening or break n something
9 having two sides or two opinions	7 quarrelsome or argumentative
11 a lawyer in an upper court in England	8 to affect or happen to
13 to be in one's best interest	9 the effect or result of something
14 an attack with weapons at once	10 the full force of something
	12 not harmful or life-threatening

Puzzle made at puzzle-maker.com

BB Word Search Puzzle BB

```
B B E N E V O L E N C E B C R S
M U X L L X T Z R L K K L K U L
X R O N F K M V H L K N X O K E
K L W Y F P C L R F D M R K G T
T P D R A H F J C B Y E C A D B
N V C F B N M X E H T M R Y B E
B N M N L Q C N P S K R R N E L
J E J J L V C Y I V A D J L N L
N Q H L T H R O L B C L X A E I
D E L O M C B N J Z Z H P U F G
N K G A O B E G R U D G E G I E
Z C R E C V R V N G W M N C R
R K L Q I M E T B J M P C I I E
K B K P V S T K T W C T B L A N
R O T C A F E N E B B K R I R T
Z B T H B Z W B Q M K Q C B Y C
```

BAFFLE	BENEFICIARY
BARRAGE	BENEVOLENCE
BEGRUDGE	BESIEGE
BEHOOVE	BILINGUAL
BELLIGERENT	BOISTEROUS
BENCHMARK	BUOYANCY
BENEFACTOR	

Puzzle made at puzzle-maker.com

CC

cabaret (cab-er-ay) n. entertainment usually offering singing and dancing. The cabaret club was very popular in the 1940s.

cache (kash) n. a storage or hiding place for things, usually of value or importance. The sailors had a cache of guns on board the ship.

cacophony (ka-kof-o-nee) n. loud, harsh, annoying sounds. A cacophony of noise came from the kitchen when all the plates fell.

cajole n. to coax or flatter someone into doing something. The boy cajoled his father into taking him to the ballgame.

calamity n. a disaster or bad situation. The calamity caused by the fire left many people homeless.

caldron (call-dren) n. a large pot for boiling. The witch stirred her potion in the caldron.

calligraphy (ke-lig-ruh-fee) n. stylistic handwriting. Calligraphy is a lost art.

callous (kal-us) adj. hard or rough; showing no emotion or sorrow. The callous brother was not upset by the hardship of his family.

camaraderie (kah-mah-rah-der-ee) n. good spirits from being with friends or around people. The man joined the club for the camaraderie of people like himself.

canal n. a channel of water connecting two other bodies of water; a channel used to carry water from place to place. The canal connecting the Atlantic and Pacific oceans is man-made.

candid adj. honest; frank; open. The politician was very candid in his opinion.

cannibalism n. eating human flesh or body parts. The stranded expedition party resorted to cannibalism.

cantilever (kan-ti-lee-ver) n. adj. v. / n. a weight-bearing beam that sticks outs and is only supported at one end. /adj. related to the cantilever design. / v. to build something with cantilevers. The balcony was cantilevered over the back of the house.

capital n. 1. the center or place of importance of something; something that is important or serious. The capital of Illinois is Springfield. 2. money or financial resources. The investors need more capital to start their business.

capitulate (kuh-pich-yu-late) v. to give in, give up, or surrender. The store's owner finally capitulated and agreed to offer more services.

capricious (kuh-pree-shus) adj. liable to change one's mind without reason. Youngsters are sometimes more capricious than adults.

caravan n. v. /n. a group traveling somewhere together; a group traveling together for safety. A caravan of bikers went down the street. /v. to travel together. The students caravanned to the stadium.

carcinogen (kar-si-no-jen) n. something that causes cancer. Radiation is a carcinogen. / **carcinogenic** adj.

cardiac adj. related to the heart. His cardiac problems have been cured.

caricature (kair-i-kah-chur) n. a picture or cartoon-like drawing that exaggerates or makes fun of someone or something; a picture symbolizing something. The student's caricature of the teacher amused the other students.

carnivore n. meat-eating animal. Bears and humans are carnivores. /**carnivorous** adj.

carpe diem (karpee dee-em) Latin term meaning "seize the day." Refers to taking advantage of one's opportunities now rather than later; live for the moment.

carte blanche (kart blonch) n. complete authority to do something. The employee thinks he has carte blanche within the company.

cascade (kas-kade) v. n. /v. to flow downward; to affect one thing after another. The water cascaded down the mountain. / n. a waterfall. The rafters rode the cascades all the way down.

caste (kast) n. a segment of a social or economic class of people; social or economic class system that people are born into and usually does not allow for upward mobility. The upper and lower castes of some countries rarely associate with each other.

castigate v. to admonish or criticize harshly. The teacher was castigated by the principal for his lack of good judgment.

cataclysm (ka-tah-kliz-um) n. a terrible event; a catastrophe affecting the earth. The tornado produced a cataclysm like no one had ever seen. /**cataclysmic** adj.

catalyst (ka-tah-list) n. something that brings about a change or reaction. Certain hormones act as catalyst for bodily functions. The fire served as a catalyst for improved safety procedures.

catastrophe (ka-tas-troe-fee) n. a horrible or devastating event. The catastrophe of war will never be forgotten.

categorical adj. without stipulations or conditions; complete; final. His response was swift and categorical. / **categorically** adv. The man categorically denied the allegations.

catharsis n. a releasing or purging of something bad causing needed metal or emotional relief. Talking things over is a good catharsis for the mind.

catty adj. nasty; trivial; spiteful. The female co-workers were competitive and catty towards one another.

caustic adj. harsh or critical in responding or communicating. The teacher's caustic reply hurt the child's feelings.

cavalier adj. 1. a lazy or uninterested manner; careless or showing no importance. His cavalier attitude toward school got him nowhere. 2. boastful; arrogant. People did not like his cavalier tone.

cavern n. a deep recess or gap; a cave. The hidden caverns were filled with bats and snakes. / **cavernous** adj. cave-like

cease (sees) v. stop doing something; to end. The boy was told to cease his complaining.

cede (seed) v. to give up; relinquish; surrender. The owner ceded his property to the government so a new road could be built.

celestial (se-le-stee-uhl) adj. relating to the sky, heavens, stars, space, or the universe; figurative for beautiful or <u>serene</u>. The celestial light illuminated the entire planet.

censor v. n. /v. to review to determine if something is acceptable or offensive and fit for public consumption. The album was censored for its graphic words. /n. a person who does such a review.

censure v. to blame, criticize or rebuke a person. The teacher was censured for his unprofessional comments.

centrifugal adj. moving away from the center. Amusement park rides such as the Flying Bobs exert centrifugal force.

centripetal adj. moving toward the center. Gravity is the centripetal force the holds the moon in orbit around the earth.

cerebral (sir-ee-bral) adj. 1. related to the brain; The accident left him with cerebral damage. 2. using reason rather than emotion. His cerebral response was well thought out.

Matching Quiz # 8	
___1. capital	a. to give something up
___2. capricious	b. completely honest
___3. cede	c. social grouping based on class
___4. catharsis	d. cancer causing
___5. cache	e. to stop
___6. catalyst	f. complete authority
___7. carcinogen	g. a channel that carries water
___8. capitulate	h. causes a change or reaction
___9. cease	i. to give in or surrender
___10. canal	j. to flatter someone to action
___11. categorical	k. a storage place
___12. carte blanche	l. money or finances
___13. cajole	m. a release of something bad
___14. caste	n. likely to change one's mind
___15. candid	o. without conditions

chagrin (shuh-grin) n. a feeling of disapproval or failure; disappointment. The chagrin of not being picked for the team ruined his day.

chalice (cha-lis) n. a fancy or ornamental drinking cup or goblet. The king drank wine from the gold chalice.

charisma (kuh-ris-mah) n. refined manner; charming or pleasing personality that attracts and influences others. The man's charisma attracted the attention of the ladies. /**charismatic** adj.

chasm (cha-zum) n. a deep gap or gorge; a deep crack or opening in the earth. The ocean is filled with underwater chasms and caves.

chastise (chas-tise) v. to <u>admonish</u>; to punish or criticize for improvement. The boy was chastised for his rude manners.

chattel n. personal property that can be taken with someone. Horses, cows, and tractors are examples of a farmer's chattel.

chauvinism (show-vi-niz-um) n. a belief that one gender is more or less capable than the other. Male chauvinism states that women cannot perform the same duties as well as men. / **chauvinist** n. person who practices chauvinism.

chicanery (shi-kay-ner-ee) n. deceit; trickery. The thief's chicanery fooled many people.

chivalry (shiv-ahl-ree) n. literally pertaining to the attributes of a good knight or proper knightly conduct; brave, honest, loyal, courteous; respectful, especially towards women. Young men today are ignorant of chivalry. / **chivalrous** adj.

circumstantial (sir-kum-stan-chel) adj. pertaining to individual circumstances; not standing alone but dependent on other factors or the circumstance. His explanation is too circumstantial to believe.

circumvent (sir-kum-vent) v. to get around; to avoid. The wealthy businessman circumvented the tax code by hiding money in an overseas bank account. Magellan circumvented the globe.

civic (siv-ik) adj. related to a city or citizens. The park is for civic use.

civics n. study of the rights and obligations of citizens. Voting is a major aspect of civics.

civil (siv-il) adj. 1. related to citizens of a city or country. 2. relating to the government of a city or country. 3. non-military. 4. related to a civilization or a civilized manner. The Bill of Rights protects many civil rights of Americans. Barbarians and murders are not civil people.

civilian n. someone not in the military. The students remained civilians during the war while others joined the army.

clandestine adj. in a secretive or deceptive manner. The cat burglar's theft of the jewels was quick and clandestine.

cliché (kli-shay) n. something such as an idea, phrase, or expression that is old and been used a lot. Car crashes in movies is a worn out cliché.

coagulate (koe-ag-yu-late) v. to make a liquid into a thicker substance. Baking soda on an open cut will coagulate the blood and stop the bleeding.

coarse (kors) adj. 1. a rough surface; not smooth. The material was coarse and scratchy. 2. crude; abrupt. The man gave a coarse reply.

coerce (ko-ers) v. to persuade by force or intimidation. The student was coerced into being in the school play. / **coercion** n.

cogent (ko-jent) adj. influential; able to persuade or convince. The salesman gave a cogent speech for buying the car today.

cognitive (kog-ni-tiv) adj. related to a mental process such as thinking, reasoning, remembering, and perception. Processing sight and sound are among the most important cognitive senses. /**cognition** n.

cognizant (kog-ni-zent) adj. to be aware; related to mental knowledge observed or perceived. The teacher was cognizant of the student's reading problem.

coherent (ko-hair-ent) adj. 1. sticking together. 2. making sense. The victim's account of the tragedy was coherent and helped police understand the accident.

cohesive (ko-hee-siv) adj. sticking or causing to stick together; united; loyal. The labor union is cohesive and will not give in on any issue.

collaborate v. to work together or cooperate. The scientists collaborated to solve the problem.

collateral n. adj. /n. something of value used to secure a loan that the bank can take if the loan is not paid. The man had to put his house up as collateral for the business loan. /adj. something extra or on the side. The explosion caused a lot of collateral damage to other buildings.

colloquial (ko-loe-kwee-al) adj. the common way of speaking in everyday life; the <u>vernacular</u>. Colloquial English is hard for foreigners to understand. /**colloquialism** n. a local word for something.

colloquium (ko-low-kwee-um) n. a conference usually of specialists or noted experts in a field. The college held a colloquium for future engineers.

combatant n. person involved in a fight or battle; someone in the combat. The observers soon became combatants when the fight got out of control.

combustible (kum-bus-ti-bul) adj. a substance capable or burning. Gasoline is a highly combustible liquid. / **combust** v. to burn. / **combustion** n. act of burning.

commensurate (ko-men-sher-it) adj. fair; in the proper amount; equal. The punishment must be commensurate with the crime.

commissary n. place where food is sold. The building's commissary offered no health foods.

commute v. n. /v. to travel from one place to another on a regular basis. The man commutes to work on the train every day. / n. the trip from one place to another. The commute took longer than usual today.

compensation n. reward given in exchange for something. The boy received a new bike as compensation for helping out his dad over the summer. / **compensate** v.

complacent adj. satisfied. The man was complacent with his job so he never looked for a better one. / **complacency** n.

comprise v. to include or be made up of. The association comprises local business people and residents.

compromise (kom-proe-mise) n. v. / n. an agreement where each side gets something and gives up something. /v. to make such an agreement. A compromise is usually the best way to settle a disagreement.

compulsive adj. against one's will or beyond one's control; under force. He has a compulsive drinking problem.

compulsory adj. mandatory; required. All states have compulsory school attendance laws for children.

conceal (kon-seel) v. to hide something. The gun was concealed in the seat.

```
                    Matching Quiz # 9

____1. chattel              a. satisfied with things
____2. civics               b. made up of
____3. chastise             c. in secret
____4. compromise           d. to force or persuade
____5. circumstantial       e. to give something in exchange
____6. chasm                f. to go around
____7. comprise             g. required
____8. compulsory           h. moveable personal property
____9. clandestine          i. personal charm and refinement
____10. charisma            j. related to citizens
____11. circumvent          k. to criticize for improvement
____12. civil               l. a deep crack
____13. complacent          m. dependant on other factors
____14. coerce              n. agreement with a sacrifice
____15. compensate          o. rights and duties of citizens
```

concede (kon-seed) v. to give in to; to admit defeat; to give up. The candidate conceded the election to his opponent.

conceited (kon-seet-ed) adj. arrogant; feeling of superiority. The millionaire is rude and conceited. / **conceit** n.

conceive (kon-seev) v. to think of; to produce or make. The scientist conceived and marketed the invention.

conceptual (kon-sep-chew-al) adj. related to thoughts or ideas; existing in the mind as an early thought. The technology does not yet exist to bring his conceptual ideas to life.

concession (kon-se-shun) n. 1. something given up. The union had to make certain concessions to get more pay. 2. food and drinks for sale. Hot dogs and soda were the only concessions available at the park.

concur (kon-kur) v. to agree with. The principal concurred with the teacher about the student's punishment.

concurrent adj. occurring at the same time. The driver received concurrent tickets for speeding and driving without a license.

condense v. to shrink or make smaller. The long essay was condensed into three paragraphs.

conducive adj. helpful in some way; leading to. Studying hard is conducive to good grades.

confederation (kon-fed-er-ay-shun) n. a loose association or alliance. The organization was a confederation of local businessmen who had the same goals.

conflagration (kon-fla-gray-shun) n. a huge devastating fire. Five houses were destroyed in the conflagration.

confute v. to prove something wrong. The lawyer confuted the evidence against the man.

congenial (kon-jee-nee-al) adj. pleasant; friendly; agreeable; likeable. The speaker was very congenial in his presentation.

congregate v. to gather. The students congregated in the hallways. / **congregation** n. a gathering

conjecture n. v. / n. an assumption; a guess or conclusion made by guessing. The scientist's theory was only conjecture and not based on facts. / v. to make an assumption or conclusion by guessing.

conjure v. to make or make happen through trickery, enchantment, or by magic. The magician conjured up a rabbit.

consanguinity (kon-san-gwin-i-tee) n. a relationship by blood or from the same ancestors. Royalty and consanguinity often go hand in hand.

connoisseur (kon-e-soo-er) n. an expert in something or some field. The chef was also a wine connoisseur.

connotation n. something that implies or suggests another meaning. His sly attitude was a connotation of something untrustworthy. / **connote** v. His suspicious answer connotes that more investigation will be needed.

consecrate v. to make holy or religious; to make sacred. The church consecrated the site of the miracle.

conservative adj. not wasteful; not flashy. She is very conservative with her money.

consignment n. 1. act of handing over something to another, especially for safekeeping. 2. transferring goods to someone but not being paid until the goods are sold. Because the bookstore bought the books on consignment, the author had to wait two months to get paid.

console v. to make someone feel better. The mother consoled the daughter over the girl's loss in the tennis match.

conspicuous (kon-spi-kyu-us) adj. 1. obvious; easy to see. 2. attracting attention. The thief looked very conspicuous with the ski mask on his head on the summer day.

conspire v. to act together secretly against someone. The rebels conspired to overthrow the king.

constitute v. 1. to form or make up. Rebellion constitutes treason. 2. to warrant or deserve. Stealing constitutes punishment.

constrict v. 1. to shorten or tighten. The snake constricted itself around the man's arm. 2. to lesson or decrease. The budget was constricted to save money.

contemplate v. to think about carefully; to consider; to ponder. The man contemplated quitting his job after a bad day at work. /**contemplation** n.

contemporary adj. n. / adj. of the current or same period in time. The style suggests a contemporary design, not one of ancient design. / n. a person living at the same time as another. Thomas Jefferson was a contemporary of Ben Franklin. / **contemporaries** n. (plural)

contiguous (kon-tig-yu-us) adj. connected; touching. Alaska is not part of the contiguous United States.

contingent (kon-tin-jent) adj. depending on something else. The game is contingent on all the players showing up.

contingency n. an unexpected occurrence. The rescuers were prepared for every contingency.

continuous (kon-tin-yu-us) adj. happening over and over; constant. The continuous rain spoiled the outing. / **continuity** n. state of being continuous, connected, uninterrupted, or whole.

contrite adj. regretful; feeling sorry or guilty for doing something wrong. The girl felt contrite after forgetting to feed her puppy.

contrive v. to plan cleverly. The detective contrived a plot to outwit the thief.

convene (kon-veen) v. to come or call together; to meet. The generals convened a meeting to discuss their strategy.

converge v. to meet or come together at some point. The streets converge on the other side of town.

convey (kon-vay) v. 1. to transfer. The man conveyed ownership of the car to his brother. 2. to explain. The parents conveyed their feelings to their children.

convoluted adj. 1. confused; complicated; not making sense. 2. twisted. His convoluted logic confused everyone.

cordial (kor-jahl) adj. friendly; polite; warm. The parents were very cordial towards their daughter's boyfriend.

corollary n. a likely or natural result. Good grades should be a corollary of studying hard.

correlate v. to make a connection to; to relate or organize one thing to another. / **correlation** n. There is a strong correlation in society between vocabulary and socio-economic status.

correspond v. 1. to agree with or be consistent with. The answers did not correspond to the questions. 2. to keep in touch with. They still correspond by mail. / **correspondence** n.

corroborate (ko-rob-or-ate) v. verify or support. The eyewitness corroborated the defendant's testimony.

Matching Quiz # 10

____1. convene	a. something given up	
____2. conceive	b. to make smaller	
____3. conceptual	c. an assumption	
____4. condense	d. to gather	
____5. conjecture	e. arrogant, stuck up	
____6. concede	f. occurring at the same time	
____7. congregate	g. confusing	
____8. conceited	h. to come together	
____9. concurrent	i. to give up	
____10. convoluted	j. obvious or easily seen	
____11. conspicuous	k. an expert about something	
____12. consanguinity	l. to carefully think about	
____13. connoisseur	m. to create	
____14. contemplate	n. relationship by blood	
____15. concession	o. related to thoughts or ideas	

---

coup (koo) n. a sudden or unexpected action. The marketing plan was a real coup for the company.

couth (kooth) adj. sophisticated. His cultured upbringing has made him quite couth.

covenant n. an important agreement or promise. The king made a covenant with his people.

covet v. to desire badly; to be jealous of. The boy coveted his brother's girlfriend.

credulous (kre-ju-lus) adj. <u>naïve</u>; gullible; ready to believe anything. The young girl was credulous in that she always believed her friend's lies.

creed n. a belief or set of beliefs; a statement of belief. Do not discriminate against someone because of his or her religious creed.

crony (kroe-nee) n. associates; friends. The manager gave all his cronies jobs.

cryptic (krip-tik) adj. coded; having a coded or secret message; not easily understood. The letters on the mummy's tomb were in some kind of cryptic language.

cryptography (krip-to-grah-fee) n. skill in coding or decoding secret information. Cryptography is used a lot by the military to keep information secret.

cultivate v. to help or prepare to grow; to nurture. The farmer cultivated his fields. The athlete cultivated his skills for many years. /**cultivation** n.

cursory adj. not thorough or complete; not careful. A cursory examination of the product was not enough to find the flaws.

customary adj. 1. according to custom. 2. what is appropriate or usually acceptable in a given circumstance. The customary greeting among men is a handshake.

cutaneous (kyu-tay-nee-us) adj. on or related to the skin. The wound was only a cutaneous cut.

cut-rate adj. at a great price; a low price. Beef was on sale for a cut-rate price.

cynical (sin-i-kel) adj. 1. not believing in the truth or honesty of something. The fanciful tale brought cynical looks from a few people. 2. judgmental; sarcastic. The cynical remark hurt the boy's feelings.

CC Crossword Puzzle CC

www.CrosswordWeaver.com

ACROSS	DOWN
1 sophisticated, cultured, or refined	1 to criticize harshly
5 to flow downward	2 place where similar things are stored
6 in the proper amount, appropriate	3 hard or rough, showing now emotion
8 not thorough or complete	4 to stop doing something
10 to agree with	6 related by blood or ancestry
12 belief that one gender is better than the other	7 to be aware of
14 to cut out something considered unacceptable	9 loud, harsh, or annoying sounds
15 a lazy or uninterested manner	11 to blame or rebuke a person
16 to punish or criticize for improvement	12 related to the stars, space, or the sky
18 related to thinking or thinking process	13 statement of belief
20 pleasant or friendly	16 to work together
21 to meet or come together at a point	17 to get around or avoid something
22 capable of burning	19 to be honest, frank, or open
23 something that causes a reaction or change	
24 related to the brain, using reason over emotion	
25 of the current or same time period	
26 to form or make	

Puzzle made at puzzle-maker.com

CC Word Search Puzzle CC

```
T L C O G N I T I V E M N G D C X R C
K P C O N S P I C U O U S H G K W O Z
J C N C A M S I R A H C C Q M V M W E
C R M C O N T I N U O U S F L M C T N
A U K S L L R C N L P M N Q E R A Y E
T E N R I T L T A R A L B N Y L W I G
A S C D C N K A V R M U S Y U R R T F
L S E N T R I L T Z C U T G H E B C R
Y I N P K C Y V W E R I A P D L A R L
S O I K T O T Q U A R O N A E T M A Y
T N T J H M I H T A C A R O A C C R D
M N S H V B M E X P H A L S G I N H K
W O E Y L U A T P Y M C T M N E X O K
G C D W R S L L R A F R Y Y K Z N V C
H J N Z T T A Q C R O V C Q T M N L R
K Z A H N I C L J P D L B R D Z K T K
F M L K F B L M H N T H T M J J N V D
Z Y C T R L D E T I E C N O C W D M W
X K N R K E R W C A P I T U L A T E X
```

CALAMITY	CHAUVINISM	CONCEITED
CAMARADERIE	CLANDESTINE	CONCEPTUAL
CAPITULATE	COAGULATE	CONNOISSEUR
CARCINOGEN	COGNITIVE	CONSPICUOUS
CATALYST	COLLATERAL	CONTINUOUS
CATASTROPHE	COMBUSTIBLE	CYNICAL
CHARISMA	COMMENSURATE	

Puzzle made at puzzle-maker.com

DD

dark horse adj. figurative for a winner who was not supposed to win. The runner from Chicago proved to be the dark horse in the race.

dashing adj. handsome; smooth; trendy. The dashing fellow always wore the latest fashions.

dastardly adj. underhanded; evil and sneaky. The surprise attack on Pearl Harbor was a dastardly act of war.

dauntless adj. not easily discouraged; brave. The mountain climber was a dauntless individual.

dearth n. a lack or shortage of something; too small of an amount. A dearth of rain hurt the farmer's crops.

debacle n. a great failure. The business idea turned out to be a huge debacle.

debase v. 1. to lower the value of; to diminish. 2. to belittle someone. The actor's image was debased by the scandal.

debauchery n. a lifestyle of sinful pleasures characterized by too much drinking, eating, or sex; lacking morality. A life of debauchery can lead to a life of regrets.

debilitated adj. weak; not as healthy as before. The stroke left him debilitated.

debonair adj. sophisticated; charming; nice to be with. The boy's debonair personality made him a favorite with the ladies.

decadent (de-kah-dent) adj. 1. sinful; lacking ethics or morality; not good. A decadent lifestyle left him unhappy and lonely. 2. decaying; falling apart.

deceit (di-seet) n. something not true or honest; the act of misleading, tricking, or lying to people. A life of deceit left him with no friends. / **deceitful** adj.

deceive (di-seev) v. to trick or make someone believe something that is not true or as it seems. The magician deceived the audience with his sleight of hand.

deciduous (di-sid-ju-us) adj. trees that lose their leaves. Not all trees are deciduous. A deciduous forest looks bare in the winter.

decimate (de-si-mate) v. to destroy most of. The disease decimated the native populations until there were almost no people left.

decipher (di-sy-fer) v. to decode; to understand something that is not clear. The scientist deciphered the hidden code.

decisive (di-sy-siv) adj. clear; unchallenged or uncontested. The team won a decisive victory.

decompose v. to decay; breakdown into parts. The dead body began to decompose.

decorum (di-kor-um) n. sense of proper conduct; good taste; politeness. The man showed no decorum when he kept interrupting everyone.

decoy (dee-koy) n. something used to distract or get the attention of. The fire alarm was a decoy the burglars used to get everyone outside.

decree (di-kree) v. n. /v. to state firmly. The king decried a new law. /n. an official statement or policy. The new decree made robbery punishable by a longer jail time.

deduce v. to figure out by going from general information to specific information. The detective was able deduce the identity of the real criminal. / **deduction** n. Her powers of deduction are impressive.

deduct v. to subtract or take away. The boss deducted money from the employee for not coming to work. / **deduction** n.

deep-rooted adj. figurative for strong. The woman had a deep-rooted sense of pride.

deep six v. figurative for dead, buried, or getting rid of something. The worker got the deep-six when he was fired.

deface v. to ruin the appearance of. The boys defaced the building with the graffiti.

de facto Latin term meaning from the fact itself, the way it really is, or as a result of (the result of something not planned or by design). Because of poverty, urban schools are often examples of de facto segregation.

default v. n. /v. failure to meet an obligation. The man defaulted on his loan. /n. The man's loan was in default.

defection n. act of leaving one's country or group to join the enemy of that group or country. The Russian spy had many opportunities for defection to the United States.

defer v. 1. to delay until a later time. The test was deferred until tomorrow. 2. to respectfully pass to someone else for an opinion. The teacher deferred the tough question to the principal.

deference n. 1. act of showing respect. Out of deference for the senior citizen, the boy offered his seat to the older man. 2. act of respectfully submitting to another's opinion.

defiance (di-fy-ens) n. refusing to obey. Staying out past curfew is an act of defiance. / **defiant** adj.

deficient (di-fish-ent) adj. lacking in something; not complete. The student was deficient in math skills.

deficit (de-fi-sit) n. a shortage of money; difference between the amount of money collected and the amount spent. If more tax money is not collected the city will face a budget deficit.

126

defile v. to make dirty or sinful; to stain; to make bad or corrupt. The cult defiled the church with satanic messages.

deforestation (de-for-e-stay-shun) n. cutting down trees; act of destroying forests by cutting down many trees. The population growth has led to deforestation in many places.

deformity n. physical imperfections on the body; broken in appearance; Webbed feet on humans is an unusual deformity.

defraud v. to commit fraud; to cheat people out of money or other possessions. The company defrauded its employees out of millions of dollars.

defray v. to pay for. The city defrayed the cost of the new subway.

degenerate v. to grow worse or make worse. The man's health degenerated over time. /**degenerative** adj.

```
Matching Quiz # 11

_____ 1.  dauntless          a.  to trick
_____ 2.  decimate           b.  showing respect
_____ 3.  decipher           c.  to ruin the appearance of something
_____ 4.  debonair           d.  a great mistake or mishap
_____ 5.  debilitated        e.  the way it really is
_____ 6.  decorum            f.  a shortage of money
_____ 7.  debacle            g.  to put off until later
_____ 8.  deface             h.  to leave one country for another
_____ 9.  deceive            i.  to grow worse
_____ 10. de facto           j.  to completely destroy
_____ 11. deficit            k.  to decode or understand
_____ 12. defer              l.  sophisticated
_____ 13. defection          m.  not easily discouraged
_____ 14. deference          n.  weakened
_____ 15. degenerate         o.  sense of proper conduct
```

degradation (deg-re-day-shun) n. a lowering in status, quality, or spirit; a worsening. The man suffered much degradation from the scandal. / **degrade** v.

dehydrated adj. to not have any water; to suffer from a lack or water or fluids. The runner was dehydrated after the race.

deism (dee-iz-um) n. belief in God or a supreme being but not believing in a particular religion. / **deist** n. person who believes in deism.

deity (dee-i-tee) n. 1. a god or goddess; a supreme religions being. Apollo was a main deity of the ancient Greeks. 2. one having divine qualities.

Copyright Laws Prohibit Reproduction

déjà vu (day-zha-voo) n. French expression for a feeling of already seeing or experiencing something before. Though the man never visited the home before, it seemed familiar, and when he walked in a feeling of déjà vu filled his body.

de jure Latin term meaning by law or by deliberate act (differs from de facto in that de jure situations are created with intent). The Jim Crow laws that made racial segregation legal in the South were examples of de jure segregation.

delegate v. n. /n. (del-e-get) a person representing another. The student council had nine delegates at the meeting. /v. (del-e-gate) to assign power or a duty to. The boss delegated the tasks among the remaining workers.

deliberate adj. v. / adj. (dee-li-ber-et) on purpose. The athlete made a deliberate attempt to hurt the other player. /v. (dee-li-ber-ate) to think over carefully and for a period of time. The jury deliberated the guilt or innocence of the man for three days.

delineate (de-lin-nee-ate) v. to clearly show or explain something using drawings or words. The vacation route was delineated on the map.

delinquent adj. failing to do something or meet an obligation. The man was delinquent on his car payments.

deliverance n. act of setting free; being freed or rescued; Passover is a celebration of the Jews' deliverance from slavery in Egypt.

delude v. to deceive one's mind or opinion. The parents deluded the child into thinking he was smarter than he really was.

deluge (del-yuj) n. v. / n. a huge flood. The deluge destroyed the crops. / v. to overcome or overwhelm. The athlete was deluged by fans.

delve v. to search tirelessly and carefully for; to seek out deep inside something. The scientist delved into the caves looking for old bones.

demure (de-myur) adj. acting more sophisticated or sincere than one really is. Her demure attitude did not fool anyone.

denigrate v. to harm the reputation of someone. The scandal denigrated the man.

denote v. to indicate. Poor hygiene often denotes poverty or poor parental supervision.

dense adj. thick or arranged close together. The dense population made it hard to find a quiet place to live.

depose v. to get rid of; to put out of power; to overthrow. The king was deposed by his angry subjects.

depraved adj. morally corrupt or bad. Many violent criminals are depraved individuals. / **depravation** n. in a depraved manner.

128

deprecate v. to strongly speak out against or to disapprove of. The parents deprecated their son's foolish plans. / **deprecation** n.

depreciate (di-pree-shee-ate) v. to lessen in value over time. Cars are a bad investment because they depreciate so fast. / **depreciation** n.

depredate v. to commit a harmful action; to destroy or ruin. Air pollution has depredated the atmosphere. / **depredation** n.

derive v. to arrive at a conclusion. The solution was derived from much thought, testing, and input from others.

derivation (der-i-vay-shun) n. 1. act of deriving. 2. the origin of something. The derivation of many English words come from Greek and Latin.

desist v. to stop doing something. After orders to desist were given, the investigators stopped following the suspect.

desolate adj. v. / adj. (de-soe-let) lifeless; deserted; barren. The moon's surface looks cold and desolate. /v. (de-soe-late) to destroy or make lifeless. The volcano desolated the surface of the earth near the eruption. / **desolation** n.

despondent adj. having lost hope, faith, or courage. The despondent team had no hope of winning the championship due to all the injuries.

despot n. an evil ruler or authority figure with much power; one who abuses his power. The boss acted like an angry despot.

destitute adj. not having necessities such as clothes, food, or place to live. The destitute family was on the verge of starvation.

detriment n. harm or loss caused by something. Smoking is a detriment to your health. /**detrimental** adj.

deviation (dee-vee-ay-shun) n. process of moving away from something; getting off track or off course from the original plan or what is expected. Going to the movies instead of dinner was a deviation from what the couple originally agreed upon. / **deviate** v.

devil's advocate a person who argues in favor of an unpopular idea so that people can understand or examine both sides of a situation. The teacher played devil's advocate by defending England during the Revolutionary War so students could better question the actions of both the colonists and the King.

devise v. to think of. The principal devised a plan to get all students to go to class.

dialect n. form of a language spoken in a particular region. Chinese has many dialects depending where you go in the country.

dialectics (dy-uh-lek-tiks) n. engaging in logical discussions or debates in an attempt to prove or disprove something. The ancient Greeks were masters of dialectics.

diaspora (dy-as-por-ah) n. the scattering of a people. The Jewish diaspora caused by the Holocaust led to the creation of the modern country of Israel.

dichotomy (dy-kot-oe-mee) n. 1. something having two parts. 2. the difference or existence of opposite ideas. The void between theory and reality in his plan creates a great dichotomy.

diction n. act of expressing words in writing or in speech. Without a good vocabulary and knowledge of the rules of English it is impossible to have proper diction.

didactic adj. teaching in a way that convers a point or moral lesson. The didactic manner of his supervision won him the respect of his workers. / **didactics** n. the art of teaching or improvement.

differentiate (dif-er-en-shee-ate) v. to understand the difference between things. They could not differentiate between the two scientific theories.

dignity n. self-respect; characteristics that are noble, sincere, and commanding of respect. A man who would do such a horrible thing has no dignity.

digress (dy-gres) v. to get off track from the main point or topic. The speaker was talking about pollution when he digressed into a speech about better education.

dilapidated adj. falling apart; neglected. The dilapidated building is old and a safety problem.

dilemma n. situation requiring a difficult choice between two bad options or solutions. Firing workers or cutting other expenses left the manager in a serious dilemma.

Matching Quiz # 12

_____1. dehydrated
_____2. devise
_____3. deliverance
_____4. depreciate
_____5. derive
_____6. deity
_____7. despot
_____8. differentiate
_____9. depose
_____10. déjà vu
_____11. delegate
_____12. denigrate
_____13. despondent
_____14. diaspora
_____15. digress

a. a scattering of people
b. having lost hope
c. understand differences between things
d. a god
e. an evil ruler
f. to overthrow
g. a familiar feeling
h. to assign responsibility
i. to come to a conclusion or figure out
j. lack of water
k. to lose value
l. to think of
m. to move away from the main idea
n. act of being set free
o. to harm one's reputation

diligence (di-li-jens) n. effort; determination. The detective's diligence resulted in him solving the mystery.

dilute v. to lessen the effect or strength of; to weaken. The alcoholic drink was diluted with water.

disarray (dis-uh-ray) n. to be in complete disorder or having no organization. The company was in disarray after the manager quit.

disavow (dis-uh-vow) v. to deny that one has any knowledge about or responsibility for something. The parents disavowed any wrongdoing on their part regarding their child.

disband v. to break up or stop associating with. The group disbanded after their goals were achieved.

disburse v. to hand out or divide up. The charity money was disbursed to the neediest people first.

discern (di-sern) v. to understand something difficult or hidden; to see clearly. The boy's father discerned the truth about his son's trouble.

disclaimer n. a release of responsibility for something. The employee had to sign a disclaimer so he could not hold the company responsible if he got hurt on the job.

discord n. disagreement over something. The discord over a new airport drove the political parties far apart.

discourse n. v. /n. a long formal spoken or written opinion about something. His discourse on a new airport won him many supporters. / v. to speak or write at length on a topic.

discrepancy n. an error caused by a lack of consistency. There was a discrepancy in the enrollment between the teacher's roster and the school records.

discretion n. exercising good judgment or careful action. The teacher showed good discretion by calling the parents first.

discretionary adj. something that is left to one's own decision; freedom to deicide for oneself. Schools should have more discretionary money that the principal can spend in a variety of ways.

disenfranchise (dis-en-fran-chise) v. to be denied the right to vote or have that right taken away. Women and African Americans were disenfranchised for many years in the United States.

disheveled adj. messy, unkempt; disorganized. The young boy's disheveled appearance surprised many people.

disparage v. to speak lowly of; try to discredit; to reduce in importance. The criminal tried to disparage the reputation of the policeman who arrested him.

disparity n. an imbalance of some type. There is a disparity between the amount of money some school districts pay teachers.

dispense v. to give out. The charity money was dispensed in a timely manner.

disperse v. to scatter. The crowd dispersed when the police arrived.

dissent n. v. / n. a difference of opinion. There was much dissent related to the new runway idea. / v. to disagree. The opponents of the airport expansion dissented with the architect's statements.

dissipate v. to cause to scatter away; to lessen the effect of. The solution dissipated the stain on the carpet.

distinguish (dis-sting-qwish) v. to tell the difference between. The boy was still too young to distinguish right from wrong.

distinguished adj. standing noticeably apart from others; obvious; important; impressive; successful. The politician had a distinguished career as an attorney before he ran for office.

distress n. a state of trouble or anxiety. The ship was in distress after the storm created large waves. The husband's gambling caused his wife much distress.

diverge v. to move apart from the same place. After meeting, the ships diverged on different courses. / **divergence** n.

diversify v. 1. to make different or create a variety. A successful person will diversify his job skills. 2. to distribute things into different locations. Successful investors diversify their investments into different funds.

docent (doe-sent) n. a chaperone or guide that conducts tours and gives information. The museum just hired three more docents to help visitors.

docile (dos-ile) adj. gentle; obedient. The dog is quite docile and friendly.

dogma n. accepted values or belief system; Much of today's educational dogma states that all children can achieve at the same level. / **dogmatic** adj.

doldrums n. feeling of depression, dullness, or boredom. The doldrums often set in on cold rainy days.

domestic adj. related to what goes on inside a home or country. Domestic violence has been on the rise. The President outlined his foreign and domestic policies.

domicile (dom-i-sile) n. place where someone lives; a house. The old man's domicile was characteristic of a European castle.

domineering adj. controlling; demanding; pushy. The boy's domineering mother decided where he would go to school.

dossier (daw-see-ay) n. collection of important papers or information, usually financial, personal, or occupational. The spy had a complete dossier of the company's assets. His dossier contained his entire work history.

dowry (dow-ree) n. assets such as money or property that a woman gives to a man when they get married. With the help of her parents, the girl had amassed quite a large dowry to bestow upon her future husband for their mutual happiness.

Draconian adj. derived from Draco, the ancient ruler of Greece, meaning harsh, severe, or very punitive. The Draconian measures the king passed were meant to help deter crime by imposing serious penalties.

dredge (drej) v. to dig out. Can you believe the dirt for the Erie Canal was dredged without modern equipment?

drudgingly adv. in a very slow difficult manner requiring a lot of work. The men worked drudgingly on the Erie Canal for years.

dual adj. two; having two parts. The solution served the dual purpose of saving money and time.

dubious (doo-bee-us) dj. not clear; not certain; not sincere or genuine. The outcome of his crazy untested plan was dubious at best. His sly and convenient answer was very dubious.

dupe n. v. / n. a person who is easily tricked, deceived, or taken advantage of. The uneducated man was an obvious dupe for the unscrupulous salesman. / v. to trick someone. He was duped by the salesman.

duplicity n. acting one way under one set of circumstances and differently under other circumstances for the purpose of tricking or deceiving people. The way he acts in public compared to the way he acts at home had everyone fooled and is an example of great duplicity. The double agent was a master of duplicity.

duress n. act of using force or coercion to get someone to cooperate. The man was under great duress when he sold his business to the criminals.

DD Crossword Puzzle DD

www.CrosswordWeaver.com

ACROSS	DOWN
2 not sincere or genuine, not clear or certain	1 accepted values or belief system
4 to state firmly	3 to grow worse
9 an imbalance of some type	5 situation requiring a choice between two bad options
14 to ruin the appearance of something	6 left to one's own decision
15 standing noticeably apart from others	7 something not honest or true
17 person easily tricked or fooled	8 to lower the value or importance, to diminish
18 process of moving away from something	10 to give out
21 to assign a duty someone else	11 lacking good taste, ethics, or morality
22 clear, unchallenged	12 using force to achieve cooperation
23 to indicate	13 lifestyle of sinful pleasure
	15 self-respect
	16 having differing or opposing ideas
	17 to create a variety
	18 to clearly show or explain
	19 to figure out using logic and reason
	20 thick or closely arranged

Puzzle made at puzzle-maker.com

DD Word Search Puzzle DD

```
N C T N J R L R R R Q W B K H R R F
Y J D C O H S I U G N I T S I D R P
L K I R Q I A E T A I C E R P E D Z
K N S G Z N T Y M Z D C R K T E B G
M L C T O W H A R N Q H M W L R N D
D M R B K B D R I J D Z R I N D X N
I R E Y W E F H G V K E B Q I L N R
S D P M X L D H D M E E C S C E J Y
C G A O Q C E E V I R D P I C V D F
R W N T X A F N G A S E Z N M R T I
E K C O K B I K T R N C E X S A T S
T G Y H Z E A E N S E G E U P L T R
I D P C T D N Z E T I V O R R Q L E
O N Z I J K C T K L F I I M N P R V
N B G D L L E M I N B R L D J K C I
A N H H L R V D H U E S R E P S I D
R D E C E I V E D G N X D V M H V M
Y L T M L P J M D I S B U R S E W J
```

DEBACLE	DEVIATION	DISPENSE
DEBONAIR	DICHOTOMY	DISPERSE
DECEIVE	DILIGENCE	DISTINGUISH
DECIMATE	DISBURSE	DIVERGE
DEFIANCE	DISCERN	DIVERSIFY
DELIBERATE	DISCREPANCY	DUBIOUS
DEPRECIATE	DISCRETIONARY	

Puzzle made at puzzle-maker.com

EE

easement n. right to use part of someone else's land in a limited way. The easement near the utility pole in the back of the house is owned by the city.

ecclesiastical (ek-lee-see-as-ti-kal) adj. having to do with a church. The ecclesiastical practices have changed since the new priest took over.

echelon (esh-e-lon) n. the ranks of power, authority, or decision-making within an organization or group. The upper echelon of managers will not agree to a pay raise for employees.

eclectic (ek-lek-tik) adj. using a variety of ideas, methods, or sources. The furniture in the apartment was modern and eclectic. The design of the building was very eclectic, using glass, brick, and steel.

ecstatic (ek-sta-tik) adj. very happy; in very good spirits. The boy was ecstatic about the chance to meet his favorite athlete.

edict (eed-ikt) n. a decree; an order issued by a public official in power. The king's edict outlawed slavery.

educe v. to bring or draw out; to bring about or cause; to <u>elicit</u>. The horrible accident educed nightmares from the children.

effervescent (e-fer-ve-sent) adj. 1. cheerful, spirited, very outgoing. 2. literally to produce bubbles of gas. The effervescent attitude of the fellow made him very popular. / **effervescence** n.

effigy (e-fi-jee) n. 1. a likeness or image of someone. 2. to burn in effigy means to burn an image of someone as a show of hatred or disapproval. The country's exiled king was burned in effigy because of all the suffering he brought to his people.

egalitarian (e-gal-li-tair-ee-an) adj. n. / adj. belief that all people are or should be equal. His egalitarian side came out when he offered a job to the homeless person. / n. a person who thinks everyone is or should be equal. The egalitarians have helped a lot of people.

egotistical adj. belief by some people that everything revolves around them; self-centered; egocentric. Famous people can be quite egotistical.

egress (ee-gres) n. v. / n. an exit or way out. The fire made only one egress possible. / v. to exit or go out. He will egress from the garage when he is finished working on the car.

elaborate adj. v. / adj. (e-la-bor-et) complicated or well thought out. The burglar worked out an elaborate plan to steal the jewels. / v. (e-la-bor-ate) to state more clearly or in more detail. The scientist had to elaborate on his plans so others could understand him.

elicit (i-li-sit) v. to draw out or bring forth. The popular speech elicited much applause from the audience.

elite (i-leet) n. adj. / n. the most important people; upper crust of society; the wealthy; the ones who are the best at something. The dinner is only the for elite of the club. / adj. Those athletes are elite within the sporting world.

elitism (i-leet-iz-um) n. favoring the most important or best. The expensive college reeks of elitism. / **elitist** n. one who believes in elitism.

eloquent (e-loe-kwent) adj. sophisticated in speech or writing. The man wrote a very eloquent poem to his wife.

elude v. to avoid. The criminal eluded the police for three days before he was caught.

elucidate (e-loo-si-date) v. to explain or make more clear. The teacher was asked to elucidate on the Dred Scott decision.

elusive adj. hard to find or catch. The thief proved to be quite elusive, hiding for two years. The cure for the disease was most elusive.

emancipate v. to set free. The dogs were emancipated from their tiny kennels when the owners returned home. / **emancipation** n. state of freedom

emasculate (e-mas-kyu-late) v. adj. literally to remove the male parts of a body, however used most frequently to mean to weaken the strength of someone or something; to lower in power or authority. The cruel boss was emasculated when his employees would not follow orders.

embellish v. to make more lively or exciting; to make something sound better. The reporter embellished the dull story by adding gory details.

emigrate v. to leave one place or country for another. His relatives emigrated from Greece.

eminent adj. something that is most important or well-known on a wide scale; above the rest. The eminent doctor was known around the world for his success.

emissary n. someone sent to do something on behalf of another. The mayor's emissary delivered the documents.

empathy n. a deep understanding of someone's feeling or thoughts. He expressed much empathy at the loss of the girl's mother. / **empathize** v.

empirical adj. based on firsthand knowledge or experience. She favors empirical evidence not scientific theory that nobody can prove.

emulate v. to achieve the same level of success; to copy something or do the same thing. The boy is trying to emulate his older brother, even on the basketball court.

enamored adj. to be very fond of or in love with; captivated by. The man is still enamored by his childhood sweetheart.

encapsulate v. literally to enclose in a capsule of some type. The documents were encapsulated in a sealed container.

enchanted v. 1. to be very happy with. He was enchanted with the way his date looked. 2. to be put under a spell. / **enchantment** n. condition of being very happy or under a magic spell.

enclave n. a small group or area surrounded by others who are different in some way. Different enclaves of unhappy citizens still exist throughout the region.

encompass v. to be made up; to contain or include. The area encompasses more than a thousand square miles.

encroach v. to go further than what is acceptable. The man encroached on his neighbor's privacy by always entering without knocking.

encumber v. to obstruct or hold back; to act as a burden or weight. The car's speed was encumbered by its weight.

endeavor (en-de-vor) v. n. / v. to make an attempt at something; to try. The boy endeavored to complete all his chores. / n. an attempt at something. Her new business endeavor was a complete success.

endemic adj. to be common or usual in a certain place or among certain things. The faulty tires were endemic to that particular model of car. Reincarnation is a belief endemic to the Hindu people.

endorse v. to support publicly. The union endorsed a candidate for governor.

endow (en-dow) v. 1. to give money to support someone or something. The parents endowed their children with money in the event of their death. 2. something given at birth. According to Thomas Jefferson, all men are endowed with certain rights.

Matching Quiz # 13

____1. elicit	a. an attempt
____2. ecclesiastical	b. favoring the best
____3. emancipate	c. believing in the equality of people
____4. effervescent	d. widely known
____5. elitism	e. right of use of someone's land
____6. egalitarian	f. the ranks of power
____7. eminent	g. knowledge based on experience
____8. easement	h. to include
____9. empirical	i. to be given at birth
____10. echelon	j. to publicly support
____11. elucidate	k. to set free
____12. encompass	l. related to a church
____13. endow	m. to explain clearly
____14. endorse	n. cheerful attitude
____15. endeavor	o. to bring out

endowment n. 1. a sum of money given to support someone or something. The school received a large endowment to build the new gymnasium.

endure v. to put up with; to suffer through. The students had to endure a boring lecture from their teacher.

engross v. to consume or captivate completely; to become totally occupied with. The family was engrossed in the interesting movie and never got off the couch.

enlighten v. to give great or important information to; to bestow truth and understanding. The student was enlightened by the teacher's explanation. /**enlightened** adj. / **enlightenment** n.

enumerate v. to list something one by one. The teacher enumerated the assignments that had to be completed.

envoy n. a representative, usually of an official; an emissary. The king's envoy delivered the speech for him.

eon (ee-on) n. a long time, usually thousands of years. The ocean's water levels have changed over the eons.

epic n. adj. / n. a very long piece of writing or drama such as a story, poem, or movie. The ancient Greeks wrote many epics about their history. / adj. something very long, impressive, or important. The military rescue was an epic event.

epicenter (e-pi-sen-ter) n. 1. the center of something. The child's carelessness was the epicenter of the parent's argument. 2. the place where an earthquake originated. The quake's epicenter was traced to Los Angeles.

epicurean (e-pi-kyur-ee-an) n. adj. / n. a person who has expensive tastes or enjoys luxurious items and much pleasure. He is an epicurean when it comes to cars. / adj. having expensive tastes or habits; indulging in pleasure and luxury. He does not have the money to support his epicurean habits.

epiphany (i-pif-ah-nee) n. a sudden exposure to knowledge or a religious encounter; a sudden enlightenment about something. When he finally thought of the right solution it seemed like an epiphany.

e pluribus unum (ee pluribis oo-num) Latin meaning, out of many, one.

equinox (ee-kwi-nocks) n. The two days per year when day and night are of equal length. The spring equinox is March 21st , and the fall equinox is September 21st.

equitable adj. fair. The brothers had an equitable arrangement where they shared the household chores.

equivalent adj. equal to. Both workers were paid an equivalent sum of money for doing the same job. Four is equivalent to two plus two.

equivocal (ee-kwi-vi-col) adj. 1. something that has two or more meanings. 2. something that is not clearly stated or decided. Stacy's thoughts were equivocal; they were contradictory and subject to examination.

erudite (air-yoo-dite) adj. educated; knowledgeable. The teacher seemed quite erudite to her students.

eschew (es-choo) v. to avoid or stay away from. Reasonable drinkers eschew drinking and driving.

esoteric adj. something that only a few people would understand; meant for select people to know; technical or complicated information. His esoteric answer was confusing and probably only understood by the professor.

espionage (es-pee-ah-nahzj) n. using spies to obtain information. Many countries were guilty of espionage during the Cold War.

espouse v. to adopt something. The woman espoused a new workout routine.

ethics n. the study of right and wrong; proper moral conduct . Some parents are not doing a good job at teaching their children proper ethics these days. /**ethical** adj. morally right or just. It was not very ethical of him to steal the money.

etiquette (e-ti-ket) n. standards of proper or sophisticated behavior. The children were never taught proper table etiquette. Standing when a woman leaves the table is proper etiquette.

etymology (et-i-mo-loe-jee) n. the study of the origin, meaning, and history of a word. Etymology and linguistics are closely related.

eugenics (yu-jen-iks) n. the study of improving the human race. New genetic advancements have given new life to eugenics.

euphemism (yu-fe-miz-um) n. a polite or delicate way of stating something. Frugal is a euphemism for cheap.

evince v. to make clear or show clearly. The athlete evinced his skills during the game.

evoke v. to bring out or draw out. The American flag should evoke a sense of patriotism.

exacerbate (eg-zas-er-bate) v. to make worse. The fall exacerbated her previous injury.

exalt v. to treat with much honor; to glorify. The king was exalted by his people.

exasperate (eg-zas-pe-rate) v. to bother or annoy greatly. The child's constant crying exasperated the babysitter.

excavate v. to dig up or out. The archeologist excavated the old bones from the ground.

excursion (eks-kur-shun) n. a short trip. The family went on a weekend excursion to Florida.

exempt adj. not required to do something. The student was exempt from her final exams because of her good grades.

exile n. v. / n. a condition of not being allowed in some place such as a country. The king is in exile. / v. to be kicked out of or not allowed in some place. The horrible king was exiled from his country.

exonerate (eks-zon-e-rate) v. to clear of guilt or responsibility. The new evidence exonerated the man who was wrongly arrested for the crime.

expedient (eks-pee-dee-ent) adj. helpful; assisting in achieving a goal. The extra workers were expedient in our desire to finish the project on time.

expedite (eks-pe-dite) v. to speed up a process. The airplane has expedited travel.

explicit (eks-pli-sit) adj. very clear or graphic; very detailed. Too many movies contain explicit sex and violence that youngsters should not see.

exquisite (eks-kwi-zit) adj. wonderful; brilliant; very pleasing. The man bought an exquisite painting for his home.

extemporaneous (eks-tem-por-ay-nee-us) adj. without planning or preparation; spontaneous. His extemporaneous ideas come out of nowhere. Some people can give an extemporaneous answer, but I must collect my thoughts first.

extraneous (eks-tray-nee-us) adj. not part of; unnecessary. Students often write down too much extraneous information that is not relevant to the discussion.

extrapolate v. to <u>infer</u> or conclude possibilities from what is already known. Good scientists can extrapolate knowledge from a little information.

Matching Quiz # 14

____1. equitable		a. very detailed
____2. equivalent		b. polite way to say something
____3. etiquette		c. proper behavior
____4. exonerate		d. using spies to get information
____5. endowment		e. equal to
____6. evoke		f. to bring out
____7. espionage		g. expensive tastes
____8. euphemism		h. to show clearly
____9. evince		i. study of right and wrong
____10. enumerate		j. a gift of money
____11. ethics		k. to give or receive knowledge
____12. epicurean		l. to list
____13. exacerbate		m. to clear from wrongdoing
____14. explicit		n. fair
____15. enlighten		o. to make worse

extraterrestrial (eks-tra-ter-es-tree-al) n. adj. /n. something not from earth. Popular science fiction movies are about extraterrestrials. /adj. More information is needed about extraterrestrial life.

extroverted adj. very outgoing; likes to be around people; Extroverted people usually have many friends, unlike introverted people who usually like to be alone. / **extrovert** n.

extricate v. to pull out of. The firemen extricated the passenger from the car.

exuberant (ek-zoo-ber-ent) adj. very happy or excited; joyful; full of energy and excitement. The children were exuberant when they learned about going to Disney World. / **exuberance** n.

142

EE Crossword Puzzle EE

www.CrosswordWeaver.com

ACROSS	DOWN
1 to list one-by-one	1 complicated, well thought out
2 hard to find or catch	2 sudden exposure to knowledge, an idea, or
4 an understanding of another's thoughts and	religious experience
feelings	3 using a variety of ideas, methods, or
5 a likeness or image of something	materials
6 to adopt or make use of something	4 something that only a few people would
9 unrelated or not part of the topic at hand	understand
12 sophisticated in speech or writing	6 to copy or to the same thing
14 without planning or preparation, spontaneous	7 very detailed or clear
15 wonderful or brilliant	8 to draw conclusions from what is already
16 to speed up a process	known
	9 likes to be around people, very outgoing
	10 to put up with or suffer through
	11 having expensive tastes or enjoying
	luxurious items
	13 to avoid

Puzzle made at puzzle-maker.com

EE Word Search Puzzle EE

```
N M E F J K M W Z L E T P K E L E H
F S X X E M E P J P V R T T Q N N W
K U P W F N K X I L P L A Q R R L N
K O E L X N D C O R Q B Y T E L I A
K E D D T N U E X N R K M H T M G I
B N I R L R M K A E E M T B I K H R
Z A T F E C M T C V J R D F D F T A
N R E A V N Y A N F O H A P U M E T
Q O N F L N X X Y E R E T R Z N I
V P M L J E C D Q X L T D B E Q R L
E M A N C I P A T E A A W D K T L A
V E V R Y D M R F R T G V H H Y H G
L T N H K Z A Q O C T T J I T D V E
M X D Q M N M B G M D X M F U R W M
K E L K E R A H E L B A T I U Q E M
Z N R O F L W K T K J D P K F X E V
H T U N E Q Y M M E X C A V A T E B
T S Y M D V N O I S R U C X E R K N
```

EGALITARIAN	ERUDITE
ELABORATE	EXACERBATE
EMANCIPATE	EXCAVATE
ENDEAVOR	EXCURSION
ENLIGHTEN	EXONERATE
EPICUREAN	EXPEDITE
EQUITABLE	EXTEMPORANEOUS
EQUIVALENT	EXTRANEOUS

FF

fable (fay-bul) n. story that teaches a lesson but is not real. Many civilizations had fables that were told to children about making good decisions.

fabricate v. to make or make up. Many pieces of electronic equipment are fabricated in other countries.

façade (fuh-sahd) n. 1. the front of a building. The building looks new since the façade was repaired. 2. something that looks real or truthful but is not as it seems. His unlikely story had the facade of a fairy tale.

facetious (fuh-see-shus) adj. displaying inappropriate humor. His facetious remarks annoy people.

facilitate (fuh-si-li-tate) v. to help or lead to. More studying facilitates better grades.

faction n. part of a group that differs from the rest. A faction of the group did not agree with the plan.

fallacy n. something that is not true. Believing that all dogs are mean is a fallacy.

famine n. having no food; starvation. Many countries in Africa suffer from severe famine.

famished adj. to be very hungry. He is always famished after a hard workout.

fastidious (fas-ti-dee-us) adj. picky; fickle; critical; tough to please or make happy. He is very fastidious when it comes to food.

fatalism n. believing that people have no control over things and that fate controls everything. Fatalism can be very depressing. /**fatalistic** adj. believing in fatalism.

fat cat n. figurative for an important or wealthy person with many privileges and high expectations. The boss and the other fat cats of the business always eat at nice restaurants.

fate n. a supreme power that controls the world and everything that happens beforehand; destiny. His fate was written when he took that dangerous job. /**fateful** adj. related to fate or figurative for beyond one's control.

fathom v. n. / v. to understand something. I cannot fathom why he would quit such a good job. / n. unit of measurement in water. A fathom is equal to six feet deep.

fatigued (fuh-teeg-ed) adj. to be exhausted or worn out from hard work. The athletes were fatigued after the hard workout.

feasible adj. possible; reasonable. It is feasible that the home team could win despite not being as good as the other team.

federation n. an association of different members. Labor unions make up many federations in this country.

feint (faint) v. n. / n. something false or deceptive. The football team's play to the right was just a feint as the ball was thrown to the left. / v. The team feinted right but threw to the left.

felicity n. great joy or happiness. The good news produced much felicity in the home.

fervor n. much emotion about something. Much fervor preceded the announcement of the winner.

fiasco n. a big, embarrassing failure. The dinner party turned into a fiasco when the host ran out of food.

fickle adj. something that is always changing without much reason; inconsistent. She is very fickle when it comes to food.

fictitious (fik-ti-shus) adj. made up; imaginary; not real. His fictitious stories of danger and adventure are quite amusing even if they never happened.

fidelity n. adj. / n 1. loyalty; faithfulness. Fidelity is a major aspect of marriage. 2. accuracy; quality of reproduction. The craftsman carved the wood with much fidelity. / adj. The machine produces high fidelity copies.

fiduciary (fi-doo-shee-air-ee) adj. something that is held in trust. A lawyer has a fiduciary responsibility to his clients.

fief (feef) n. a piece of land used by someone in return for services to the owner of the land. Fiefs were a major part of feudalism.

fiend (feend) n. and evil person or spirit. What kind of fiend would steal money from a child? /**fiendish** adj.

figment n. something that is made up. The UFO was just a figment of your imagination.

figurative adj. a non-literal meaning or interpretation of something; an alternate meaning not taken from the word for word description; a representation of something. Some poems are meant to be read in a figurative manner because they do not make sense when read literally.

figurehead n. a person who is in charge by name only but has no real power or ability. The boss is just a figurehead because the assistant is the one who really runs the business.

finesse (fi-nes) n. skill in doing something; skill in handling a delicate situation or job. A doctor must have much finesse when he operates. Politicians must often use finesse when dealing with reporters.

finite (fy-nite) adj. a limited number or amount. The money available for the project is finite. We only have a finite amount of paper for copies.

fiscal (fis-kal) adj. related to money or finances. The company's fiscal report is due out next week.

fission n. the splitting of things in two such as atoms or cells. Current nuclear power is achieved by fission, which is the splitting of an atom into two separate atoms.

fissure n. a long deep crack in something, most commonly the earth. The earthquake produced huge fissures in the ground.

fixate v. to become preoccupied with something; to think about one and only one thing. The boy fixated his eyes upon the pretty girl. The scientist was fixated by the new idea. / **fixation** n.

flagrant (flay-grent) adj. obviously done on purpose or without regard. Stealing a car is a flagrant violation of the law.

fledgling (flej-ling) adj. struggling to succeed or new at something. The fledging business just started to make a profit. / **fledgling** n. literally a bird just learning to fly.

Matching Quiz # 15

_____ 1. facetious
_____ 2. fidelity
_____ 3. facilitate
_____ 4. figurative
_____ 5. famine
_____ 6. fastidious
_____ 7. feasible
_____ 8. fabricate
_____ 9. figurehead
_____ 10. facade
_____ 11. federation
_____ 12. finite
_____ 13. fledgling
_____ 14. fixate
_____ 15. fiscal

a. related to money
b. person with no real power
c. likely or possible
d. to make something
e. outward appearance
f. not seriously
g. hard to please
h. a limited amount
i. struggling to succeed
j. faithfulness
k. lack of food
l. association of members
m. to help or lead to
n. to become preoccupied
o. non-literal interpretation

---

fleece (flees) v. 1. The wooly covering of a goat and imitated by other materials to make certain soft clothes. 2. to trick or cheat somebody out of something. The con artist fleeced him out of a thousand dollars.

fleeting adj. not lasting; passing; temporary. He had a fleeting hope of winning the lottery.

flippant adj. slightly rude or disrespectful. The student made a flippant comment to the teacher.

flog v. to whip somebody. The prisoner was flogged until he released the information. /**flogging** n. He received a flogging yesterday.

flounder v. to struggle in a clumsy manner. He floundered around for hours trying to put the toy together. / **flounder** n. literally a type of fish.

flourish v. to do or grow quite well. The student flourished in the new school. Flowers flourish in the springtime.

fluke n. a lucky occurrence. The team is really not that good; it was a fluke they won the championship.

flux v. n. / v. to change. The light bulb fluxed from bright to dim. / n. a condition of change. The staff is an a state of flux because so many new people were hired.

foliage n. leaves from plants or trees. We could not see the house clearly because of all the foliage.

forage v. to search for something. Small animals always forage for food.

forbearance (for-bair-ens) n. the act of restraining oneself or keeping from doing something through self-control. The assertive employee held his tongue in an unusual case of forbearance.

forebode v. to predict or warn. The clouds forebode of bad weather.

foregone adj. known or finalized ahead of time. It was no surprise when the frustrated worker quit as it was a forgone conclusion.

foreign (for-in) adj. 1. belonging or related to a different country. Too many people buy foreign cars. The President has changed our foreign policy again. 2. different or out of place. That seems like a foreign idea.

forensic adj. the application of science, scientific test, and medical knowledge to investigate crimes and used in courts of law. A forensic medical expert explained the evidence to the judge.

forestall v. to avoid or prevent something by acting in advance. The child forestalled a punishment by telling his parents what happened before they found out on their own.

forge (forj) v. n. / v. 1. to make or shape something through effort and skill. The deal was forged between two rivals. 2. to heat metal and shape it. The gun was forged by hand. / n. an instrument where metal is heated then hammered into shape. A forge was used to make the horseshoes.

formative adj. that which develops something. Ages one to six are formative years in a child's mental and character development.

formidable adj. challenging; hard to accomplish. Even though the team had a losing record, they were a formidable opponent.

forte (for-tay) n. a special skill at something; a strength. She was not good in math, but science was her forte.

fortify v. to make stronger or protect. The soldiers fortified the city before it was attacked again.

fortitude n. ability to deal with pain, hardship, or challenges; courage; determination. The young lady displayed much fortitude in recovering from the horrible car accident.

fortuitous (for-tu-i-tus) adj. occurring by luck or chance; not planned. It was fortuitous to run into an old friend at the store.

148

forum n. 1. an opportunity for public debate or discussion. A forum was held to discuss the airport's expansion. 2. public meeting place.

foster v. to help grow or develop; to take care of or encourage. Kindness fosters more kindness.

franchise n. 1. a right to do or sell something. The man was granted a restaurant franchise in the airport. 2. The right to vote.

fresco n. a colorful painting on walls or ceilings usually made with watercolors. Some of the most beautiful frescos are in Italy.

fringe n. the edge or border; the outer limits of something. He is on the fringe of being fired. The fringes of the city are uninhabited.

frontier n. undiscovered or unsettled territory. The American frontier was always advancing. The frontier was settled by brave men and women.

frugal adj. not wanting to waste things; careful with the way one spends money or time; cheap. He is very frugal when it comes to clothes.

fruition n. state of completion, conclusion, or achievement. The plan finally came to fruition after much debate. Years of work finally came to fruition with the award she won.

fulcrum n. an object that acts as a support for a lever to lift a heavy object. The box of books was used as a fulcrum to lift the bookcase.

full-fledged adj. with the most effort; all the way; complete. A full-fledged attempt was made to get the project finished on time.

fundamental adj. basic; essential; very important; formative; Proper hygiene is a fundamental aspect of good health.

furlough (fur-loe) n v. / n. a permitted or approved leave of absence. General Sherman granted his men a furlough after the capture of Atlanta. / v. Upon being furloughed, many of Sherman's men went home to vote for President Lincoln.

fuse (fyuz) v. to combine or put together, sometimes by heat. The doctor fused the broken bone.

fusion (fyuz-shun) n. 1. the process of fusing things (combining or melting together). 2. the combining of two atoms into one. The sun uses nuclear fusion for power.

futile (fyu-til) adj. pointless; useless; without hope of achievement. Going on strike would be futile since there is no money to give the workers a raise.

futon (foo-ton) n. a cushioned or padded floor mat used as a bed by the Japanese. A futon is not as uncomfortable as it looks.

Matching Quiz # 16

____	1. forbearance	a.	already known
____	2. foreign	b.	a special skill
____	3. foregone	c.	state of change
____	4. frugal	d.	hard to accomplish
____	5. forte	e.	to cheat or trick
____	6. forge	f.	by chance, lucky
____	7. flux	g.	slightly rude
____	8. formidable	h.	outside edge
____	9. fleece	i.	conservative with money
____	10. formative	j.	state of completion
____	11. fortuitous	k.	basic
____	12. flippant	l.	outside the country
____	13. fringe	m.	to make something
____	14. fundamental	n.	self-restraint
____	15. fruition	o.	that which develops

FF Crossword Puzzle FF

www.CrosswordWeaver.com

ACROSS	DOWN
1 to struggle in a clumsy manner	1 to grow and do quite well
2 opportunity for public discussion	2 ability to deal with pain, hardship, or challenges
3 worn out from hard work	4 to lead, help, or oversee something
6 belief that people have no control over things	5 temporary, passing, not lasting
7 pointless, without hope of achievement	6 non-literal meaning of something
8 to understand	9 something that is not true
9 something that is held in trust	10 figurative for an importance person with many privileges
10 something obviously done on purpose or without regard	
11 imaginary, not real, made up	
12 skill at handling a delicate or tough situation	

Puzzle made at puzzle-maker.com

FF Word Search Puzzle FF

```
H T N A R G A L F R C F X F H L
Y W N M W F K W F R O N T I E R
F M R N Z R F R V P T X M N L H
P I V Q N K C R T M S L I B K N
R M C W K L P R U U M M G V F Z
K K G T M R H C O G A R E R I D
H B M N I T T T H F A M T F G E
R S L F A T I G U E D L A O U L
N T I M C U I C K N B L C R R B
G K Q R T L N O Q L W F I M A A
I M L R U F P H U M L T R A T D
E G O B I O G N X S N H B T I I
R F C N G D L R K Q R R A I V M
O F I P F F T F N T L H F V E R
F T L N K C H R J Q G L B E R O
E K F U N D A M E N T A L M P F
```

FABRICATE	FINITE	FORMIDABLE
FAMINE	FLAGRANT	FORTUITOUS
FATIGUED	FLOURISH	FRONTIER
FICTITIOUS	FOREIGN	FRUGAL
FIGURATIVE	FORMATIVE	FUNDAMENTAL

Puzzle made at puzzle-maker.com

GG

gaffe (gaf) n. a mistake. Being rude to the boss was a huge gaffe on his part.

gale n. a powerful wind. The gales rocked the boat for hours.

gallant (gal-ant) adj. sophisticated or proper; noble; brave in spirit and action. Not many men are as gallant as he. /**gallantry** n.

gallivant (gal-i-vant) v. to roam around looking fun, excitement, or pleasure. Since he retired all the man does is gallivant around town. / **gallivanting** v.

gallows n. 1. a wood frame used for hanging people. 2. a place where criminals are hung as punishment. He will be sent to the gallows for stealing.

galoshes (guh-los-es) n. rain boots. The children put their galoshes on before leaving for school.

galvanize v. 1. to energize or spur to action. The tragedy galvanized the community to a new level of commitment. 2. literally to charge with electricity.

gamut n. a range of something. The bright dress ran the gamut of colors.

gangly adj. tall and thin with the look of weakness or awkwardness. The basketball player looked gangly until he put on some weight.

gape n. v. /n. a wide opening. He walked with a large gape [between his legs]. /v. to open wide, such as a mouth. The audience gaped at the magician's trick. /**gaping** adj. There is a gaping hole in the side of the boat.

garb n. one's dress or clothes. His garb went out of fashion twenty years ago.

garish (gair-ish) adj. too showy or flashy; gaudy; too bright or tacky. That garish painting is still on their wall.

garnish v. 1. withholding money from someone as payment for a debt. The company garnished his wages for a month.

gaudy (gawdy) adj. cheap and tacky looking; not in good taste; bright and showy. She wore that gaudy jewelry again.

generality n. an unspecific description; something lacking details. The professor spoke in generalities, assuming the students already knew a lot.

genre (zshahn-ra) n. type or classification. The drama genre is very popular with readers.

genteel (jen-teel) adj. from the sophisticated or polite class. Their children were brought up to be very genteel.

Gentile or gentile (jen-tile) n. a non-Jewish person. The Jews and the Gentiles have rich histories to share with each other.

gentry (jen-tree) n. the noble, sophisticated, or wealthy class. The gentry tried to control European society after the Dark Ages.

gentrify (jen-tri-fy) v. to make wealthier; to have wealthier people move into an area. Some low-income parts of the city have begun to gentrify.

geriatric adj. having to do with old age or elderly people. The hospital has a good reputation for geriatric care. / **geriatrics** n. the study and medical care of elderly people.

germane adj. of importance to; related to. The evidence is not germane to the case.

germinate v. to grow or develop, especially as related to seeds and flowers. The seeds will not germinate if the weather does not cooperate. Good deeds germinate from good thoughts.

gesture n. v. / n. a communication made by a physical rather than verbal statement. That thing he did with his hand was a strange gesture. /v. to communicate using physical rather than verbal cues. He gestured to the waitress with his hand that he was ready for the check.

geyser (gy-zer) n. an opening in the earth that shoots up hot water and steam. "Old Faithful" is a famous geyser in Yellowstone National Park.

ghastly (gast-lee) adj. horrible; upsetting; frightening. The group witnessed a ghastly accident while waiting for the bus.

ghoulish (goo-lish) adj. horrible; demonic; evil; spooky; A ghoulish figure appeared in the window and scared everyone.

gilded adj. 1. something appearing better than it is. 2. something shinny and nice. 3. covered with a precious metal such as gold. The gilded cup was really only lead with gold plating.

glutton n. a greedy person who eats or wants a lot of something. He was a glutton for chocolate cake. He must be a glutton for punishment because he is always in trouble.

gold digger n. figurative for a person who is after someone's wealth or possessions. He is nothing but a gold digger because he is just after her money.

gradient (gray-dee-ent) n. the angle by which a slope, such as a road, goes up or down (often expressed as a percent); the grade. Trucks must be careful of steep gradients, especially in bad weather. The road has a two percent gradient.

grandeur (gran-jur) n. importance, greatness. Arrogant people often have delusions of grandeur.

grandiose (gran-dee-oes) adj. impressive; on a big scale. Grandiose ideas have often changed the world.

154

grapple v. 1. to wrestle or have a hard time with something. The man grappled with the tough decision for days. 2. to grip something. The climber grappled the safety line.

grass-roots adj. having to do with the common people. The politician's campaign had a large grass-roots following. His success was owed to a grass-roots movement. / **grass roots** n. The grass roots supported him.

gratis adj. adv. /adj. complimentary; free. The hotel room was gratis. /adv. The repairs to the room were performed gratis.

gratitude n. being thankful for something. He bought dinner for his friend out of gratitude for all the help.

gratuitous (gruh-too-i-tis) adj. given for no apparent reason or for free. The movie contained a lot of gratuitous violence.

gratuity n. a tip. The waiter's gratuity was included in the bill.

grave adj. very serious or thoughtful. A grave moment in his life occurred when he thought he would never return home.

gravitate v. to drift toward something; to be attracted in a certain direction or toward something. The athletes gravitated toward each other at the school dance.

Matching Quiz # 17

_____1. gallant	a. the wealthy class
_____2. gaudy	b. non-Jewish person
_____3. gaffe	c. covered with gold
_____4. generality	d. free
_____5. garnish	e. noble
_____6. gamut	f. polite and sophisticated
_____7. genteel	g. a tip
_____8. gentry	h. of the common people
_____9. Gentile	i. cheap looking
_____10. gentrify	j. a range
_____11. gilded	k. to withhold money
_____12. gratis	l. a mistake
_____13. gratuity	m. to have a hard time with
_____14. grass-roots	n. to make wealthy
_____15. grapple	o. not specific, lacking details

Greco adj. related to Greece or Greek-like. The Greco-style painting attracted much attention.

gregarious (gre-gair-ee-us) adj. outgoing; happy to be around others. The movie star was quite gregarious.

grievance (gree-vens) n. legal complaint about something done wrong. The workers filed a grievance against their boss.

grievous (gree-vus) adj. serious in an bad or upsetting way; causing harm. Driving drunk is a grievous offense.

grueling adj. difficult; exhausting. The competition was a grueling test of endurance.

guild (gild) n. a group of people organized together for a common purpose or benefit. The writer's guild approved a new union contract.

guillotine (gil-uh-teen) n. a device once used in France for cutting people's heads off by dropping a blade across the back of the neck. The guillotine was a cruel tool of terror.

guru (goo-roo) n. an expert or leader in something; a spiritual leader or someone with much influence. The weight loss guru achieved much fame and acceptance.

GG Crossword Puzzle GG

www.CrosswordWeaver.com

ACROSS	DOWN
1 to energize or spur into action	1 of importance or related to the topic
2 free	3 happy to be around others, outgoing
4 the noble, wealthy, or sophisticated class	4 given for no apparent reason or free of charge
5 importance, greatness	8 group of similar people or workers organized together for a common benefit
6 spiritual or influential teacher in something	
7 type of category or classification	
8 to withhold money as payment for a debt	
9 roam around looking for excitement	
10 serious in a bad or upsetting way	

Puzzle made at puzzle-maker.com

GG Word Search Puzzle GG

```
M F X L L N R Y E K P K
C R E D U T I T A R G G
R N B Z G K A I N K R R
G Y G U Q T R L Q H A A
M R I R I K L A P G T N
H L I V A E G R R N U D
D U A E E N D E L I I I
F R R T V V D N N L T O
G H N U N A Y E J E O S
M E H Y G W N G U U U E
G B L L N D L C R R S T
N M G E S T U R E G L L
```

GENERALITY	GRATUITOUS
GENTEEL	GRAVITATE
GESTURE	GRIEVANCE
GRANDEUR	GRUELING
GRANDIOSE	GUILD
GRATITUDE	GURU

Puzzle made at puzzle-maker.com

HH

haggard adj. looking worn out or tired. The runner appeared haggard after the race.

haggle v. to negotiate over price or terms. The woman haggled with the car dealer for hours.

haphazard (hap-haz-ard) adj. by luck or random; not thorough. It was an haphazard attempt.
/**haphazardly** adv.

harangue (hah-rang) v. n. / v. to speak loudly or for a long time. The students harangued in the halls all day. / n. a long loud speech or noise.

harbor v. to protect, hide, or give shelter to. The criminals were harbored in another country.

hedonism (hee-do-niz-um) n. seeking pleasure or self-indulgence. Hedonism can lead to a lifestyle of excess. / **hedonistic** adj.

hegemony (he-je-mo-nee) n. the domination by a country or government over another. The hegemony that existed between the Soviet Union and Eastern Europe was cruel and repressive.

herbivore n. a plant-eating animal. Herbivores often have different teeth than carnivores.

heredity n. the passing of genes including physical and metal characteristics from one generation to the next. Hair color and intelligence can be determined by heredity. / **hereditary** adj. passing from parent to offspring.

heretofore (here-to-for) adv. adj. /adv. up to this point; before now; until now. Heretofore, not much was known about the genetic code. / adj. The heretofore impatience of the public must be understood.

heritage (hair-i-tij) n. belonging to one's family or ancestors; from one's past. Immigrants often try to retain their cultural and linguistic heritage.

heterogeneous (he-te-roe-jee-nee-us) adj. different; not alike or of the same kind. Heterogeneous plants might not grow well in the same climate.

heuristic (hew-ris-tik) adj. eager for or leading to discovery or the quest for more information. Teachers are very excited when they have heuristic students.

hiatus (hy-ay-tus) n. a temporary pause or gap; a suspension of action. Reruns fill the channels during television's summer hiatus.

hierarchy (hy-er-ar-kee) n. an ordering of things according to importance. The business is a hierarchy of managers. / **hierarchical** adj.

hinder v. to obstruct or hold back. The student was hindered by his poor math skills. /**hindrance** n.

historiography (his-tor-ee-ah-grah-fee) n. the study of the methods or writing and researching of history; historical methods. Good historiography will avoid many common errors in the telling of history.

hoard (hord) v. to keep or take many things greedily. The corrupt organization hoarded the people's money.

holistic adj. taking all the aspects of something into account; complete. Holistic medicine concerns the well-being of the entire body. A holistic approach to understanding students would be to study their home, academic, and interpersonal backgrounds.

holocaust n. something terrible; a terrible event. The earthquake was a holocaust for the town.

homeopathy n. the use of small amounts of drugs to treat a disease. Homeopathy is a conservative approach to medicine. /**homeopathic** adj.

homeostasis n. the tendency for something to remain balanced or neutral. The cells returned to a state of homeostasis after the electric charge was removed. /**homeostatic** adj.

homogeneous (hoe-moe-jee-nee-us) adj. similar; alike; of the same kind. Homogeneous trees are often found grouped together.

homogenize (hoe-mo-je-nize) v. to make the same or similar. The military tends to homogenize people.

homogenous (hoe-mo-je-nus) adj. similar in condition or characteristics; similar in biological content. The speaker lectured about diversity to a homogenous group.

hooligan n. slang term for troublemakers. The hooligans are up to no good again.

horde n. a large group. A horde of buffalo ran through town.

hors d'oeuvre (or-dervs) n. light, often fancy, appetizers such as finger sandwiches, cheese, crackers, or vegetables. Hors d'oeuvres are at six, dinner is at seven.

horticulture n. the science of growing plants. Horticulture is a lost art.

hostel n. temporary place to stay while passing through. Europe is of full of inexpensive hostels for travelers on the move.

hubris (hew-bris) n. excessive pride; arrogance. His hubris kept him from admitting to his mistakes.

humanitarian adj. n. /adj. concerned with the well-being or good treatment of human beings; proper treatment of people. She is always engaged in humanitarian causes. / n. a person who is concerned with the well-being of people or proper treatment of people.

humdrum adj. dull; boring. Lighthouse attendants probably led humdrum lives.

hybrid n. adj. / n. a product created from the combination of two different things; an organism created from the breading of two different species or races. /adj. having the qualities of a hybrid; of mixed descent or creation. Hybrid cars combine gasoline and electric power for locomotion.

hyperbole (hy-per-boe-lee) n. exaggeration; a statement containing exaggeration. Writers use a lot of hyperbole to create the desired effect.

hypochondriac (hy-poe-kon-dree-ak) n. person who falsely believes he is always sick. He is a hypochondriac. / **hypochondria** n. the obsessive and false belief that one is always sick or injured.

hypocrite (hip-oe-krit) n. a person who preaches one thing but acts against what he preaches about. Anyone who warns against stealing but steals himself is a hypocrite. /**hypocritical** adj.

hypodermic (hy-poe-der-mik) adj. under the skin. The vaccine was given with a hypodermic needle.

hypothesis (hy-po-the-sis) n. an assumption based on what is known but not a proven theory yet. The hypothesis that a meteor killed off the dinosaurs is yet to be proved. /**hypothetical** adj. / **hypothesize** v. to form a hypothesis.

Matching Quiz # 18

_____ 1. hedonism
_____ 2. heredity
_____ 3. haggle
_____ 4. heretofore
_____ 5. haggard
_____ 6. holistic
_____ 7. heterogeneous
_____ 8. hinder
_____ 9. homogenous
_____ 10. horde
_____ 11. hubris
_____ 12. hybrid
_____ 13. hors d'oeuvre
_____ 14. hoard
_____ 15. hyperbole

a. to take things greedily
b. exaggeration
c. warn out
d. to hold back
e. of the same kind
f. of a different kind
g. a large group
h. excessive pride
i. a light fancy appetizer
j. up to now
k. seeking pleasure
l. concern with the whole
m. a combination of two things
n. passing of genes to offspring
o. to negotiate price

HH Crossword Puzzle HH

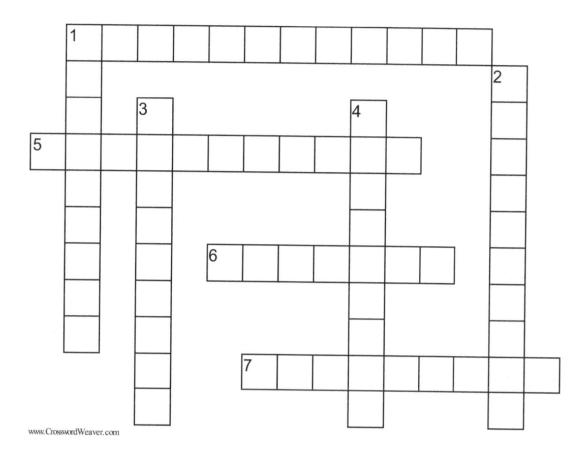

www.CrosswordWeaver.com

ACROSS	DOWN
3 person who does not do as he tells others to do	1 up to this point
4 eager for more information or to learn for themselves	2 concerned with the well-being or good treatment of people
6 tendency to remain balanced, stable, or neutral	3 ordering of things according to importance
7 careless, not thorough	5 looking worn out or tired

Puzzle made at puzzle-maker.com

HH Word Search Puzzle HH

```
S  W  T  S  U  A  C  O  L  O  H  F  F  N  H
I  N  R  C  J  G  L  E  K  N  B  R  X  Y  H
S  P  S  I  X  X  J  L  M  L  P  T  L  E  E
A  H  I  T  L  W  Y  G  D  H  X  V  T  T  K
T  O  S  S  Q  J  Y  G  K  I  U  E  I  L  W
S  M  E  I  N  R  B  A  T  Y  R  R  K  Z  L
O  O  H  L  R  T  M  H  T  O  C  B  B  B  R
E  G  T  O  R  K  T  I  G  O  N  K  Y  I  C
M  E  O  H  N  T  D  E  P  R  H  F  B  H  S
O  N  P  M  R  E  N  Y  C  R  Z  J  F  C  B
H  E  Y  N  R  E  H  T  B  N  Z  D  Y  B  G
G  O  H  E  O  P  C  H  E  R  I  T  A  G  E
K  U  H  U  G  X  N  L  K  B  P  R  T  N  J
M  S  S  H  U  M  A  N  I  T  A  R  I  A  N
M  Y  H  C  R  A  R  E  I  H  W  H  L  Q  P
```

HAGGLE	HOLISTIC	HURBIS
HEREDITY	HOLOCAUST	HYBRID
HERITAGE	HOMEOSTASIS	HYPOCRITE
HETEROGENEOUS	HOMOGENEOUS	HYPOTHESIS
HIERARCHY	HUMANITARIAN	

Puzzle made at puzzle-maker.com

II

Icarian adj. something careless or reckless. It was an Icarian move on his part to drive into oncoming traffic.

iconoclast n. 1. person who destroys or does not believe in worshipping icons or other religious symbols. 2. a person who goes against established religious beliefs or policies. Martin Luther was an iconoclast in many ways because he spoke out against the Catholic Church in the 1500s. / **iconoclastic** adj.

ideology n. a belief system; a set of beliefs; a philosophy. The Republican ideology regarding economics is quite different than the Democrats' ideology.

idiosyncrasy (i-dee-oe-sing-kra-see) n. a strange habit or character trait. Among her many idiosyncrasies was washing her hands every ten minutes.

ignominious (ig-noe-mi-nee-us) adj. embarrassing; humiliating. The worker's ignominious actions did not sit well with his boss.

imbecile (im-be-sile) n. a very stupid person. He acts like an imbecile sometimes.

immerse v. 1. to put into water or liquid until covered. The tools were immersed in water for cleaning. 2. to be completely engaged in something. The students were immersed in their work. /**immersion** n.

immigrant n. a person who comes from another country to live. Immigrants often come to the United States for a better life.

imminent adj. about to happen; unavoidable. The newscaster predicted an imminent storm.

immunity n. 1. resistance to disease. The patient has much immunity to the sickness. 2. freedom or protection from something. The prisoner was promised immunity from prosecution if he cooperated with the police. / **immune** adj.

immutable adj. unchanging. His immutable views on the death penalty frustrated many people.

impair v. to hold back or obstruct; to interfere with. Alcohol impairs vision, reflexes, and judgment.

impeccable (im-pek-ah-bul) adj. very neat; orderly; without flaw. She has impeccable taste when it comes to decorating.

impede (im-peed) v. to hold back or obstruct; to interfere with. Procrastination impedes progress. / **impediment** n. His speech impediment hindered his communication skills.

impel v. to cause, make, or force. Her good conscience impelled her to tell the truth.

impending adj. upcoming. The impending investigation should reveal the truth.

imperative (im-pair-uh-tiv) adj. very important; much needed. It is imperative that you get to a doctor right away.

impertinent adj. not showing respect; rude. The student's impertinent reply angered the teacher.

impervious adj. protecting or shielding by not letting things through. The man seemed impervious to pain.

impetus n. something that leads to or causes something. Money is a good impetus for work.

impinge (im-pinj) v. to act upon, touch, or contact wrongfully or without permission. The new law impinged upon a person's right to free speech.

implausible adj. not plausible; not believable or likely. Alien abduction was an implausible reason for being late.

implicate v. to accuse of wrongdoing. The employee implicated her boss in the cover-up.

implicit (im-pli-sit) adj. implied; something that is meant but not clearly or openly stated. The polite letter was an implicit warning to leave.

implore v. to beg for a helpful reason. The woman implored her husband to go to the doctor.

impose v. to force upon. The new law was imposed upon the people without their consent.

impregnable adj. very secure or safe; not able to be attacked or defeated. The soldiers held an impregnable position on the hill.

improvise v. to make up as one goes along; to do without necessary preparation; to make use out of what is available. The men had to improvise when they did not have the right tools to complete the job.

impudent adj. not showing respect; rude and without shame. The boy's impudent actions embarrassed his parents.

impugn (im-pyoon) v. to challenge the credibility or truth of something. The attorney impugned the evidence against the man.

impunity (im-pyoo-ni-tee) n. freedom or protection from punishment. Children often have a certain degree of impunity that adults do not have.

inadmissible (in-ad-mis-i-bul) adj. 1. not allowable. 2. not capable of being used in a court of law. The evidence was inadmissible because it was obtained illegally.

inadvertent adj. accidental; not done on purpose. It was an inadvertent mistake.

inalienable (in-ay-leen-ah-bul) adj. not capable of being taken away. According to Thomas Jefferson, all people have certain inalienable rights.

inane adj. ridiculous; foolish. He had an inane idea that would never work.

inanimate adj. containing no life; not alive. Inanimate objects do not feel pain.

incapacitated (in-ka-pas-i-tay-ted) adj. of limited power or ability. He was incapacitated for weeks after the accident. / **incapacitate** v.

incendiary (in-sen-dee-air-ee) adj. 1. causing fire. Incendiary bombs were used a lot during WWII. 2. stirring up trouble or emotion. His incendiary comments only made matters worse.

incipient (in-si-pee-ent) adj. just staring out; early on or in a beginning stage. The parents put a stop to the child's incipient misbehaving.

incoherent adj. not clear; not making sense; illogical. The medicine made her drowsy and her statements incoherent.

Matching Quiz # 19

_____1.	imminent	a. causing or leading to something
_____2.	impel	b. system of beliefs
_____3.	implicit	c. to obstruct
_____4.	idiosyncrasy	d. having no mistakes
_____5.	inadvertent	e. freedom from punishment
_____6.	immerse	f. to force
_____7.	incoherent	g. person from another country
_____8.	immigrant	h. not making sense
_____9.	impair	i. strange habit
_____10.	ideology	j. weakened
_____11.	impetus	k. not able to be taken away
_____12.	impeccable	l. not on purpose
_____13.	incapacitated	m. implied but not clearly stated
_____14.	impunity	n. about to happen
_____15.	inalienable	o. completely engaged in

---

incontrovertible adj. not able to be proved false or denied; very clear and certain. The evidence against the man was incontrovertible.

incorporate v. to bring into; to include. The plan incorporated ideas from many people.

incorrigible (in-kor-ej-i-bul) adj. something bad that is not capable of change. His incorrigible behavior was a sad reflection on his parents.

incredulous (in-kre-ju-lus) adj. not believing; skeptical. The man was quite incredulous regarding flying saucers.

incremental adj. in increments; a little bit at a time. The man made incremental improvements.

166

incursion (in-kur-shun) n. an unwarranted move into something. Telemarketers are an incursion on privacy.

indemnify (in-dem-ni-fy) v. to compensate for loss. The insurance company indemnified him for the house fire 2. to protect from loss. Home insurance is a good way to indemnify one's property.

indict (in-dite) v. to charge with a crime. The men were indicted for their role in the robbery. /**indictment** n.

indifference n. lack of care or concern about something. His indifference over his grades is disappointing. /**indifferent** adj.

indigent (in-di-jent) adj. n. / adj. not having the basic necessities of life such as food, clothing, and shelter. The indigent people of poor countries suffer great hardship. / n. a person lacking those necessities.

indignant (in-dig-nant) adj. being very upset with something that is not right or fair. The people were indignant over the harsh treatment of the animals.

indomitable adj. something that cannot be overcome or defeated. The team was an indomitable force to reckon with.

induce v. to cause or bring about. The spoiled food induced an upset stomach.

inebriated (in-ee-bree-ay-ted) adj. drunk; intoxicated. The inebriated man made a fool out of himself.

infallible (in-fal-i-bul) adj. not making any mistakes. The boy thinks he is infallible and capable of no wrong.

infamous adj. memorable in a very bad way; horrible and disgraceful. We shall never forget that infamous day when Pearl Harbor was attacked. /**infamy** n.

infer v. to deduce or conclude from what is known. One must infer from the evidence that is known, that the man is guilty. /**inference** n. a conclusion based on what is known.

infidel n. a non-believer in something, particularly a religion. Some religions deal with infidels cruelly.

infidelity n. unfaithfulness. Infidelity is terrible in marriage.

infrastructure n. the basic and necessary elements of a structure. A country's infrastructure refers to its roads, bridges, buildings, and other transportation and communication systems.

infringe (in-frinj) v. to violate by going beyond what is proper or acceptable. The law infringes upon one's personal freedoms. / **infringement** n.

ingenious (in-jee-nee-us) adj. clever; good at making or inventing things. The ingenious device saves everyone a lot of time. /**ingenuity** n.

ingratiate (in-gray-shee-ate) v. to make people pleased with oneself. He ingratiated himself with the woman with flattery and expensive gifts.

ingress n. entrance. Our only ingress was in the front of the building.

inherent adj. naturally part of; born with or coming naturally. She has an inherent tendency for perfection.

inhibit v. to restrict or hold back. Her shyness inhibits her ability to meet people. /**inhibition** n.

iniquity n. something most unfair, unjust, or unequal. There have been many iniquities in the way some races have been treated throughout history.

initial adj. first. The woman's initial plan was to take the day off work to have her car serviced.

innocuous (i-nok-yu-us) adj. harmless. The remark turned out to be innocuous.

innovation n. a change or improvement made to something that already exists. The Bessemer process was an innovation in the steel industry. /**innovative** adj. / **innovate** v.

inquisitive (in-kwi-si-tiv) adj. asking many question; curious. The inquisitive youth always challenged her teacher.

inscrutable (in-scroo-tah-bul) adj. something that cannot be understood because not much is known about it. The inscrutable circumstances left everyone bewildered.

insidious (in-sid-ee-us) adj. trying to trick or trap; secretly trying to do something. The detective's insidious questions did not fool the criminal.

insolvent adj. not able to pay bills or debts; having no money. After being open for five years, the business became insolvent.

intangible (in-tan-ji-bul) adj. 1. hard to understand. The idea seemed too intangible to many people. 2. not capable of being touched.

integral adj. an important part of; essential; necessary part of. Good people skills are an integral part of being a manager.

integrate v. to combine or include. The machine's design integrated all that was known about mechanics. / **integration** n.

integrity n. 1. honesty; willingness to do what is right and proper; respectability. He is a man of great integrity. 2. solidness or completeness. The structural integrity of the building must not be compromised.

Matching Quiz # 20

_____ 1. initial	a. to combine
_____ 2. innocuous	b. to bring into or include
_____ 3. integral	c. asking many questions
_____ 4. incorporate	d. unfaithfulness
_____ 5. infringe	e. very clever
_____ 6. incremental	f. an important part of
_____ 7. inherent	g. born with
_____ 8. innovation	h. not understandable
_____ 9. indifferent	i. little bit at a time
_____ 10. incursion	j. first
_____ 11. intangible	k. harmless
_____ 12. infidelity	l. showing no concern
_____ 13. ingenious	m. an unwarranted move or action
_____ 14. inquisitive	n. to go beyond what is proper
_____ 15. integrate	o. improvement on something

intelligentsia (in-tel-i-jen-see-ah) n. the educated people within a country; the intellectuals. The country's intelligentsia will solve the nation's problems.

intercede (in-ter-seed) v. to come between or interfere in an effort to make things better. The teacher interceded on behalf of the student who got in trouble. /**intercession** n.

interdict v. to forbid or keep from doing something. The policed interdicted just as the man was about to be assaulted. / **interdiction** n.

interlude n. anything that fills up time between events. The interlude between games included entertainment and music.

intermittent adj. not constant; starting and stopping. The intermittent rain was just enough to ruin the picnic.

intrigue n. a situation that is curious and interesting; situation characterized by suspense, mystery, or secrecy. The case of the disappearing diamonds was filled with much intrigue.

intrigued v. to cause an interest in something. The mystery intrigued the girl.

intriguing (in-tree-ging) adj. suspenseful, curious, or interesting. The mystery was intriguing.

intrinsic adj. inherent; naturally part of or belonging to. Loyalty is intrinsic to faithfulness.

introspection n. the examination of one's own thoughts, feelings, or actions; self-reflection. Introspection is a good way to improve oneself. / **introspective** adj.

introvert n. person who likes to be alone or do his own thing. He is not unfriendly, just an introvert. / **introverted** adj.

intuition (in-too-i-shun) n. sudden knowledge about something based on experience or a feeling, rather than reason. Women are said to have better intuition than men. His intuition told him not to go to work that day. /**intuitive** adj.

inundate v. to overcome or overflow. The team was inundated with autograph requests.

invertebrate n. an animal with no backbone. Many creatures are invertebrates.

invoke v. to call or bring into effect. The king invoked a new law.

ipso facto Latin term meaning by the fact itself. Murder is an ipso facto evil. Supply and demand is an ipso facto aspect of capitalism.

ironic adj. something that is opposite of what would be expected. It is ironic that many people who criticize teachers know nothing about teaching. / **irony** n. Oedipus was a tragic tale of irony.

isometric adj. having equal measurements or sides. The walls are isometric.

isthmus (is-mus) n. a narrow stretch of land, with water on each side that connects two larger pieces of land. An isthmus is usually a perfect place to build a canal.

ivory tower figurative for a place or state of mind where people are not aware of reality or what really goes on in everyday practical life. People in ivory towers often think their ideas are great, but they don't often see their ideas tested in real situations. Does the ivory tower scientist actually think his idea will work outside the science lab?

Matching Quiz # 21

_____ 1. invoke   a. the educated class
_____ 2. intriguing   b. knowledge based on feeling
_____ 3. intrinsic   c. having equal measurements
_____ 4. intermittent   d. self-reflection
_____ 5. interdict   e. something that fills up time
_____ 6. introspection   f. likes to be alone
_____ 7. isometric   g. interesting, curious, suspenseful
_____ 8. interlude   h. to step in and act
_____ 9. introvert   i. to bring into effect
_____ 10. ironic   j. starting and stopping
_____ 11. ipso facto   k. part of
_____ 12. inundate   l. where one is not aware of reality
_____ 13. intuition   m. by the fact itself
_____ 14. intelligentsia   n. opposite of expected outcome
_____ 15. ivory tower   o. to overflow or overcome

II Word Search Puzzle II

```
X L N V I N F A L L I B L E
B N E L B I G I R R O C N I
Y Y T I L E D I F N I T R Z
P K I N A L I E N A B L E E
R E L I Q T V F D E N C T C
N T J R W J F L S O I A T R
Y A Q O G H T I I S R H F T
T R T N Y W V T N O L Q R K
I G N I Z O I I P V B N V V
N E M C R U R R C M O M Z X
U T D P T T O Y H Z R K R V
M N M N N C K F T N F W E Z
M I I I N Q U I S I T I V E
I Y T I R G E T N I L Y K L
```

IMMUNITY	INFALLIBLE	INTRINSIC
IMPROVISE	INFIDELITY	INTUITION
INALIENABLE	INQUISITIVE	INVOKE
INCORPORATE	INTEGRATE	IRONIC
INCORRIGIBLE	INTEGRITY	

Puzzle made at puzzle-maker.com

JJ

jaded (jay-ded) adj. disillusioned; upset with; worn out. The jaded university student liked community college much better.

jaundice (jawn-dis) n. an unhealthy condition characterized by a yellowing of the skin. The man looked horrible after jaundice set in.

jaunt (jawnt) n. v. /a short trip or journey. The boys made a quick jaunt down the street. / v. to make a short trip.

jihad (jee-hahd) n. literally means "struggle" in Arabic, but often refers to a Muslim holy war against opponents or non-believers. The jihad has claimed many innocent lives.

jocular (jo-kyu-lar) adj. not serious; in a joking manner. She was quite pleasant and jocular today.

Jolly Roger n. a black flag with a skull and cross-bones on it used by pirates. A pirate is known by his Jolly Roger.

jovial adj. outgoing; friendly; good-natured. The girl is always caring and jovial.

jubilant adj. very excited or happy. The children were jubilant upon hearing the good news.

judicious (jew-dish-us) adj. having or exercising good judgment. The policeman was most judicious about the whole incident.

jurisprudence (jur-is-pru-dens) n. the study of law or its application. the study of law or its application. Jurisprudence dictates the way the judge could interpret the law.

juxtapose (jux-tah-pose) v. to put close together or side-by-side so things can be compared. You must juxtapose the two pieces of evidence. /**juxtaposition** n.

KK

kindred adj. n. /adj. related; of the same family; similar. Kindred spirits stick together. / n. a relative.

kinesiology (ki-nee-see-o-loe-jee) n. the science of human motion. Kinesiology is very important to doctors of professional athletes.

kismet n. destiny; fate. If not for kismet, they never would have met.

knave (nave) n. a liar or dishonest person. Cheaters and knaves have few morals.

kudos (koo-does) n. praise. Kudos to the winner of the race.

Matching Quiz # 22

_____ 1. jaded	a. praise
_____ 2. jaundice	b. jokingly
_____ 3. jaunt	c. very excited
_____ 4. kinesiology	d. friendly
_____ 5. jocular	e. showing good judgment
_____ 6. Jolly Roger	f. upset with
_____ 7. jovial	g. yellowing caused by bad health
_____ 8. jubilant	h. side by side
_____ 9. judicious	i. from the same family
_____ 10. jurisprudence	j. fate
_____ 11. juxtaposition	k. a liar
_____ 12. kindred	l. science of human motion
_____ 13. kismet	m. pirate's flag
_____ 14. knave	n. a short trip
_____ 15. kudos	o. application of the law

LL

laborious (luh-bor-ee-us) adj. requiring much hard work or effort. Stacking those boxes was laborious work.

laconic (luh-ko-nik) adj. not using many words when speaking or writing. His laconic style appealed to many readers.

laden (lay-den) adj. loaded with; weighted down with. The car was laden with suitcases and bags. He is laden with bad habits.

laity (lay-it-y) n. 1. people associated with a church who are not part of the clergy or priesthood. The laity organized the church event, not the priests. 2. regular people not part of a professional order.

lambaste (lam-baist) v. to severely scold or speak harshly to someone. The employee was lambasted by his boss for being late again.

lame duck figurative term for a politician or another important figure who has no real authority anymore because they will soon be out of power. Second-term presidents are usually lame ducks.

lament (luh-ment) v. to feel bad about something. The boy lamented about hurting his best friend's feelings. / **lamentation** n.

lampoon v. n. / v. to make fun of insultingly. The students lampooned their teacher for his out of fashion clothes. / n. something that pokes fun at something.

languish (lang-qwish) v. to become weak over time; to struggle. The horse languished do to a lack of exercise.

larceny (lar-se-nee) n. theft. The criminal was convicted of fraud and larceny.

latitude n. 1. figurative for freedom to act or think. The boss gave the worker a lot of latitude in making decisions. 2. distance north or south of the equator signified by horizontal lines on a map and measured in degrees. The lines of latitude are easy to find on a map.

laudable (law-dah-bul) adj. something deserving notice or praise. The man made a laudable attempt to be at all of his child's school functions.

legitimate (le-gi-ti-met) adj. 1. real; official; valid; accepted. Community service was a legitimate punishment for the violation. 2. born to married parents.

lethargic (le-thar-jik) adj. drowsy; sluggish; acting tired. The medication made her lethargic. / **lethargy** n.

leviathan (le-vy-uh-thon) n. 1. a large sea monster. 2. a large or powerful person or thing. That truck is a real leviathan.

levity (le-vi-tee) n. act of not taking something seriously; taking things lightly. No one was alarmed due to the levity of the situation.

levy (le-vee) v. n. / v. ordering that something be paid or collected. The government levies taxes to collect <u>revenue</u>. /n. something that is ordered or collected. A new city levy was passed.

lexicon (lek-see-kon) n. the words used in a language or a subject. The lexicon of chemistry is quite confusing.

liaison (lee-ay-zon) n. 1. a secret or secure connection or meeting between people or things to ensure cooperation. 2. a person performing such duties. The U.S. liaison to the oil company brokered a deal.

libel (ly-bel) n. written expressions harming someone's reputation or character. Newspapers have often been sued for libel.

liberal adj. n. /adj. having open minded or progressive ideas about things; not favoring many restrictions. The school is pretty liberal with its dress code. / n. a person with those attributes.

liberate (li-ber-ate) v. to set free. The animals were liberated from their cages.

limber adj. flexible; easily bent or adjusted. The muscles of athletes are usually pretty limber.

lineage (li-nee-ij) n. line of descent from one's ancestors. His lineage speaks of royalty and wealth.

linear (li-nee-er) adj. in a straight line; in one direction; along one plane. Her thought process is very linear and ordered.

linguistic (lin-gwi-stik) adj. related to languages or the study of languages. The linguistic characteristics of both ancient words are similar. / **linguist** n. person who studies languages.

litany (li-ta-nee) n. 1. a large number or collection of things. A litany of old books was found in the attic. 2. anything related or occurring in a repeated order.

literal adj. taking something word for word; deriving the meaning from something exactly the way it was said or written; without error or exaggeration. Do not look for a literal meaning in the poem. /**literally** adv. Many poems are not meant to be read literally.

literary (li-ter-air-ree) adj. related to writings or literature. The literary critic reviewed the book.

litigation (li-ti-gay-shun) n. legal proceedings in court. The accident required litigation.

litmus test n. literally a way of testing for acid but refers to the true test of something's quality. The trial of the new invention will be the litmus test of the theory.

livid adj. very upset or angry. The man was livid with his son for staying out all night.

loathe (loeth) v. to hate or detest. The girl loathes the taste of spinach. /**loathsome** adj.

locale (lo-kal) n. location of something. The southern locale is perfect for a vacation.

locomotion (loe-keo-moe-shun) n. movement; the act of moving or being in motion.

logistics (lo-ji-stiks) n. 1. the actual planning or carrying out of tasks. 2. the science or art of careful planning and carrying out of duties. Good logistics requires much forethought and anticipation of potential problems. /adj. Feeding a thousand people will take a logistical miracle.

longevity (long-je-vi-tee) n. act of living or lasting for a long time. Cars don't seem to have much longevity anymore.

longitude (long-ji-tood) n. distance east or west on the earth measured in degrees along vertical lines. /**longitudinal** adj.

loquacious (lo-kway-shus) adj. talking a lot. She is a loquacious youth.

lore (lor) n. information including facts, myths, or stories about something old. The lore surrounding the castle was quite interesting.

Matching Quiz # 23

____ 1. larceny
____ 2. legitimate
____ 3. liberal
____ 4. loathe
____ 5. locale
____ 6. laden
____ 7. logistics
____ 8. livid
____ 9. liberate
____ 10. laborious
____ 11. lambaste
____ 12. litmus test
____ 13. loquacious
____ 14. literal
____ 15. lethargic

a. word for word
b. to set free
c. sluggish
d. talking a lot
e. very angry
f. requiring hard work
g. location of something
h. theft
i. official or real
j. to scold harshly
k. test of quality
l. planning out of duties
m. open minded
n. loaded with
o. to hate

---

lubricate (loo-bri-kate) v. to oil or grease with something so it moves smoothly. Car engines must be lubricated often.

lucid (loo-sid) adj. aware; coherent; making sense. The man was lucid even after the blow to his head. /**lucidity** n.

lucrative adj. money-making; profitable. The students started a lucrative business.

luminous (loo-mi-nus) adj. giving off its own light. The sun is luminous.

lurid (lur-id) adj. horrible, terrible; <u>ghastly</u>. Rape is a lurid and despicable crime.

luster (luh-ster) n. a bright finish or shine on something. Cars in warm climates retain their luster very well.

lycanthropy (ly-kan-throe-pee) n. a mental disorder in which the person thinks he is a wolf. Cases of lycanthropy have been documented for centuries.

Lyceum (ly-see-um) n. an ancient outdoor area in Greece where students studied philosophy.

lyceum (ly-see-um) n. a place where lectures and other educational gatherings take place.

LL Crossword Puzzle LL

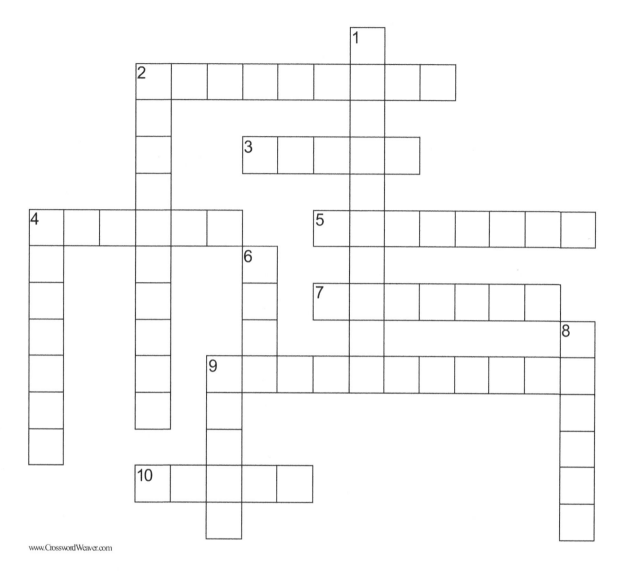

www.CrosswordWeaver.com

ACROSS	DOWN
2 the planning and carrying out of tasks	1 legal proceedings, process of legal action
3 aware, coherent, making sense	2 talking a lot
4 large number of things	4 line of descent from one's ancestors
5 freedom to act or think	6 to require that something be paid
7 secret meeting between people	8 place where lectures and other educational gatherings take place
9 mental disorder in which a person thinks he is a wolf	9 unpleasantly vivid, shocking, explicit
10 people associated with a church but not part of the priesthood	

Puzzle made at puzzle-maker.com

MM

macabre (muh-kob) adj. grotesque in an evil or horrible way. He has a macabre sense of humor.

Machiavellian (mah-kee-ah-ve-lee-an) adj. related to the notion that a person or leader should do whatever is necessary to get or keep power. His boss has employed Machiavellian methods from time to time.

machination (mak-i-nay-shun) n. the act of scheming or planning something evil or underhanded. The corporation's profit driven machinations have left many people poor and unemployed.

machismo (muh-chees-moe) n. a Spanish word referring to manliness or masculine ability; being macho. His machismo always got him into trouble.

magna cum laude (magna coom laud) refers to the second highest degree of merit one can graduate college with. She graduated magna cum laude from Harvard in 1971.

magnanimous (mag-na-ni-mus) adj. of great or noble spirit (intentions); unselfish and forgiving. Helping those who have hurt you in the past is quite magnanimous. / **magnanimity** n.

magnitude n. importance or size; the degree of something. The magnitude of the crime requires a severe punishment.

major-domo (may-jer doe-moe) n. a live-in paid person in charge of a large or wealthy household; a butler. The major-domo made all of the arrangements for the house party.

maladapted adj. not adapted to something; unfit for something. The maladapted worker could not perform his job very well.

maladroit adj. not good at something; clumsy or awkward. The maladroit painter got paint all over the place.

malaise (muh-laze) n. a sickened, disturbed, or uncomfortable condition. A malaise overcame the room when the layoffs were about to be announced.

malcontent adj. n. / adj. unhappy, unpleased, or unsatisfied. The malcontent employees were even more upset after the bad news. / n. All the malcontents gathered to protest the layoffs. / **malcontented** adj.

maldevelopment n. undeveloped or not developed properly. A maldevelopment occurred in the child's infancy.

maldistribution n. not being rightly, fairly, or effectively distributed. The company suffered from a maldistribution of funds.

malediction n. the act of speaking bad or evil things about someone. The old woman was quite skilled in malediction directed at her family.

malevolent (muh-le-vo-lent) adj. wishing bad things upon someone. His malevolent personality will come back to get him some day.

malfeasance (mal-fee-zens) n. wrongdoing by an official or other person held in public trust. The government worker was guilty of gross malfeasance when he misused public money.

malice (ma-lis) n. ill will; intent to cause harm. He has malice in his heart and vengeance in his mind. / **malicious** adj.

malign (muh-line) v. to talk badly about someone. The innocent boy was maligned by his neighbor.

malignant v. harmful; causing death. Fortunately, the tumor was not malignant and can be easily removed.

malleable (ma-lee-ah-bul) adj. able to be shaped or bent; flexible; adaptable. Metal is malleable when heated. She is quite malleable when it comes to learning new things.

mandamus n. a law or order handed down from a higher authority to a lower authority requiring that a certain act be done. The Supreme Court handed down a mandamus to the school board to change its admissions policy.

mandate n. v. / n. something that is required or ordered. The new mandate calls for higher graduation requirements. /v. to order or require. The school board mandated a new graduation requirement.

manifest v. to become a part of; to appear. The legend manifested itself in the minds of an entire generation.

manifesto (ma-ni-fes-toe) n. a public statement in written or oral form about one's opinions or intentions. The politician's manifesto clearly outlined his goals.

maritime (mair-i-time) adj. related to the water or sea. The Eastland disaster was a terrible maritime incident in Chicago history.

martyr (mar-ter) n. a person who dies for a cause he or she believes strongly in, often becoming an even more popular or important person after death. The death of the group's leader made a martyr out of her.

masochist (ma-so-kist) n. a person who likes to inflict pain or discomfort upon himself. Only a masochist would go ice swimming.

materialize (muh-teer-ee-ah-lize) v. to happen or come about. The plans to build a new school never materialized.

matriarch (may-tree-ark) n. the mother or female elder who is head of a family. The grandmother is the matriarch, and she still makes the rules for the household.

matriculate (ma-tri-kyu-late) v. to advance to the next level or to be admitted to school. Students must meet certain requirements before they matriculate to the next grade. / **matriculation** n.

180

maturation (ma-chur-ay-shen) n. act or process of maturing or developing. The maturation period for some people is quite a long time.

median (mee-dee-an) n. 1. the middle of something. 2. with numbers, median refers to a number that has just as many numbers above it as below it. The median score on the test was 93% where ten people scored higher than 93% and ten people scored below 93%.

mediate (mee-dee-ate) v. to get involved in a disagreement and help solve it. The teacher was asked to mediate the problem between the two students./ **mediation** n.

mediocre (mee-dee-oe-ker) adj. average; not very good but not real bad. She is a mediocre tennis player. /**mediocrity** n.

meek adj. quiet, kind, forgiving, and gentle. The meek little boy turned out to be one of the most powerful individuals in the country.

megalith n. a large great stone. The ancient Egyptians left behind many megaliths for people to envy. Many ancient buildings were constructed with megaliths.

megalomania (me-guh-loe-may-nee-ah) n. an obsession, often a mental illness, associated with personal power and greatness. Hitler suffered from megalomania. /**megalomaniac** n. Hitler was a megalomaniac.

melancholy (me-lan-ko-lee) adj. a depressing or sad feeling; unhappy; gloomy. Rainy days often bring melancholy thoughts.

melodramatic (me-loe-drah-ma-tik) adj. showing exaggerated emotions for effect. Her outburst was a bit melodramatic.

menagerie (me-na-jer-ree) n. a collection of wild animals for display. The menagerie had some very exotic animals.

Matching Quiz # 24

_____1. magnitude
_____2. maladroit
_____3. malevolent
_____4. macabre
_____5. malcontent
_____6. magnanimous
_____7. malignant
_____8. malice
_____9. malleable
_____10. Machiavellian
_____11. matriculate
_____12. martyr
_____13. melancholy
_____14. materialize
_____15. mediate

a. to come between and help
b. harmful
c. wanting to cause harm
d. flexible, shapeable
e. to come into being
f. a sad feeling
g. grotesque
h. of great spirit
i. wishing bad things
j. one who dies for a cause
k. not good at something
l. unhappy with something
m. philosophy of keeping power
n. degree or size
o. to advance to the next level

mendacious (men-day-shus) adj. untruthful; lying. The mendacious students came up with a story to protect themselves from punishment.

menial (mee-nee-al) adj. referring to the lowest ranks; becoming of a servant. The professor thought he was above menial labor such as sweeping floors.

Mensa n. an international organization for people of very high intelligence. People must take intelligence tests before they can become members of Mensa.

mercantile (mer-kan-tile) adj. related to commerce or trade. The mercantile system in the U.S. usually works quite well.

mercenary (mer-se-nair-ree) n. a soldier who is paid to fight for a foreign army. Mercenaries fight for money, not for a cause.

mercurial (mer-kyer-ree-uhl) adj. 1. liable to change easily. His mercurial temperament finally got him in trouble. 2. quick; always moving. The mercurial youth was always first in line.

Messiah n. savior of the Jews (Jesus in Christianity)

messiah n. any person considered a savior of people. People in bondage often look for a messiah to lead them to freedom.

Messianic (messianic) (mes-ee-a-nik) adj. related to a messiah or having a messiah's characteristics.

metamorphosis (me-tuh-mor-fah-sis) n. a change in structure or appearance. Butterflies undergo a complete metamorphosis before they are mature. People usually undergo a metamorphosis during their teenage years.

methodical adj. slow and deliberate; displaying much care and method; following a set procedure. The surgeon was very methodical in his actions.

meticulous (me-ti-kyu-lus) adj. very neat and orderly; clean. Their home is so meticulous it seems as if no one lives there.

metropolis (me-tro-poe-lis) n. the largest or most important city in a country or region. Chicago is the metropolis of the Midwest.

microcosm (my-kro-koz-em) n. a small world or universe. Cities are a microcosm of diverse people. Bathrooms are often a microcosm of germs.

migrate (my-grate) v. to move from one place to another. Many animals migrate for food. /**migration** n. / **migratory** adj.

migrant. adj. n. related to migration. /adj. The migrant animals searched for food. /n. one who migrates. The migrants were paid less than the native born citizens.

militant adj. eager to use force or violence; aggressive. The militant protestors destroyed the building.

millennium n. period of a thousand years.

milieu (mil-yu) n. environment; surroundings. Arizona's dry climate is just the milieu the man needed for his allergies.

misanthropy (mis-an-throe-pee) n. a deep hatred or mistrust of people. Some loners suffer from misanthropy. /**misanthrope** n. person who dislikes or mistrusts people.

misnomer (mis-noe-mer) n. a wrong way of describing something. Hot is a misnomer for ice.

missionary (mi-shun-air-ree) n. a person who tries to spread religion or convert people to another religion. Spanish missionaries tried to teach Christianity to many American Indian tribes in the 1500s.

mitigate v. to lessen or make less severe. The judge mitigated the juvenile's punishment. The medicine mitigated the fever.

mnemonics (new-mon-iks) n. related to memory or ways to improve memory. Mnemonic strategies like rhyming and association work well for some people.

mogul (moe-gul) n. an important person within an industry; person of great power or achievement. The movie moguls spend millions of dollars to promote their films.

momentous (moe-men-tus) n. of great importance; memorable. College graduation is a momentous occasion.

monastery (mo-nah-stair-ee) n. a place or building where monks live. Monasteries have served many important religions and educational purposes in European history.

monastic (mo-na-stik) adj. related to the life of a monk. Some monastic rules require much devotion on the part of the monk.

monk n. a person who devotes himself entirely to God by living in a monastery and spending his days in prayer and finding ways to serve God. Monks often take vows of poverty and remain isolated from the everyday world.

monogamy n. the practice of being married to or having sexual relations with only one person at a time. Monogamy and polygamy do not go hand in hand. / **monogamous** adj.

monolith n. a huge piece of stone, often used in building ancient structures or monuments. Many monoliths were used to build ancient temples. /**monolithic** adj.

monotheism (mo-noe-thee-iz-um) n. the belief in one god. The ancient Greeks and Romans did not practice monotheism because they had a different god to explain many things in nature, such as the god of war and the sun god.

morals n. having standards of right and wrong, good and bad; <u>ethical</u>. A lack of morals leads to a selfish society with many social problems.

morality n. related to the morals of a thought or action; being good or bad, right or wrong. Many people think our current society lacks enough proper morality.

morale (mor-al) n. mental spirits or condition. The soldiers had high morale after the victory. The morale of the staff is quite low because of all the layoffs.

morose adj. gloomy; macabre. The story was quite morose and displeasing to hear.

mortify (mor-ti-fy) v. to harm one's feelings or embarrass someone through improper actions. The student's rude outburst at the assembly mortified his teacher.

mosaic (moe-zay-ik) n. artwork or design made from a colorful arrangement of small tile, stone, or glass. The mosaic on the floor of the museum impressed visitors.

motif (moe-teef) n. the main idea or subject in an artistic work, such as in literature, drama, music, art, or cinema. The artist's motif was hard to detect in the painting.

mutation (mu-tay-shun) n. a change in the structure or appearance of something. Exposure to radiation can cause genetic mutations.

myriad (meer-ee-ad) n. a large number. There are a myriad of reasons to explain why some children do not perform well in school.

```
Matching Quiz # 25

____1.  meticulous          a. of the lowest ranks
____2.  metamorphosis       b. savior
____3.  methodical          c. a small world
____4.  mercurial           d. attitude or spirit
____5.  menial              e. important business person
____6.  messiah             f. one who spreads religion
____7.  microcosm           g. place where monks live
____8.  monotheism          h. very important
____9.  mercenary           i. a paid soldier
___10.  morale              j. very clean and neat
___11.  mogul               k. complete change in appearance
___12.  missionary          l. eager to use force
___13.  monastery           m. slow and careful
___14.  momentous           n. belief in one god
___15.  militant            o. likely to change one's mind
```

mystify (mi-sti-fy) v. to confuse. The man's answer to the problem mystified his co-workers.

mystique (mis-teek) n. a quality of mystery, suspense, or intrigue. The musician's mystique made him even more popular.

MM Crossword Puzzle MM

www.CrosswordWeaver.com

ACROSS	DOWN
1 importance, size, or degree of something	1 to help solve a disagreement between people
3 showing exaggerated emotions for effect	2 having a quality of mystery or intrigue
4 public statement, often written, of one's beliefs	5 able to be shaped or influenced, adaptable
5 wrongdoing doing by elected officials or those held in public trust	6 to lesson or make less severe
6 obsession associated with one's own power or greatness	7 belief in one god
9 paid, live-in person in charge of a large household or estate	8 a large number or variety of something
10 artwork made from arranging colorful tiles	9 wrong way of describing something
11 change in structure or appearance	11 the theme or main idea in an artistic work
12 standards of right and wrong and good and bad	
13 being married to or having sexual relations with only one person	

Puzzle made at puzzle-maker.com

MM Word Search Puzzle MM

```
M E L A N C H O L Y P F T C M
M L C H H M E T H O D I C A L
X A C J Y T M D M P M M H Q M
M L T L X E A M K E R O S L A
N T W E C I Y X T R D R U M T
W P R I R S C I X B R A O L R
N N L Y T I C M J A T L T R I
B A M I X U A K F C L E N Y C
M P Q L L R J L F A D B E F U
K U B O U N H K I M T W M Y L
E D U C J G W N T Z R D O L A
R S K L W Y O P F Q E J M M T
L K F N L T V M R T P Y R P E
T Y F K J S C I N O M E N M K
N Z G M A L I G N A N T T M L
```

MACABRE	MELANCHOLY	MOMENTOUS
MALICE	METHODICAL	MORALE
MALIGNANT	METICULOUS	MYRIAD
MATERIALIZE	MNEMONICS	MYSTIQUE
MATRICULATE	MOGUL	

Puzzle made at puzzle-maker.com

NN

naïve (nah-eev) adj. not experienced in the ways of the world; not aware of things. The naïve young girl did not realize that the boy liked her.

narcissism (nar-si-siz-um) n. great love of oneself. His narcissism knows no limits as he is completely preoccupied with himself. /**narcissist** n.

NASA National Aeronautics and Space Administration.

naturalize v. to make an immigrant an official citizen of a country. Visitors to the United States do not have the same rights as people who have been naturalized. / **naturalized** adj.

nebulous (ne-byu-lus) adj. 1. literally not having a solid form; gas or cloud-like. 2. confusing; not clear or certain; vague; obscure. His thoughts on politics are nebulous at best.

necrophilia (nek-roe-fee-lee-ah) n. an obsession with or attraction to dead bodies. Necrophilia must have its roots in a mental or emotional disorder.

nefarious (ne-far-ee-us) adj. evil; treacherous; underhanded. The group organized a nefarious plot to overthrow the company.

negate v. to cancel out. One good deed does not negate a lifetime of bad habits.

nemesis n. a foe or enemy who punishes or overcomes another; a person who delivers punishment or retribution to evildoers.   Elliot Ness was Al Capone's nemesis.

neophyte (nee-oe-fite) n. a beginner; someone who is new to something. Teenagers and other neophytes to university life have a lot to learn.

nepotism n. showing favoritism to one's relatives. In an obvious display of nepotism, the boss gave all his family members company jobs.

nihilism n. 1. the negative view that life is useless and only full of suffering and death with no objective sense of right and wrong. 2. the negative view or rejection of established beliefs of a society such as government or religion.   3. the belief that violence and terror are acceptable means of achieving a goal. Nihilism found a voice in many philosophers. /**nihilistic** adj.

nimble (nim-bul) adj. coordinated and quick.   The nimble cat eluded capture for an hour.

Nirvana (nirvana) n. state of ultimate peace, happiness, or complete awareness; heaven or the ultimate reality as believed by the Hindus and Buddhists. Nirvana filled the room when the good news was heard.

nocuous (nah-kyu-us) adj. harmful; poisonous. The nocuous fumes chased everyone out of the room.

nonchalant (non-shah-lahnt) adj. a calm, casual manner. He approached the woman in nonchalant manner that <u>intrigued</u> her. / **nonchalantly** adv.

nonentity (non-en-ti-tee) n. something that does not exist or have or any meaning or value. As far as she was concerned, her ex-boyfriend was a nonentity.

nonpareil (non-puh-rel) adj. n. /adj. unmatched or unequaled. / n. something that has no equal in quality. The nonpareil of jewels is the Hope diamond.

nonproliferation (non-pro-lif-er-ay-shun) n. 1. the containment of something to keep in from spreading or increasing.   Attempts at nonproliferation did not keep the rumors from circulating.
2. the attempt to stop the spread of nuclear weapons through agreements. The U.S. and the Soviet Union embarked on nonproliferation too late. (also see <u>proliferate</u>).

Norse adj. referring to ancient Scandinavia or its people. Thor is a legendary Norse god.

Nordic (nor-dik) adj. referring to the Scandinavian or Germanic people or region of northern Europe. Nordic people often have similar physical characteristics such as blond hair and blue eyes.

nostalgia (nos-tal-jah) n. having fond feelings for the past or for older or far away things. A sense of nostalgia often overcomes people when they see movies set in the past. /**nostalgic** adj.

notarize v. to have an authorized person certify that a document is valid or <u>authentic</u>. The politician had to have his petition signatures notarized.

novice n. a beginner; someone new, inexperienced, or unskilled at something. It takes a novice a while to learn to ski well.

noxious adj. harmful; poisonous; deadly. The noxious gas left a foul odor in the room.

nuance (new-ons) n. a subtle (slight) difference in the way something looks or acts. One could tell he was in pain just from the nuances of his motions.

nullify (nul-li-fy) v. to render something useless or invalid; to void something. A state cannot nullify a federal law. /**nullification** n. act of nullifying.

NN Crossword Puzzle NN

www.CrosswordWeaver.com

ACROSS	DOWN
1 in a calm and casual manner	1 to make an immigrant an official citizen of the country
3 not experienced in the ways of the world, too trusting	2 showing favoritism to one's relatives
6 fond feelings for the past	3 to render something useless or invalid
8 poisonous or harmful	4 great love of oneself
9 noxious, harmful, poisonous	5 a beginner, someone not good at something because they are new to it
10 unclear or uncertain, vague	7 a beginner
11 slight difference in the way something looks, acts, or functions	

Puzzle made at puzzle-maker.com

OO

objective n. adj. / n 1. a goal. Her objective was to get into a good college. / adj. free from bias or personal judgment; clear-cut, not open to much interpretation. A fact is objective, and an opinion is subjective.

obligatory (o-blig-ah-tor-ee) adj. something required by obligation. His appearance in court was made obligatory by the summons.

oblivious (o-bliv-ee-us) adj. completely unaware. The man was oblivious to the consequences of his actions.

oblique (oe-bleek) adj. not straight or in one direction; indirect. He drew an oblique line on the page depicting the path of the car. Her oblique confession did not satisfy her mother.

obscure (ob-skyur) adj. 1. not clear or easy to understand; not well-known. 2. odd; out of place. His obscure comment left everyone confused.

obsequious (ob-see-kwee-us) adj. politeness out of duty or hope of future reward or fear of punishment. The secretary's obsequious manner did not sit well with her boss.

obsolete adj. outdated; no longer useful. The old computer is obsolete.

obstinate (ob-sti-net) adj. stubborn. The obstinate student was always tardy.

obtrusive adj. overstepping one's bounds; interfering when not asked. The obtrusive employee invited himself to the party.

odious (oe-dee-us) adj. despised; unfavorable. The odious comment was rude and uncalled for.

olfactory adj. related to the sense of smell. The olfactory nerves affect the sense of smell.

olive branch figurative for a gesture of peace. A bouquet of flowers from a man to his upset wife is a good olive branch.

ominous adj. treacherous; unfavorable; dangerous. The waves were quite ominous for the boaters.

omnipotence (om-nip-oe-tens) n. state of being all-powerful. The omnipotence of the military should not be abused. /**omnipotent** adj.

omniscience (om-nish-ens) n. state of being all-knowing. His omniscience of the situation made it seem like he was watching the entire time. /**omniscient** adj.

omnivorous adj. eating everything. Bears can be omnivorous animals.

onerous (on-er-us) adj. hard to handle or agree with. Studying day and night can be quite onerous even though it pays off in the long run.

190

ontological (on-to-loj-i-kal) adj. related to the philosophy concerned with the study of reality. Descartes' ontological pursuits made him a legend among philosophers. / **ontology** n.

onus n. responsibility. The onus to get the homework done on time rests with the student.

opaque (oe-pake) adj. not allowing light through. The opaque shades kept the room cool in the summer.

Matching Quiz # 26

____1. obtrusive	a. not letting light through
____2. oblivious	b. gesture of peace
____3. obscure	c. stubborn
____4. obligatory	d. all-powerful
____5. olive branch	e. overstepping one's bounds
____6. obstinate	f. not well-known
____7. objective	g. all-knowing
____8. obsequious	h. eating everything
____9. ontological	i. free from personal opinion
____10. opaque	j. politeness out of desire for reward
____11. onus	k. treacherous, dangerous
____12. omnipotence	l. responsibility
____13. ominous	m. related to the study of reality
____14. omniscience	n. completely unaware
____15. omnivorous	o. out of obligation

---

opulence n. wealth. The house boasted of opulence. /**opulent** adj.

oracle (or-ah-kahl) n. a wise person or mystic person who reveals truths; a place where truths are magically revealed. The oracle predicted a great famine.

oration n. a public speech. The politician's oration attracted many people. /**orator** n. / **oratory** n. skill in public speaking. Socrates' oratory was legendary.

orchestrate (or-ke-strate) v. to manage or arrange things. The politician orchestrated his own campaign.

ordain v. 1. to officially make someone a priest. 2. to officially make a law or pass an order. The state legislature ordained a new seatbelt law.

ordinance n. a law for a local town, city, or municipality. The new skate-boarding ordinance was passed yesterday.

ornate adj. heavily decorated or colorful. She wore very ornate jewelry.

orthodox adj. traditional; commonly accepted. His throwing motion was quite orthodox among curve ball pitchers. /**orthodoxy** n.

oscillate (os-si-late) v. to move or swing back and forth or to vary between two points. The desk fan provided a cool breeze as it oscillated back and forth. Electrical waves oscillated on the screen of the oscilloscope.

osmosis (oz-moe-sis) n. process by which something is taken in by absorption. Plant leaves consume moisture by osmosis.

ostentatious (os-ten-tay-shus) adj. done for show. His interrupting with facts about the subject was quite ostentatious.

ostracize (os-trah-size) v. to make unwanted. The boy was ostracized by the team for cheating.

outlandish adj. crazy; farfetched; absurd. His idea was outlandish and will never work.

overbearing adj. dominating; pushy. The boy's overbearing mother made his life very uneasy.

overwhelm v. to overcome completely. She was overwhelmed with support from her friends.

oxymoron (ahk-see-mor-on) n. statement that contains a contradiction. A dry rainy day is an oxymoron.

OO Crossword Puzzle OO

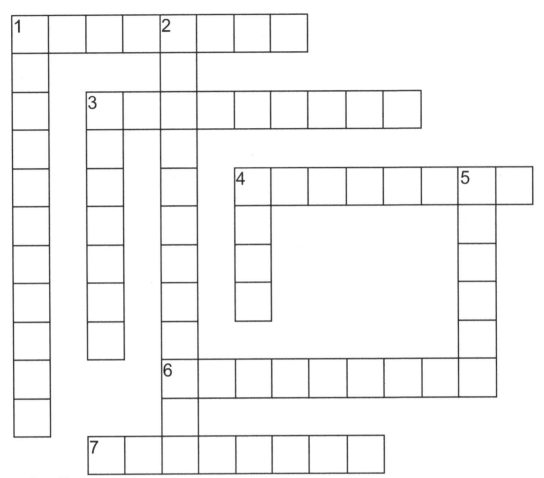

www.CrosswordWeaver.com

ACROSS	DOWN
1 traditional, commonly accepted	1 to manage or arrange things
3 interfering when not asked	2 done for show
4 statement that contains a contradiction	3 hard to handle
6 to make unwanted or push out	4 responsibility
7 outdated, no longer useful	5 mystic person who reveals truths

Puzzle made at puzzle-maker.com

PP

pacifist (pa-si-fist) n. a person who is opposed to violence or war. The pacifists in Congress voted against a declaration of war.

pacify (pa-si-fy) v. to satisfy or make a person calm. The angry customer was pacified by a free meal for the poor service she received.

pagan (pay-gan) n. a person who worships many gods. The ancient Romans were pagans because they worships many individual gods, such as the god of war and the goddess of love.

palatial (puh-lay-shee-al) adj. large and luxurious, like a palace. The rooms at the four-star hotel were very palatial.

panacea (pan-uh-see-ah) n. a cure for many problems or diseases. New genetic discoveries should lead to a panacea in medicine.

pandemic adj. covering a large area, country, or continent. AIDS has become a disease of pandemic proportions.

paradox n. a statement or situation that appears to have opposite meanings. Going back in time to prevent your birth would be a paradox. / **paradoxical** adj.

paramount adj. of most importance. It is paramount that the letter be there by tomorrow.

paraphernalia (pair-ah-fer-nay-lee-ah) n. personal belongings. His money and other paraphernalia were taken when he was robbed.

parasite n. 1. any living creature that attaches itself to another for food and nourishment. Tapeworms are parasites. 2. Figurative for a person who selfishly takes advantage of others on an ongoing basis.

parenthetical adj. something that further explains something else, as if it were in parentheses. / **parenthetically** adv. Tom doesn't go to movies a lot, unless, parenthetically, it's a Star Wars movie.

pariah n. anything that is considered a problem and looked down upon. Alcohol abuse has become a pariah in our society.

parlay v. to reinvest a profit into another venture. The restaurant owner parlayed his money into a new pizzeria.

parsimonious (par-si-moe-nee-us) adj. not wanting to spend money; cheap; frugal. The General Assembly had no choice but to approve the parsimonious budget.

partisan adj. support for a particular person or group, often based on tradition or allegiance. Partisan politics between the Democrats and Republicans have slowed the political process. /**partisanship** n.

pasteurize (pas-chur-ize) v. to kill bacteria with heat in certain foods, such as milk. Milk is pasteurized before it gets to the store.

pastoral adj. 1. pertaining to the raising of farm animals or livestock. 2. animal husbandry. Pastoralism is a branch of <u>agriculture</u> that deals with the raising of farm animals or livestock. **pastoralism** n.

paternal adj. like a father. The man's paternal instincts took over when his son was faced with danger.

paternalism n. acting like a father over a child in the way one treats others or manages the affairs of a business or country. Many <u>colonial</u> rulers used paternalism to justify the way they treated the native inhabitants of some countries. / **paternalistic** adj.

patriarch n. the father or male elder of a group who is considered to be the ruler or leader. The tribal patriarch forbid contact with outsiders. / **patriarchal** adj.

patron (pay-tron) n. person who is a costumer at a place of business. Three other patrons were in the coffee shop while we were there. / **patronize** v. to give business to a store by being a regular customer.

patronage (pay-tron-ij) n. 1. the awarding of jobs to people through personal connections. The politician filled many positions through patronage.

peak n. v. / n. the highest point of something. Snow was found on the mountain's peak. /v. to reach the highest point. Unemployment rates in our country peaked during the Great Depression.

pedagogy (pe-dah-goe-jee) n. teaching practices or methods. Teachers should stay abreast of new trends in pedagogy. / **pedagogical** (pe-dah-go-ji-kal) adj.

pedantic adj. showing off one's knowledge. The professor likes to be pedantic when she has an audience.

pedigree n. ancestral history; family <u>lineage</u>. The dogs on display come from a fine pedigree.

pedophile n. an adult who is sexually attracted to children. The man's reputation was ruined when he was accused of being a pedophile. / **pedophilia** n.

pejorative adj. likely to make matters worse. His pejorative manner combined with his questionable judgment does not make him a good candidate for the job.

penance (pen-nens) n. punishment for a wrong. The student's penance for misbehaving was an apology to the teacher and a Saturday detention.

penitence n. sorrow for a sin or wrongdoing. The man showed no penitence for his crime. /**penitent** adj. showing sorrow for a wrong.

pensive adj. engaged in serious but somber (gloomy) thought. The man was quite pensive about the possibility of seeing his son, whom he had not seen in several years.

per diem (dee-em) Latin term meaning per day. She was paid $75 per diem.

perennial adj. for an entire year; every year; for a long time. The woman received perennial <u>compensation</u> payments.

perfidy n. betrayal or treachery. The king's perfidy against his subjects was well documented. /**perfidious** adj.

perilous adj. dangerous. The hikers made a perilous climb to the top of the mountain.

peripheral adj. associated with; connected with. The computer's peripheral equipment, such as the printer, was outdated.

periphery n. on the sides. The periphery of the field was secured.

permeable adj. allowing something to pass through. The permeable material covering the temporary roof allowed water to seep in. /**permeate** v. to pass through, penetrate, or spread throughout. The illegal misuse of funds permeated the entire department.

pernicious (per-ni-shus) adj. causing much damage or harm. The pernicious drinking habits of some people have destroyed many families.

personification n. 1. the perfect example of something; the embodiment of something. Mother Theresa was the personification of kindness and unselfishness. 2. to speak about a material object as if it were alive, as in "The sky cried heavy tears of rain." / **personify** v.

persona non grata Latin term referring to a person who is not accepted by others in certain situations. The boy wanted to play ball with the adults, but persona non grata, he was not welcome.

pertinent adj. related to the matter at hand. Asking how much repairs might cost is always a pertinent question when buying a piece of used equipment.

Matching Quiz # 27	
____1. pandemic	a. like a father
____2. paradox	b. organism that lives off another
____3 panacea	d. person who worships many gods
____4. pejorative	c. large and luxurious
____5. pacifist	e. supporting a particular group
____6. palatial	f. not wanting to spend money
____7. parlay	g. not as strong as it appears
____8. parasite	h. to kill bacteria with heat
____9. pagan	i. covering a very large area
____10. partisan	j. likely to make matters worse
____11. parsimonious	k. to reinvest profits
____12. paper tiger	l. person opposed to violence
____13. paternal	m. a customer
____14. pasteurize	n. containing opposite statements
____15. patron	o. cure for many problems

philanthropy (fi-lan-throe-pee) n. love of mankind, often displayed through the donation of time or money to a good cause. One could argue that Andrew Carnegie was a firm believer in philanthropy. / **philanthropist** n. one who gives money to worthy causes.

196

pinnacle n. the highest point. Graduating from Harvard was the pinnacle of success for the girl.

pious (py-us) adj. religious in belief or action. Pious people attend church often. / **piety** (py-e-tee) n.

pittance n. a small amount. The boy was only paid a pittance for cutting the grass on a weekly basis.

placate (play-kate) v. to calm someone by giving in to them; to <u>pacify</u> or <u>appease</u>. The coach placated the aggressive parent by making sure all the players got into the game.

placid (pla-sid) adj. calm and quiet; <u>tranquil</u>. The campers found a placid location near the stream to sleep for the night.

plagiarism (play-jer-iz-um) n. to use someone else's words, thoughts, ideas, or information as one's own without acknowledgment. The professor warned the students carefully about the penalty for plagiarism.

plat n. a map of land, property, streets, or buildings. By studying a plat of the city, planners discovered the best location for a new library.

plebeian (plee-bee-an) adj. n. / adj. related to the average or common person. It is quite an accomplishment when plebeian ideas make their way into mainstream society. / n. Alexander Hamilton warned against letting the plebeians vote or hold office as he thought only the educated elite should run the government.

plenary adj. 1. complete. The plenary resources of the military were used in the attack. 2. with everyone present. A new marketing plan was revealed at the monthly plenary meeting of the board of trustees.

pliable (ply-ah-bul) adj. able to be easily bent or shaped; flexible; adaptable. Rubber is a pliable material. Jodie is a hard worker, as well as being pliable when it comes to trying new methods.

pneumatic (new-ma-tik) having, using, or being filled with air. A pneumatic pump operates the machine's moving parts.

poignant (poin-yant) adj. intense; sharp. The victim made a poignant plea for justice.

polarize v. to separate or move apart to opposite ends (poles). The Dred Scott decision of 1857 polarized the Democratic Party as some members were in favor of it, and others were against it.

polygamy (po-li-gah-mee) n. practice of having more than one wife at the same time. Polygamy is still practiced within some religions and cultures.

polytheism (po-lee-thee-iz-um) n. the belief in many gods. The ancient Greeks and Romans practiced polytheism.

pompous adj. acting too important; arrogantly proud; conceited. Some people considered the movie star unfriendly and pompous.

ponder v. to think over carefully. The woman pondered her promising employment possibilities.

portico n. a roof or porch supported by columns. The decorative portico gave the home a lot of curb appeal.

postulate v. to assume something as fact without real proof. The newspaper postulated who the winner of the election would be.

practical (prak-ti-kol) adj. ideas or plans that actually work in practice or during the actual process of doing something instead of things that sound good in theory but might not work in reality. Expecting all the people who might show up to all fit in one room was not very practical.

pragmatism (prag-ma-ti-sm) n. school of thought based on finding solutions to problems that are practical given the situation. Favoring a practical approach to issues or problems rather than solutions based on ideals or theories that might not work in the real world. Sometimes a pragmatic approach is the best approach. / **pragmatic** adj./ **pragmatist** n. Teddy Roosevelt was a pragmatist.

precarious (pre-kair-ee-us) adj. dangerous or uncertain. The traveler was put in the precarious position of having to drive home in the snow storm or find a hotel somewhere.

precedence (pre-se-dens) n. something that comes before another in the order of importance. Safety should always take precedence over fun.

precedent (pre-se-dent) n. a previous example that serves as a guide or rule for similar circumstances in the future. Many courts have relied on a precedent to make their decisions.

precocious (pre-koe-shus) adj. occurring or developing sooner than normal. A precocious interest in reading led the child to the head of her class in reading scores.

predicate v. to base a statement or thought on something. The notion that dinosaurs came before man is predicated by early fossil records.

predisposed v. having a natural or general tendency toward something. The girl is predisposed to having allergies. /**predisposition** n.

prelude (pree-lude or prey-lude) n. something that comes before or introduces something else. The thunder was a prelude to rain.

premise (pre-mis) n. the background or setting of a situation. The premise of the movie was a boy who was raised by wolves.

preponderance n. a greater quantity; a quantity that is greater than another. Only a preponderance of the evidence was needed to find the defendant guilty.

prestige (pres-teej) n. fame or acknowledgement for a skill or accomplishment; notoriety. The doctor's prestige was elevated after successfully performing the first operation of its kind. /**prestigious** adj.

pretense (pree-tens) n. 1. a false reason. The boy called the girl under the pretense that he needed help with his homework. 2. a claim.

pretentious (pree-ten-shus) adj. displaying one's skills or accomplishments openly to draw attention to oneself. The pretentious magician never passed up a chance to show off his tricks.

pristine (pris-teen) adj. like new. Critics have challenged the single-bullet theory related to the assassination of president Kennedy because the bullet seemed too pristine to have been fired.

proactive adj. assertive; willing to make the first move. Some employers like a proactive staff, others simply want their employees to do only as they are told.

pro bono short for pro bono publico, which is a Latin term meaning for the public good or welfare; refers to a service that is performed free of charge. The lawyer took the case pro bono.

procure (proe-kyure) v. to acquire or obtain something. The couple procured financing for the business from the bank.

prodigious (proe-di-jus) adj. immense; large; of great importance. Climbing Mount Everest was quite a prodigious accomplishment.

prodigy (pro-di-jee) n. a gifted or amazingly skilled person. The child prodigy was a chess champion by fifteen years old.

profiteer n. one who profits or benefits from something. Al Capone was a profiteer of illegal alcohol sales.

profound adj. very important or significant. The scientist made a profound discovery yesterday.

progeny (pro-je-nee) n. offspring or descendants. The progeny of ancient Egyptian pyramid builders must have been proud of their ancestors' work.

proliferate v. 1. to increase in number; to multiply. 2. to spread or filter into other areas. The rumor proliferated throughout the office. /**proliferation** n.

prolific adj. producing a lot. Stephen King is a prolific writer.

prominent adj. well-known and important within an area or community. The prominent politician returned to the town where she was born.

propagate v. to increase in number. The rumors were propagated by a recent newspaper article.

propensity n. a natural tendency toward something. The boy has a propensity for fixing things.

propitious (proe-pi-shus) adj. favorable; likeable. The teacher made a propitious comment about the quality of the student's work.

Matching Quiz # 28

_____1. plagiarism		a. to satisfy someone
_____2. plebeian		b. a false reason
_____3. pliable		c. small amount
_____4. pious		d. using air
_____5. pompous		e. to think about
_____6. predicate		f. like new
_____7. placate		g. to steal words or ideas
_____8. pretence		h. to base something on
_____9. pittance		i. religious in belief or action
_____10. pneumatic		j. order of importance
_____11. pristine		k. common person
_____12. ponder		l. easily shaped
_____13. precedence		m. arrogant
_____14. polarize		n. to obtain
_____15. procure		o. to separate to opposite sides

proprietor (proe-pry-e-tor) n. an owner of a business or property. The store's proprietor was sued for negligence. /**proprietary** adj. owned by someone. Pennsylvania was a proprietary <u>colony</u>.

prorate v. to distribute something in relation to another. The real estate taxes were prorated according to the number of months the owner lived in the house. / **proration** n.

proselytize (pros-le-tize) v. to convert (change) a person's opinion on something. The street corner preacher tried to proselytize everyone who walked near him.

prostrate v. 1. to lay flat. The criminal was prostrated on the ground by the police. 2. to weaken. The virus prostrated the man.

protégé (proe-te-zhay) n. one who is under the guidance and care of another, especially for the purpose of learning a skill or trade; one who studies under close care and guidance of another; an apprentice. Many great artists and architects were a protégé of another.

protocol n. proper procedure for doing something. Protocol dictates that students evacuate a school as soon as possible when the fire alarm is sounded.

prototype (proe-toe-type) n. something that is the first of its kind; the original; the original design of something. The prototype of the new engine was tested many times before being mass-produced. / **prototypical** adj. like a prototype.

protrude v. to stick out. The building had an ugly sign protruding from its south wall.

proverbial adj. well-known, often recited as in a famous proverb (a story that teaches a lesson). The debate brought up the proverbial "chicken and the egg" argument.

providence n. 1. proper care for the future. 2. under the protective care of God or divine power. Providence would dictate that a greater conservation effort for the earth's environment is needed.

provisional adj. temporary. A provisional government was established after the <u>revolution</u>.

prowess n. great skill at something. The archer showed his prowess with the bow and arrow.

proxy n. through a substitute. The board of directors managed the company by proxy.

prudent adj. exercising good judgment; wise, careful in thought. The Founding Fathers of the United States were very prudent individuals. /**prudence** n.

pseudo (sue-doe) adj. similar to but not exact; giving a false appearance; not real. A pseudo apology was offered by the country's government.

psyche (sy-kee) n. the mind; the state of mind. One's psyche can be affected by a terrible event.

psychosomatic (sy-koe-soe-ma-tik) adj. related to the physical effects of mental activities on the body. A person's face turning red when that person becomes embarrassed is an example of a psychosomatic event.

pulmonary adj. having to do with the lungs. Breathing is a function of the pulmonary system.

pungent (pun-jent) adj. smelling very bad. A pungent odor filled the room.

punitive adj. characterized by punishment. The management chose punitive measures, such as demotions, rather than corrective measures for the under-performing workers.

purge (purj) v. to empty out or expel. The programmer purged the corrupted files.

putrid adj. rotten; very bad smelling. A putrid smell came from the closet.

Matching Quiz # 29

_____1. pseudo	a. to expel
_____2. provisional	b. related to the lungs
_____3. purge	c. to change a person's mind
_____4. proprietor	d. well-known
_____5. pulmonary	e. state of mind
_____6. protocol	f. wise
_____7. proselytize	g. to stick out
_____8. protégé	h. characterized by punishment
_____9. proverbial	i. by substitute
_____10. psyche	j. temporary
_____11. prudent	k. bad smelling
_____12. protrude	l. similar but not exact
_____13. punitive	m. owner of a business
_____14. proxy	n. proper procedures
_____15. putrid	o. one who learned from another

PP Crossword Puzzle PP

ACROSS	DOWN
1 great skill at something	1 assume something is true without real proof
2 of great importance	2 on the sides
4 related to the matter at hand	3 teaching practices or methods
5 to satisfy or make a person calm	6 personal belongings, especially needed for a specific activity
6 allowing something to pass through	7 of greater quantity
9 likely to make matters worse	8 having a general tendency or attitude toward something
13 favoring a practical approach to problems	10 to increase in number, to spread or promote
15 to spread into other areas	11 dangerous
16 occurring often or over a long period of time	12 per day
	14 complete, with everyone present

Puzzle made at puzzle-maker.com

QQ

quagmire (kwag-my-er) n. 1. a soft, gel-like substance lacking definite form. That quagmire you are eating is Jell-O. 2. soft, wet ground. Quick sand is an example of a quagmire. 3. Figurative for being in a tough situation. He is in a real quagmire this time for lying to the teacher.

qualitative (kwol-li-tay-tiv) adj. related to the quality of something. Teachers should be more concerned with qualitative assignments rather than how many assignments they give.

quantitative (kwan-ti-tay-tiv) adj. related to quantity or numbers. Students should not be as concerned with quantitative facts as they should with the quality of their facts.

quantum adj. figurative for a large or major change or advancement, specifically refers to the quantum theory of the change in state from one energy level to another. The school achieved quantum leaps in its test scores.

quarantine (kwar-an-teen) v. n. / v. to seal off or keep away from others to protect people from danger or disease. The doctors quarantined the sick patient. /n. the act of separating people for safety. A quarantine was ordered for the third floor.

quarry (kwar-ee) n. 1. the prey of a hunter. Fish are among an eagle's favorite quarry. 2. place where rocks and stones are mined or cut. The stone for the wall came from the nearby quarry.

quash (kwahsh) v. to crush, destroy, or put down. The boy's hopes of a new bike were quashed when he brought home a bad report card.

quasi (kwah-sy) adj. something like the real thing; partial. The man gave a quasi-answer. A quasi agreement was reached by some members of the department.

quell (kwell) v. to quash or put down. The request for more money was quelled by the budget director.

quench (kwench) v. to satisfy a need. The fresh water quenched the runner's thirst.

query (kweer-ee) v. n. /v. to inquire about something; to ask about. The organization queried people with a survey. /n. an inquiry; the act of asking or looking into something. A query was made into the rise in taxes.

quibble (kwi-bul) v. to lightly argue about something. The boys quibbled over the toy.

quid pro quo Latin term for getting one thing in return for another. A quid pro quo agreement was worked out.

quintessence (kwin-te-sens) n. the very nature of something; the purest form of something; the best example of something. A Ferrari is the quintessence of a sports car. /**quintessential** adj.

quirk (kwirk) n. an oddity; something strange or out of place. Of all his weird habits, washing his hands over and over is his wildest quirk.

quota (kwoe-tuh) n. a predetermined number that must be reached. The salesman's quota was five cars per month.

Matching Quiz # 30

_____1. quarantine
_____2. quantitative
_____3. quarry
_____4. quagmire
_____5. quash
_____6. quasi
_____7. quench
_____8. quell
_____9. query
_____10. qualitative
_____11. quid pro quo
_____12. quintessence
_____13. quibble
_____14. quirk
_____15. quota

a. a set number
b. something strange
c. related to quality
d. something in return for another
e. related to quantity
f. purest form of something
g. to argue lightly
h. to keep away from others
i. to ask questions
j. to satisfy a need
k. prey of a hunter
l. to crush
m. to stop or put down
n. soft gel-like substance
o. partial or somewhat

RR

racketeering n. the obtaining of money from people by illegal means such as blackmail, intimidation, violence, or threats. The gangsters were convicted of racketeering.

radiant (ray-dee-ent) adj. shining brightly. The radiant glows of the fire lit the room. The girl had a radiant smile on her face.

radical adj. n. /adj. extremely different from the norm. The man's radical ideas got him a lot of attention. / n. a person who has radical ideas or characteristics. The radicals are always stirring up trouble with their crazy ideas. /**radicalism** n.

radius (ray-dee-us) n. the distance from the center of a circle to the outside of the circle. Many mathematical formulas and engineering principles require knowledge on figuring out a radius.

RAM Random Access Memory. One should decide on what computer to buy based on the amount of its RAM.

rambunctious (ram-bunk-shus) adj. playful and noisy; unable to sit still or calm down. The rambunctious youth was always doing something.

ramification (ram-i-fi-kay-shun) n. the result or consequence of one thing on another. The loss of the man's job had serious ramifications for his entire family.

rampart n. 1. a fortification made of dirt or other material built up around something, such as a fort, for increased protection. 2. anything built to protect something. The ramparts gave way as the soldiers overcame the fort.

rancid (ran-sid) adj. spoiled. The meat was rancid after being left out all day.

rancor (rang-kor) n. hatred toward someone. There was no loss of rancor between the two men. /**rancorous** adj.

rapacious (ruh-pay-shus) adj. taking something by force. The theft was a rapacious act.

rapport (rah-por) n. the way in which one gets along with another. Effective teachers must have good rapport with their students.

rapprochement (ruh-proech-ment) n. the creating of a good relationship with someone; establishing a good rapport. The belligerent nations finally reached a stage of rapprochement.

ratio (ray-shee-oe) n. the proportion (relation) of one thing to another. To say that one girl runs twice as fast as another girl would be to say that the ratio of the speed between the faster girl and the slower girl is 2 to 1 (which can also be expressed as 2:1 or 2/1).

ration (rash-un) n. v. / n. the portion of a total amount of something allotted to someone; the amount of something someone can receive. Each group of students was given a small ration of crayons to use. / v. to give out a set amount. Gasoline and rubber were rationed during WWII.

rational (rash-uhn-uhl) adj. something that is thought out or that makes sense; reasonable. A rational person would never resort to violence as the only way to solve a problem. /**rationally** adv.

rationale (rash-uh-nal) n. the reason behind something. The student's rationale for quitting the softball team was that she could now spend more time on her homework.

rationalize (rash-euh-nuh-lize) v. 1. to explain something in a rational manner. The girl's teammates tried to rationalize why their friend would quit the team. 2. to justify one's thoughts or actions. The man rationalized spending a lot of money on a new car by saying he wanted to get rid of the old car before anything started going wrong.

reactionary adj. acting out of emotion in response to something rather than logically or <u>rationally</u>. The violent attack resulted in a reactionary response by the members of the community.

realist n. a person who is very realistic and practical about matters. The visionary architect's new plans were questioned by the realists who believed the building would be too big for the location and would never be finished within the budget.

realm (relm) n. 1.an area, domain, or field of study. 2. kingdom. Looking for fossils falls within the realm of paleontologists and archeologists.

rebuttal (ri-but-ahl) n. the reply to a statement in a debate; a statement of disagreement. The architect's rebuttal to the accusations made against his design influenced the members of the committee.

recalcitrant (ri-kal-si-trent) adj. unruly; refusing to obey; hard to control. The recalcitrant student was always in the Dean's office.

recant (ree-kant) v. to take back a statement. The witness recanted his previous testimony.

recidivism (ri-si-di-viz-um) n. tendency to repeat an act (especially an act of crime) or to relapse into a past behavior. If his past recidivism is any indication of future behavior, he will probably be arrested again.

reciprocal (re-sip-ro-kal) adj. something in return for another. The feeling of animosity between the two women was reciprocal. /**reciprocity** n.

reciprocate (re-sip-ro-kate) v. to do or give something in return for something else. The women reciprocated driving each other to work every week. If someone gives you a gift, it is polite to reciprocate.

recluse (re-kloos) n. a person who keeps to himself and does not like to go out in public or socialize with people. The recluse has lived in that old house for years and hardly anyone ever sees him. /**reclusive** adj.

reconstitute (ree-kons-ti-toot) v. to rebuild or put back together. After ten years of not being used, the old plan was reconstituted.

redeem (ree-deem) v. to take or get something back. The customers redeemed their coupons at the front counter. The girl redeemed her reward for finding the lost dog.

redress (ree-dres) v. to make things right or to fix something that is wrong. The estranged father had to redress his relationship with his family.

redundant adj. unnecessary. Saying that rain is wet is a redundant statement.

refuge (ref-yuj) n. a place of safety or protection. The hikers looked for refuge from the rain in a cave.

refugee (ref-yu-jee) n. a person who has escaped to safety in another country. Refugees from Cuba continue to risk their lives by crossing over to the U.S. in unsafe boats.

refurbish (ree-fer-bish) v. to restore the condition of something. The woman refurbished the wood on her favorite dresser rather than get rid of the dresser.

refute (ree-fyut) v. to prove something is wrong or false. The driver refuted the police officer's accusation that he had no insurance.

regime (ri-zheem) n. the government, group, or system that is in control. The company's new regime likes to fire people.

reign (rain) v. n. /v. to rule over something. The queen reigned over her country for fifty years. / n. the period of rule by someone. The queen's reign lasted fifty years.

reminiscent (re-mi-nis-ent) adj. reminding of, or bringing up past memories or experiences. This vacation is reminiscent of the vacation we took five years ago.

remorse n. guilt or sorrow; regret. The criminal showed no remorse for his crimes.

remuneration (re-myu-ner-ay-shun) n. monetary compensation. The girl received a twenty-dollar remuneration for her dog-walking services.

Matching Quiz # 31

_____ 1. recidivism	a. illegally obtaining money
_____ 2. radical	b. relationship with people
_____ 3. rampart	c. spoiled
_____ 4. radius	d. making sense
_____ 5. rapport	e. people in control
_____ 6. ramification	f. tendency to repeat a behavior
_____ 7. rapprochement	g. establishing good relations
_____ 8. rancid	h. response based on emotion
_____ 9. racketeering	i. hard to control
_____ 10. rational	j. regret
_____ 11. reactionary	k. walls built for protection
_____ 12. recalcitrant	l. extreme
_____ 13. regime	m. a consequence
_____ 14. remorse	n. distance from center of circle
_____ 15. rationale	o. reason for something

renaissance (re-ne-sans) n. refers to a new beginning or rebirth of something. The study of art experienced a renaissance with the building of the new museum.

repeal (ree-peel) v. to cancel or take back. Congress repealed the 18th Amendment.

repent v. to express sorrow for a sin or wrongdoing and ask to be forgiven. The righteous man repented to his best friend for his mistakes. /**repentance** n.

reprehensible (rep-ree-hens-i-bul) adj. deserving of blame. Stealing is a reprehensible act.

reprieve (ree-preev) n. a suspension from punishment for a wrongdoing; a second chance at something. The defendant asked the judge for a reprieve. The team got a reprieve from the rain and was able to finish the game.

reprisal (ree-prys-ahl) n. a wrong committed in return for a wrong. As a reprisal for being wrongly fired, the employee stole money from the company.

reprise (ree-prys) v. to do something again. The actor reprised his role in the play.

reproach v. to express disapproval or disappointment. The boss reproached his employee for not giving him all the necessary information. / n. Their kind actions were beyond reproach.

repudiate (ree-pyu-dee-ate) v. to disregard or reject. The girl repudiated her right to a reward because she thought it was her duty to do the right thing.

repugnant adj. unpleasing, especially to the senses. The garbage dump has a repugnant smell.

requiem (re-kwee-um) n. a service in honor of the dead. The requiem included a poem written for the family of the deceased.

rescind (re-sind) v. to cancel or take back. The woman rescinded her offer to buy the business.

residual (ree-zij-yu-ahl) adj. referring to what is left over. The residual value of the car after the lease was $13,000.

resilience (ree-zil-ee-ens) n. ability to spring back from an injury or setback; ability to overcome or recover. The athlete displayed remarkable resilience by returning to the sport after his major accident. /**resilient** adj.

resolve n. v. / n. a determination to do something. The boy showed resolve by studying every day so he could pass the test. / v. To set one's mind upon something and follow it through. The boy resolved himself to getting an "A" on the test. /**resolved** adj. His resolved attitude paid off.

resurgence (ree-surj-ens) n. a revitalization in something. The team experienced a resurgence in fan support once they started winning more games.

resuscitate (ree-sus-i-tate) v. to revive or bring back to life. The paramedics resuscitated the accident victim at the scene.

reticent (ree-ty-sent) adj. quiet; not speaking much. The girl was reticent as a child, but now she is the public spokesperson for the company.

retort v. n. / v. to reply in a short, rude, or unfriendly manner. The man retorted unwisely to the police officer. / n. His retort was uncalled for.

retrospect n. a look back at the past. In retrospect, the plan seemed like a good idea. /**retrospective** adj.

revel (re-vel) v. to receive enjoyment from something. The girl reveled in the opportunity to meet her favorite musician.

revenue n. money collected from something; income. The revenue from the candy sale was enough to send the students on a trip.

reverberate v. to reflect sound. The music reverberated off the back walls and filled the room.

reverence n. a high regard or respect for someone or something. The man was held in high reverence within the community for his philanthropy.

revolution n. a complete movement around something. The earth's revolution around the sun takes one year.

rhetoric (re-tor-ik) n. 1. words used in writing or speaking. 2. ability to use words to influence people. All his rhetoric about environmental pollution persuaded many people to take action.

ROM Read Only Memory. The amount of information a computer can permanently save is known as ROM.

rostrum n. a stage for public speaking. The rostrum was not high enough because the audience in the back of the room could not see the speaker.

Rotary Club an association of local business people within a community. The Rotary Club met to select a candidate for mayor that they would endorse.

rudimentary adj. basic; the basics of something. A rudimentary knowledge of the rules is necessary before one can play the game.

rural adj. pertaining to the country or country life; away from the city. Rural citizens often have different viewpoints on things compared to urban city dwellers.

RR Crossword Puzzle RR

www.CrosswordWeaver.com

ACROSS	DOWN
2 high regard or respect for someone or something	1 place of safety or protection
4 playful and noisy	2 to do or give in return for something else
6 ability to recover from a setback	3 basic, the basics of something
7 quiet, not willing to speak much	4 deserving of blame
9 to prove something is wrong or false	5 rebirth or a new beginning
10 referring to what is left over	8 something that makes sense, reasonable
11 to take back or cancel	
12 to take or get back	
13 to justify one's thoughts or actions	

Puzzle made at puzzle-maker.com

RR Word Search Puzzle RR

```
R U D I M E N T A R Y L L T C L R
C L R W Y Q M D T V J W T N K L P
E T A T I C S U S E R X N Z R N C
R Z X T M M R B K D J F A L E J M
R A R D M L N Q F L F Y I L S W E
A N P R R E P R I S A L D L I K M
T R W P M P S Q Q C N H A W L N I
I Z E L O U E J T G J R R C I Z G
O B H S I R K U I M E K R I E L E
N B J D I L T E N B E E N R N V R
A X A N R D R W U E S E K O C J F
L R B X L X U T T O V W D T E P M
E R Z H B X T A L B T E T E N T C
K K D C M A F V L T J C R H R Y B
H J Y Q L M E T R H M M T R C R G
K Y Z R A M I F I C A T I O N V P
X N D E T A C O R P I C E R K Y N
```

RADIANT	RECIPROCATE	RESILIENCE
RADIUS	REDEEM	RESOLVE
RAMIFICATION	REGIME	RESUSCITATE
RAPPORT	REIGN	REVENUE
RATIONALE	REPRISAL	RHETORIC
REBUTTAL	RESIDUAL	RUDIMENTARY

SS

sabbatical n. a temporary rest or leave from work. The teacher took a sabbatical from teaching to pursue another degree.

sacrificial lamb n. one who is sacrificed for the benefit of another. The music department became the sacrificial lamb when the school board cut some courses to keep others operating.

salient (say-lee-ent) adj. standing out or noticeable. The salient characteristic of Wrigley Field are the vines on the outfield walls.

salutary (sal-yu-tair-ee) adj. leading to improvement. The boss provided her workers with some salutary advice.

sanctify (sang-ti-fy) v. 1. to make something holy. The priest sanctified the grounds of the church. 2. to make something right or acceptable. The government sanctified the actions of its military.

sanguine adj. happy, confident, or optimistic by nature. The girl's sanguine personality made her popular.

sapience (say-pee-ens) n. wisdom. The sapience of her idea was not appreciated until much later. /**sapient** adj.

sardonic adj. showing much disapproval or contempt. The sardonic look on the mother's face explained everything.

saunter v. n. / v. to walk in a slow casual manner. The man sauntered through the department store. / n. a slow casual walk. His saunter showed how relaxed and unhurried he was.

savoir-faire (sav-wah fair) n. the skillful ability to say or do just the right thing at just the right time. She displayed her savoir-faire at the dinner party where she charmed the guests and made business connections. James Bond seems to possess a great deal of savoir-faire.

savvy n . adj. / n. sharp intelligence and perception. A great deal of savvy is needed in the real estate business. / adj. She is a very savvy individual.

scant (skant) adj. a small amount. Only a scant amount of food was left over after the party.

scapegoat (skape-goat) n. One who is made to take the blame for something he or she did not do. Hitler made the Jews scapegoats for Germany's problems.

scenario (se-nair-ee-oe) n. literally the story of a play or movie but often refers to a plan or situation. Some scenarios call for more security at the front doors.

schematic (skee-ma-tik) n. a technical drawing. The engineer drew a schematic of the machine.

schism (skizh-um or sizh-um) n. the separation into opposite groups that are hostile towards each other. The religious schism of 1054 refers to the spilt between the Catholic and Eastern Orthodox religions.

scrupulous adj. very careful to do the right thing. The scrupulous girl made sure the wallet she found was returned to its owner.

scrutinize v. to examine something carefully, looking for anything that might be wrong. The architectural plans for the new City Hall were scrutinized by the mayor. /**scrutiny** n.

secede (se-seed) v. to formally withdraw from a group or association. Eleven Southern states seceded from the United States during the Civil War period of American history. /**secession** n. the act of seceding.

secular (se-kyu-lar) n. related to worldly matters and not matters of religion. Experts in the Middle East disagree over whether a secular or religious solution is needed to solve the problems between the Israelis and the Palestinians.

seismic (size-mik) adj. related to earthquakes. The seismic destruction extended twenty miles from the epicenter of the quake.

semantics n. the study and use of meanings of words. The jury became confused with the attorney's semantics.

semblance n. the appearance of something. The house had a semblance of Victorian charm.

seminary n. a school where people are trained to be priests. Latin is studied at the seminary.

sentimental adj. influenced by emotion rather than reason, especially pertaining to older objects or the past, which might have some emotional significance to someone. The man has sentimental memories of his childhood home. / **sentimentalist** n.

sentinel n. a person who stands guard or watches. The sentinel alerted the police when he heard something unusual.

sequential (see-kwen-shuhl) adj. occurring in a sequence or particular order. The resumes were reviewed in sequential order.

sequester (si-kwe-ster) v. to take away or hold or kept separated. The court sequestered the driver's car because of a reckless driving record. The jury was sequestered during the trial.

serendipitous (se-ren-di-pi-tus) adj. by chance or luck. The entrance to the secret cave was a serendipitous discovery. / **serendipity** n.

serene (se-reen) adj. quiet and peaceful. The serene environment was just what the man needed for his stress. /**serenity** n.

shaman n. a medicine man or priest with healing or other magical powers. The tribe called upon the shaman to deliver rain from the gods.

simian (sim-ee-an) n. adj. an ape or ape-like. Charles Darwin believed that humans evolved from simian-like creatures.

simpatico adj. in harmony or right for one another. A simpatico situation arose when the two scientists started working together.

simultaneous (sy-mul-tay-nee-us) adj. occurring at the same time. The explosion caused a simultaneous fire across the street. / **simultaneously** adv.

slovenly adj. sloppy, dirty, or unkempt. The homeless man was slovenly dressed.

smitten v. to be greatly affected by something. The man was smitten with anger when he learned that he did not get the promotion.

snafu n. a major mistake, error, or problem. A snafu in the program caused the computer to crash.

sociopath (soe-see-o-path) n. a person who does not have any sense of right or wrong or moral responsibility to other people. Some violent criminals are sociopaths because they do not care if they hurt others.

sojourn n. a brief journey or stay someplace. The family took their yearly sojourn to Arizona to visit their relatives.

Matching Quiz # 32

_____1. savoir-faire
_____2. scapegoat
_____3. salient
_____4. scrutinize
_____5. sabbatical
_____6. savvy
_____7. sentimental
_____8. sequential
_____9. seismic
_____10. schematic
_____11. sojourn
_____12. simultaneous
_____13. serene
_____14. seminary
_____15. scenario

a. a brief journey
b. plan or situation
c. occurring in an order
d. related to earthquakes
e. sharp intelligence
f. a technical drawing
g. occurring at the same time
h. quiet and peaceful
i. where priests are trained
j. noticeable
k. one who takes the blame
l. temporary leave from work
m. influenced by emotions for the past
n. to examine carefully
o. doing the right thing at right time

---

solace (soe-les) n. a comforting feeling. The man found solace in the knowledge that his family would be looked after while he was away on business.

solemn (sol-em) adj. serious or resulting in serious thoughts. A solemn look on her face expressed her sorrow when visiting the accident site.

solidarity (so-li-dair-i-tee) n. feeling of unity or cooperation from having something in common. A strong sense of solidarity swept through the labor union when it came time to negotiate a new contract.

214

soliloquy (soe-li-li-kwee) n. a speech made to oneself. The actor's soliloquy is legendary.

solitude n. act of being alone. The man prefers solitude over social interactions and large crowds.

sophist (soe-fist) n. a person who engages in clever but deceptive reasoning. The word "sophist" is derived from the Sophists, who were highly skilled speakers and teachers of philosophy in ancient Greece.

sovereign (sov-ren) adj. independent; free from rule or control by another. The United States became a sovereign nation in 1776. /**sovereignty** n.

speculate (spe-kyu-late) v. to invest money in something in hopes of making a profit; to wager, bet, or guess on something. The man risked a lot of money when he speculated on the stock market. /**speculator** n. person who speculates. / **speculation** n. /**speculative** adj.

static adj. unchanging or not progressing; not moving. His career has been static for ten years.

statistics n. numerical information (using numbers) that provides information on various things. Statistics show that smoking increases a person's chances of getting cancer. / **statistical** adj. related to statistics. Charts are sometimes the easiest way to understand statistical information.

status quo (sta-tus kwoe) the way things are now. The manager tried to maintain the status quo in the company instead of looking for new ideas and methods.

statute n. a formal rule or law written by a law-making body and contained in an official document. The state's statutes on certain crimes are very clear. /**statutory** adj.

stave off v. to keep away, put off, or delay something. Insect repellent can stave off mosquitoes. The new tax increase was passed to stave off a budget shortfall.

steward n. a person who takes care of another's property or well-being. The steward aboard the cruise ship made sure the passengers always had a clean room. /**stewardship** n.

stigma (stig-muh) n. a mark denoting something negative or that something is wrong. The poorly timed strike was a stigma on the union's reputation. /**stigmatize** v.

stipulate v. to demand something as part of an agreement. The contract stipulated that the workers would get a pay raise only if they agreed to work some weekends.

stoic (stoe-ik) adj. not showing emotion, especially pain or pleasure; always calm. The woman always had a stoic look on her face.

stringent (strin-jent) adj. not flexible; strict; rigid. The school rules were very stringent regarding such things as fighting and cheating.

studious adj. serious about learning or one's study. The girl was very studious all through high school.
stymie (sty-mee) v. to block something. Progress was stymied by a lack of money.

subjective adj. open to personal interpretation or various judgment; based on opinion more than fact. The question was subjective because it did not have a clear right or wrong answer, and the answer could depend on one's personal experience. It is not right to ask subjective questions when you are looking for objective answers.

subjugate v. to expose to or place under another's control. The prisoner was subjugated to cruel punishment.

subliminal adj. pertaining to the subconscious; not realized by the conscious mind. Subliminal advertising is illegal because it can be so powerful and persuasive without the consumer even being aware of anything.

subsequent adj. coming after or next in occurrence. The boy lost his drivers license subsequent to another speeding ticket. /**subsequently** adj.

subservient adj. tirelessly and obediently serving the needs of someone. The king's people were subservient to their beloved monarch.

subside v. to stop. The rain finally subsided after four hours.

subsistence n. what is needed to stay alive or support oneself; the act or process or staying alive or supporting oneself. The family's only means of subsistence was charity from their friends.

substantiate (sub-stan-shee-ate) v. to prove, support, or verify. The archeologist had to substantiate her claims to the discovery of the ancient city.

subterranean (sub-ter-ray-nee-an) adj. underground, below the surface. The campers found a subterranean cave while hiking through the forest.

subversive adj. attempting to overthrow, undo, or undermine something. The group was being watched by the FBI for possible illegal and subversive activity directed against the government.

subvert v. to overthrow. The king was subverted by a military faction of his government that opposed his rule. /**subversion** n.

succinct (suh-sinkt) adj. short, clear, and to the point. The senator's speech was succinct.

succumb (suh-kum) v. to give into, to fall victim to, or to die from something such as disease or injury. The man succumbed to his injuries. The mayor succumbed to the pressure for him to resign.

sullen adj. quiet from being angry or upset. A sullen attitude came over the child when the picnic was cancelled because of the rain.

superficial adj. not thorough or complete; pertaining to what only appears on the surface. A superficial understanding of economics is not enough to understand the nation's financial problems because an in depth knowledge of solid economic principles is needed.

superfluous (su-per-floo-us) extra; more than is needed. A superfluous amount of food was prepared for the party.

superlative adj. the best; very good. The movie was given superlative reviews.

supersede v. to override; to take the place of. The general's orders superseded those of the other officers.

supplant v. to take the place of. Air travel has supplanted train travel to a large degree.

supposition n. the act of supposing or basing something on a possibility. The jury's initial supposition of innocence was based upon the defendant's proof that he was out of town when the crime occurred.

```
                        Matching Quiz # 33

____ 1.  speculate           a. not changing
____ 2.  stewardship         b. being alone
____ 3.  stringent           c. to take the place of
____ 4.  sovereign           d. underground
____ 5.  solidarity          e. invest money with risk
____ 6.  stave off           f. the way things are now
____ 7.  static              g. act of caring for something
____ 8.  status quo          h. to keep away
____ 9.  solitude            i. free and independent
____ 10. subterranean        j. strict
____ 11. subjective          k. unity and cooperation
____ 12. supplant            l. more than is needed
____ 13. superfluous         m. numerical information about things
____ 14. statistics          n. open to personal interpretation
____ 15. substantiate        o. to prove or support
```

surreptitious (ser-ep-ti-shus) adj. acting with secrecy or without permission. A surreptitious attempt was made to obtain more money for the project.

surmise v. to assume based on information; to <u>infer</u>. Since the couple was extremely late and had not called to verify the appointment, we surmised they were not coming.

sustenance n. means of staying alive or what is needed to stay alive, such as food; sustaining oneself. The ship-wrecked crew had to rely on fish and fruits for their sustenance.

Svengali (sven-gah-lee) n. figurative for a person with extraordinary persuasive or hypnotic powers, especially over women. The man was a real Svengali when it came to meeting women. The man was a real Svengali when it came to talking his way out of speeding tickets.

swank adj. showing much class or expense. The reception at the five-star hotel downtown was very swank.

syllogism (sil-oe-jiz-um) n. reasoning based on <u>deduction</u>. Some ancient Greek philosophers were known for their syllogisms.

symbiotic (sim-by-o-tik) adj. serving a mutually beneficial purpose. Many life forms on earth have a symbiotic relationship. / **symbiosis** n. / **symbiont** n. one who is in a symbiotic relationship.

symmetrical (sim-e-tri-kal) adj. of equal measure, shape, or appearance. The sides of the building were symmetrical.

symposium (sim-poe-zee-um) n. a conference to discuss a particular subject. A symposium on global warming was held at the university.

synagogue (syn-uh-gog) n. a Jewish church or place of worship. The marriage ceremony took place at the local synagogue.

synergy (sin-er-jee) n. energy, power, or effort working together to achieve a greater outcome. The construction project was the result of political, financial, and architectural synergy.

synonymous (sin-on-i-mus) adj. the same or similar in meaning or effect. Hard work is synonymous with effort. Obeying laws is synonymous with being a good citizen. / **synonymously** adv.

synthesis (sin-the-sis) n. the putting together of things, such as ideas or information, to make a whole. The synthesis of new genetic research will surely lead to a cure for more diseases.

synthesize (sin-the-size) v. to put things together to make a whole. The student had to synthesize the information she learned to answer the essay question correctly.

systematic (sis-te-ma-tik) adj. according to a certain order, method, plan, or procedure. A systematic attempt was made to work out the problems in the computer program.

systemic (sis-te-mik) adj. related to or affecting the whole system. The problems in the accounting office were systemic because they resulted in budget mistakes for the entire company.

SS Crossword Puzzle SS

ACROSS	DOWN
1 the study and use of meanings of words	1 serving a mutually beneficial purpose
3 to demand something as part of an agreement	2 acting with secrecy or without permission
5 by luck or by chance	3 a small amount
9 a formal rule or law written by a law-making body	4 something that denotes something negative
12 short and to the point	6 to prove, support, or verify
13 related to worldly matters and not related to religion	7 to withdraw from a group or association
14 means of staying alive or sustaining something such as food or water	8 pertaining only to what appears on the surface
15 wisdom	10 coming after or next in order of occurrence
16 showing no emotions or feelings	11 having strong feelings of affection or attraction

SS Word Search Puzzle SS

```
B N J D J S U O I D U T S G N
Y R E S U P E R F I C I A L B
Z N T Y S H J C X T N Y T S R
S V A S Y O B J R L R M U M S
P N I T R L L Y J J O T T U
E O T E Y A M I H X E M I R O
C I N M Z I S H D N D P K R U
U T A A G T K I A A U K C F L
L I T T C N W T S L R I D F F
A S S I C E L Z A E M I F N R
T O B C M U Z T B E H B T R E
E P U C M Q E M T N H T W Y P
Q P S I D E N S D P W N N G U
G U S T R S Y Y V T H N N Y S
V S Z K T S K S O J O U R N S
```

SEQUENTIAL SIMULTANEOUS SOJOURN SOLIDARITY SPECULATE	STIPULATE STUDIOUS SUBSTANTIATE SUPERFICIAL SUPERFLUOUS	SUPPOSITION SYNTHESIS SYSTEMATIC SYSTEMIC

Puzzle made at puzzle-maker.com

TT

taboo adj. looked down upon by society; deemed unacceptable. Smoking is more taboo now then it was thirty years ago.

tacit (tas-it) adj. assumed or implied without being directly stated. The women established a tacit agreement to cooperate.

tactile (tak-til) adj. related to touching or the sense of touch. Many students learn better through tactile activities such as in science labs.

tangential (tan-jen-tial) adj. in addition to but deviating from the main idea at hand./ **tangentially** adv. Trees use photosynthesis to make food and give off oxygen; tangentially, Bill likes oak trees.

tangible (tan-ji-bul) adj. something that can be seen, felt, understood, or experienced; real. The women came up with the only tangible solution.

tantamount adj. the same as, equal to. Not paying your bills is tantamount to being irresponsible.

taxidermy n. the act of stuffing and mounting dead animal bodies. It takes a special person to work with dead animals and practice taxidermy.

taxonomy n. study or act of classifying things; classification. The scientific taxonomy related to living species can be confusing.

tectonic (tek-ton-ik) adj. geological term referring to the earth's crust. The study of earthquakes requires tectonic knowledge.

telekinesis (tel-e-kin-ee-sis) n. the ability to move objects with the power of the mind. Many movies have featured people with telekinesis, but real life examples of this power have turned out to be hoaxes.

temperance n. exercising restraint or moderation in something, such as drinking liquor. The temperance movement reached a pinnacle with the passage of the 18th Amendment, which made the sale of alcohol illegal.

temperate adj. between hot and cold; moderate; comfortable. Some places in the U.S. have a temperate climate year round.

temporal adj. not lasting forever; mortal; for a short time; temporary; related to human life rather than the afterlife. Many people warn against sacrificing lasting happiness for temporal pleasures.

terminology n. words that are used when referring to a specific area of knowledge. The medical terminology used to explain some diseases can be confusing.

tenable adj. something that can be protected. The fort's tenable location gave it an advantage.

tenacious (te-nay-shus) adj. not giving up; resolved; holding strong. The boy had a tenacious desire to win the race. /**tenacity** n.

tenderfoot n. 1. a person not experienced at something. 2. a person not ready for harsh living conditions. Many tenderfoots find camping an unpleasant experience.

tentative adj. not completely finalized or agreed upon; temporary; experimental; not fully worked out. The workers and the management reached a tentative agreement.

tenuous (ten-yu-us) adj. not firm or serious; weak. The girl had a tenuous excuse for being late.

tepid adj. a bit warm but not hot. He was running a tepid fever. The tepid water was just right for swimming.

terra firma Latin term for ground or earth. Airline passengers usually welcome returning to terra firma.

terrestrial (te-res-tree-al) adj. pertaining to the earth; from earth. Space aliens are not terrestrial beings.

terse (ters) adj. not using many words; brief. The man's terse answer was evidence that he was busy.

textile (teks-tile) n. clothing, garments, or other fabrics woven together. The textile industry was one of the first industries to benefit from the industrial revolution.

thespian (thes-pee-an) n. an actor. A local thespian was featured in the paper last week.

thwart v. to defeat; to overcome a competitor; to stop. The detective thwarted the burglar.

token (toe-ken) n. something that represents something else. Many arcade games now use tokens rather than real money.

topography (to-pog-rah-fee) n. the surface of something, usually land and all its characteristics such as hills, mountains, flats, etc. The flat topography of the area makes for a perfect place to build a home. /**topographical** adj.

torque (tork) n. turning or twisting power. When a motor does not have enough power to turn a gear, more torque is needed.

toxemia (tok-see-mee-ah) n. a poisoning of the blood. Many chemicals cause toxemia.

trajectory (truh-jek-ter-ee) n. the angle of flight of a moving object. Scientist use complicated equations to figure out the trajectory of rockets and spaceships.

tranquil (trang-kwil) adj. quiet and peaceful; relaxing. Many people consider the sound of ocean waves or rain tranquil noises.

transcend (tran-send) v. to go beyond; to surpass. A good magical illusion transcends explanation. / **transcendental** adj. beyond normal reason or experience.

222

transcendentalism (tran-sen-den-tuh-liz-um) n. philosophy that emphasizes the importance of thought and reason over experience. Transcendentalism worked its way into American literature in the 19th century. / **transcendentalist** n.

transgress v. to do something wrong; to break a law. One is sure to wind up with many tickets if one continues to transgress driving rules. / **transgression** n.

transient (tran-see-ent or tran-shent) adj. passing by; not lasting or permanent; not important. Thomas Jefferson spoke about transient causes in the Declaration of Independence.

translucent (trans-lu-sent) adj. letting light through. Stained glass is translucent but not <u>transparent</u> because light passes through stained glass, but people cannot see through it clearly.

transmute v. to change from one form to another. Batteries transmute chemical power into electrical power.

transom n. a small tilting window or opening over a door to let air into a room. Transoms were popular in older buildings.

transparent adj. 1. able to see through. Glass is a transparent substance. 2. figurative for easy to understand. The man's transparent personality made it easy to see that his apology was not sincere.

traverse v. to move or travel across. The jeep traversed the rough terrain with no problem.

trepidation n. fear; uneasiness about something. The job interview caused a lot trepidation.

triad n. a group of three. A triad of ships appeared on the horizon.

tribulation n. great problem or obstacle. The tribulations of poor uneducated people are hard to overcome and should not be taken lightly.

Matching Quiz # 34

_____ 1. torque
_____ 2. trepidation
_____ 3. tangible
_____ 4. tenacious
_____ 5. textile
_____ 6. thespian
_____ 7. temperance
_____ 8. terrestrial
_____ 9. taboo
_____ 10. temporal
_____ 11. tribulation
_____ 12. transgress
_____ 13. tranquil
_____ 14. transparent
_____ 15. tactile

a. woven fabrics, clothes
b. restraint or moderation
c. an actor
d. a great problem
e. to do something wrong
f. not lasting
g. twisting power
h. looked down upon
i. fear
j. not giving up
k. able to be understood
l. quiet and peaceful
m. related to touch
n. able to be seen through
o. of the earth

trinity n. a group of three. A trinity of workers showed up to complete the job.

triumvirate (try-um-ver-et) n. a government or other organization run by three people. The three managers make the department function as a triumvirate.

trifle (try-ful) adj. not important; small in value. The program resulted in trifle benefits to people.

trilogy n. a series of three works such as plays or stories with a related theme. Some of the most popular movies have been part of a trilogy.

trivial adj. not that important. One should not lose sight of the present by focusing on trivial problems.

tsunami (tsu-nah-mee) n. Japanese name for a huge tidal wave. The tsunami destroyed many ships in Tokyo Bay.

tumultuous (too-muhl-chew-us) adj. causing a great disturbance; noisy; disorderly. The tumultuous event affected the entire family.

typhoon n. a hurricane that occurs in the Pacific Ocean.

typical adj. representing a normal type of something. The typical baseball game lasts about three hours.

typify (tip-i-fy) v. to be an example of. Smoking typifies an unhealthy lifestyle.

tyranny (teer-ah-nee) n. harsh, cruel, and unfair use of power or authority. The Founding Fathers spoke out against governmental tyranny. /**tyrannical** adj. /**tyrant** n. person who engages in tyranny.

TT Crossword Puzzle TT

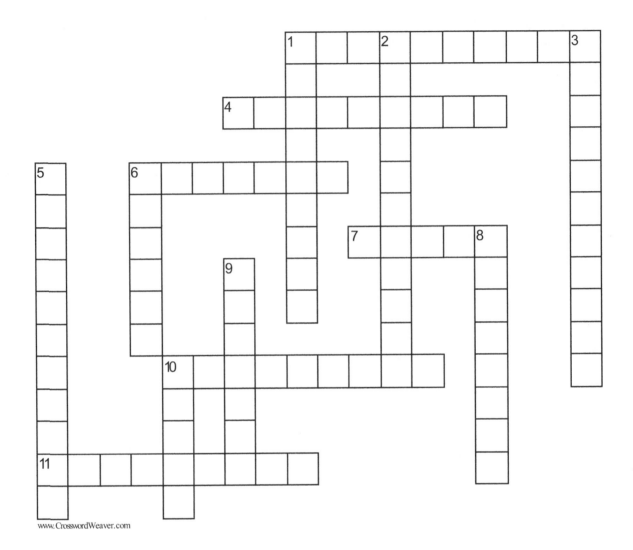

www.CrosswordWeaver.com

ACROSS	DOWN
1 means the same as	1 no finalized or official yet
4 not giving up	2 great problem or obstacle
6 not that important	3 fear or uneasiness about something
7 assumed or implied without being directly stated	5 government or organization run by three people
10 not lasting or permanent, passing	6 to be an example
11 to go beyond or to surpass	8 the act of classifying things
	9 able to be defended, maintained, or protected
	10 not using many words, brief and unfriendly

Puzzle made at puzzle-maker.com

UU

ubiquitous (yu-bik-kwi-tus) adj. existing or present in all places at all times. Death and taxes are unfortunately ubiquitous aspects of life.

ulterior (uhl-teer-ee-er) adj. something not yet revealed; kept secret or having another purpose. The co-workers thought Bill had ulterior reasons for being nice to the boss, such as hoping for a promotion.

unabashed adj. bold; not embarrassed by or ashamed of. The students were remarkably unabashed when they were caught cheating on the test.

unabated (un-uh-bait-ed) adj. not weakened or lessened in some way. His unabated temper got him in trouble with the police.

unadulterated adj. pure; not changed, affected, or contaminated by anything. Listening to the music was unadulterated enjoyment.

unbridled (un-bry-deld) adj. uncontrolled; not held back or restrained. Her unbridled quest for adventure took her on expeditions all over the world.

uncouth (un-cooth) adj. not <u>couth</u>; not sophisticated. Screaming when you see an insect can be considered quite uncouth.

undermine v. to weaken someone's authority or position by going above or around them. The worker undermined the authority of the manager by going straight to the owner of the company.

unequivocal (un-ee-kwi-vo-kuhl) adj. clear and without doubt or exception. Her final position on the subject was the unequivocal support of the plan.

unilateral (yu-ni-la-ter-uhl) adj. one-sided; supported by or affecting only one side. The negotiations were unilateral.

universal (yu-ni-ver-suhl) adj. widely accepted or known; existing all over. Environmental pollution is a universal problem.

unprecedented adj. never happening before. Hitting eighty home runs in a season will be an unprecedented event.

unscrupulous (un-scru-pyu-lus) adj. displaying a lack of concern over what is right and wrong; not careful. The businessman is unscrupulous in his methods.

unsubstantiated (un-sub-stan-shee-ay-ted) adj. not supported by any proof or evidence. The rumors were unsubstantiated and turned out to be false.

urban adj. related to a city. Large urban centers such as Chicago usually have traffic problems during rush hour.

urbane adj. having a sophistication associated with a city (<u>urban</u>) lifestyle such as good manners, proper etiquette, and knowledge of the arts.

usurp (yu-surp) v. to take power away from someone, usually without that person's permission. The manager was usurped by his new boss. / **usurpation** n. the act of usurping.

usury (yu-zur-ee) n. the act of charging extremely high interest on loans. Usury is a common abuse against uneducated or desperate people.

utilitarian (yu-til-uh-tair-ee-an) adj. serving a purpose or being useful. Some architects think the design of a building should be purely utilitarian, while others believe that a building should look good as well.

utopia (yu-toe-pee-ah) n. a perfect place; a place where no problems exist; an ideal existence. Finding or creating a utopia on earth would be quite difficult given all the differences of opinion and behavior that exist in the world. /**utopian** adj.

utter v. to speak or make a sound. The men uttered their opinions to themselves.

utterance n. the act of uttering; the act of speaking. Not an utterance of discontent was heard after the meeting.

UU Crossword Puzzle UU

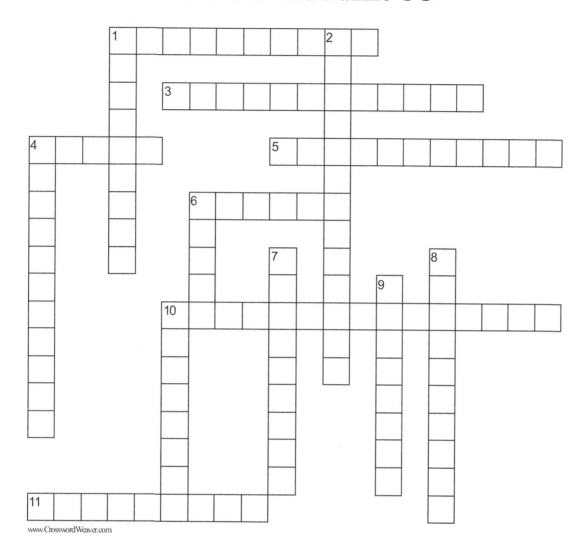

ACROSS	DOWN
1 existing in all places at all times, very common	1 to weaken one's authority by going around them
3 showing a lack of concern for others	2 never happening before, very unusual
4 taking power away from someone without permission	4 serving a purpose or being useful
5 clear and without a doubt or exception	6 related to a city
6 having a sophistication associated with a city	7 uncontrolled or not restrained
10 without any proof or evidence	8 one-sided
11 widely accepted or known, existing all over	9 not weakened or diminished
	10 having another purpose, sometimes a hidden purpose

Puzzle made at puzzle-maker.com

VV

vacillate (vas-i-late) v. to hesitate or change one's mind often because one is unsure about something. The boss vacillated for weeks over the new program.

vagabond n. a person who wanders around with no permanent residence. The vagabond hopped trains from city to city.

vagrant (vay-grent) n. a wondering person who has no job or skills. The alley is a gathering place for vagrants. /**vagrancy** n.

valiant (val-yent) adj. brave. Saving the child from drowning was a valiant act.

valor adj. courage; bravery. The firemen displayed great valor in extinguishing the fire.

vanguard (van-gard) n. the leaders, innovators, or protectors of something. The vanguard of the new social movement were upset with the lack of attention their ideas were getting.

vassal n. 1. a person who was allowed to farm a portion of someone else's land in return for military service under the <u>feudal</u> system in medieval Europe. Vassals often only received a small plot of land to work. 2. a person who is controlled in some way by another. The boss's assistant is nothing more than a vassal.

vaudeville (vawd-vil) n. a live entertainment show consisting of different acts such as magic, singing, dancing, and comedy routines that were popular before television. Many of the stars of vaudeville became the first television stars.

vehement (vee-e-ment) adj. firm; showing a lot of emotion. The mother was vehement about her son attending college.

vendor n. a person who sells something. The hotdog vendors made a lot of money at the ballgame.

venerable (ven-er-uh-bul) adj. respected, important; deserving merit because of quality, age, or accomplishment. The venerable artist was rarely seen in public anymore.

Venetian (ve-nee-shen) adj. related to or having the characteristics of the Italian city of Venice. Venetian architecture is very popular in some parts of the country.

venison n. deer meat. Many hunters like venison.

veracity (ve-ras-i-tee) n. the correctness or truthfulness of something. The scientist's veracity was questioned when the experiment failed.

verbatim (ver-bait-im) n. word for word; exactly as it appears. The student was expected to recite the poem verbatim.

verbiage n. the use of too many unnecessary words. Legal documents seem to have too much verbiage in them, yet a lawyer will defend the use of such exact wording.

verbose adj. using too many words. The drama writer is quite verbose in her work. /**verbosity** n.

vernacular (ver-na-kyu-ler) n. the common everyday words of a language; the words related to a particular region or profession. The best way to really learn the vernacular of a foreign language is to spend time in that country. The vernacular of medicine is quite confusing.

vertebrate n. an animal with a backbone. Humans are vertebrates.

vertigo n. medical condition causing dizziness. People who suffer from vertigo often complain that the room is spinning.

vested adj. in the care or control of another. The town vested their trust in the new mayor.

vested interest standing to lose or gain from the participation in something. Repair men who rely on positive word of mouth for their business have a vested interested in doing a good job.

vexed adj. annoyed; agitated. The man looked vexed after leaving the car dealership. /**vexing** v.

viable (vy-uh-bul) adj. able to work or be accomplished; possible; realistic. The committee came up with a viable solution to the problem. /**viability** n.

vicarious (vy-kair-ee-us) adj. experiencing something through another; indirect. Watching his son play baseball is a vicarious way for the man to enjoy sports. / **vicariously** adv. He is living vicariously through his son.

vicissitude (vi-sis-i-tude) n. a change in the condition or situation of something. The vicissitudes of politics can easily turn an unpopular candidate into the most popular candidate.

vigilance (vij-i-lens) n. state of caution or alertness. The nation's intelligence agencies are at a new level of vigilance. /**vigilant** adj.

vindicate v. to prove correct or clear from a negative accusation. The doctor was vindicated after the patient made a full recovery. /**vindication** n. The patient's complete recovery was a vindication of the doctor's methods.

vindictive adj. favoring revenge or retribution. The man was vindictive after being fired.

vintage (vin-tij) adj. something of a particular time period that was popular or has certain special qualities. The man's hobby is vintage cars.

virtuosity (ver-chu-os-i-tee) adj. having a special skill or interested in some aspect of the fine arts or high culture, such as music or art. The woman's virtuosity impressed everybody.

virtuoso (ver-chu-oe-soe) n. person skilled or knowledgeable in something specific such as art or music. The violin virtuoso performed with the city's symphony.

virulent adj. very harmful or poisonous. The virulent disease spread quickly through the town.

230

visceral (vis-er-al) adj. figurative for emotional or affecting feelings rather <u>rational</u> thought. The lovely music had a visceral influence on the audience.

vivacious (vy-vay-shus) adj. lively; spirited. It was pleasing to see the senior citizens so happy and vivacious.

vivid adj. very clear; detailed; intense; graphic; lifelike. The woman gave a vivid account of her travels.

vogue (voeg) adj. n. /adj. to be popular, fashionable, or accepted. Long hair was vogue during the 1970s. / n. The vogue in the 1950s was the beehive hairdo.

voracious (vo-ray-shus) adj. having a big appetite for something. Large animals can be voracious eaters. She has a voracious interest in science.

vortex n. an area where there is a lot of activity and movement, which is hard to avoid or escape. The swimmers were caught in the whirlpool's vortex.

Matching Quiz # 35

_____ 1. vagrant
_____ 2. venerable
_____ 3. vivid
_____ 4. vacillate
_____ 5. vendor
_____ 6. vanguard
_____ 7. vernacular
_____ 8. vivacious
_____ 9. viable
_____ 10. vested
_____ 11. vindicate
_____ 12. verbatim
_____ 13. vintage
_____ 14. valor
_____ 15. vindictive

a. very clear
b. able to work
c. favoring revenge
d. in the care of another
e. word for word
f. to prove correct
g. homeless person with no skills
h. of a popular time period
i. to hesitate
j. respected
k. bravery
l. person who sells things
m. lively
n. everyday words of a language
o. leaders of something

VV Crossword Puzzle VV

www.CrosswordWeaver.com

ACROSS	DOWN
5 to hesitate or waver, to change one's mind often or to be indecisive	1 state of caution or alertness
6 brave, showing much effort or courage	2 person who wanders around with no permanent home
8 experienced through the actions or feelings of another	3 firm, forceful, not backing down
9 the correctness or truthfulness of something	4 person who is controlled by another in some way
10 annoyed, agitated, frustrated	5 person highly skilled in something specific, such as music or others arts
	7 affecting feelings rather than rational thought
	8 using too many words

Puzzle made at puzzle-maker.com

WW

warmonger n. a person who loves war or is always in favor of war or military force. Putting warmongers in charge of the military can be a dangerous move.

Waterloo n. a devastating loss or defeat (from Napoleon's final defeat at Waterloo in 1815). The team's Waterloo finally came during the playoffs.

watershed event n. an event that changes something dramatically or has important consequences. The battle of Gettysburg was a watershed event in the Civil War.

wedlock n. marriage. Many people are happier in a state of wedlock.

whim (wim) n. a sudden idea or spontaneous action. He flew to Florida on a whim. /**whimsical** adj.

white elephant n. refers to any object that no one really wants or has no real value. The building has been vacant for so long that it is now just a white elephant.

wholesale adv. adj. / adv. 1. refers to the buying or selling of items in large quantities or at discounted prices. The girl bought her car wholesale from the dealer. / adj. The wholesale price of a something is always cheaper than retail price. 2. the price from the manufacturer.

wretched (rech-ed) adj. very bad; terrible; in a bad condition. The animals were living in wretched conditions.

XYZ

Xanadu (za-nah-doo) n. a large noble residence; a place of pleasure. The king's Xanadu is his castle.

xenophobia n. fear or hatred of foreigners. His xenophobia kept him from enjoying new cultural experiences with the people from Europe.

Yankee n. adj. / n. refers to a person from the Northern states of the U.S. or to a person from the United States in general. The Southerners must have thought the Yankees had a strange accent. / adj. The Yankee soldiers sounded strange to the Confederates.

yeoman (yoe-man) n. 1. a common or unimportant small landowner. Many yeoman farmers of the 1600s found it hard to support themselves. 2. a petty officer in the U.S. Navy.

yoke n. 1. a wood device put around an animal's neck so it can pull a plow or wagon. The yoke the ox was wearing was attached to a cart. 2. figurative for anything that binds things together. 3. a burden. The yoke of cruelty tarnished the country's reputation.

yokel (yoe-kol) n. a local rural person. The yokels don't like <u>Yankees</u> from the city looking around.

zeal (zeel) n. an enthusiasm for something. His zeal for chess was unmatched. / **zealous** (zel-us) adj. full of zeal or enthusiasm.

zealot (zel-ot) n. a fanatic; having too much enthusiasm or <u>zeal</u> for something. The war zealots could destroy the earth.

zenith (zee-nith) n. figurative for the highest point; the highest point of achievement. The zenith of her efforts was receiving her doctorate.

zephyr (ze-fer) n. a light, calm wind. A zephyr graced the field and brought the flowers to life.

Matching Quiz # 36	
_____ 1. white elephant	a. a small farmer
_____ 2. whim	b. enthusiasm for something
_____ 3. Xanadu	c. terrible
_____ 4. watershed event	d. a burden
_____ 5. yeoman	e. person who favors war
_____ 6. wretched	f. a calm wind
_____ 7. zeal	g. highest point of achievement
_____ 8. zephyr	h. something with no value
_____ 9. zealot	i. having drastic consequences
_____10. yoke	j. large noble residence or place
_____11. warmonger	k. a fanatic, one with much zeal
_____12. zenith	l. a local person
_____13. Waterloo	m. a sudden idea
_____14. yokel	n. a major defeat
_____15. xenophobia	o. fear of foreign people

Advanced Vocabulary Part I

Most of the following words are college and graduate level words and great to study for the SAT®, ACT®, and other standardized tests as well as more complex readings. Many, but not all of the words are also in the General Vocabulary Building section but are definitely worth reinforcing.

abrogate (a-broe-gate) v. to repeal or cancel a law. The city was forced to abrogate the soda tax because people were so mad.

accouterments (uh-koo-ter-ments) n. personal belongings, equipment, or skills. The accouterments of successful business people include a good vocabulary, good communication skills, the ability to read and write well, determination, and good people skills.

acumen n. intelligence, understanding, and strong skills, especially in a particular field. The man's scientific acumen led him to the top of his field.

altruistic (all-true-is-tik) adj. genuine, often unselfish concern for others. The man displayed his altruistic side when his neighbors were in need.

anathema (a-na-the-mah) n. someone whom others hate; a source of loathing and detest. Once the scandal broke, the politician became an anathema in political circles.

apologist (uh-po-li-jist) n. a someone who defends or supports a controversial point of view of another person or idea. The scientist had many apologists for his new theory.

austerity n. strictness or sternness in one's manner or appearance; seriousness. Everyone knew by the austerity in the woman's voice that she was not joking. The government enacted austerity measures during the economic downtown. / **austere** adj.

beguile (bee-gile)) v. to confuse, deceive, or trick; to misrepresent or mislead; to be dishonest or shady. The salesman beguiled the customer about the warranty. / adj. to be confused.

bellicose (be-lee-koes) adj. quarrelsome; argumentative; confrontational. The bellicose coach was disliked by the parents.

bucolic (byu-ko-lick) adj. beautiful and peaceful; pleasant. The vast property had beautiful gardens that many potential buyers found bucolic.

burgeon (ber-jen) n. to grow out rapidly. New restaurants have burgeoned all over town.

capricious (kuh-pree-shus) adj. liable to change one's mind without reason or on a whim. Youngsters are sometimes more capricious than adults.

castigate (kas-ti-gate) v. to scorn or reprimand severely and harshly. The mother castigated her child in front of all his friends.

categorical adj. without stipulations or conditions; complete; final. His response was swift and categorical. / **categorically** adv. The man categorically denied the allegations.

Multiple Choice Quiz # 1

1. Someone who defends a controversial point of view of another person
   a. devil's advocate   b. sophist   c. romantic   d. apologist

2. To *beguile* means to
   a. confuse   b. upset   c. scare off   d. deny

3. A person's intelligence and skills for something are also known as
   a. acumen   b. characteristics   c. tools   d. traits

4. *Altruistic* means
   a. fake   b. real   c. genuine   d. selfish

5. Another word for *bellicose* is
   a. kind   b. belligerent   c. quiet   d. altruistic

6. *Abrogate* means to
   a. extend something   b. increase   c. cancel   d. decrease

7. All the terms below mean the same as *bucolic*, except
   a. beautiful   b. peaceful   c. pleasant   d. ugly

8. *Austerity* means
   a. strictness   b. kindness   c. pleasantness   d. anger

9. The boy had all the _____ of a baseball player, including hat, glove, and bat.
   a. tools   b. accouterments   c. characteristics   d. knowledge

10. An *anathema* is someone whom others
    a. love   b. loath   c. don't want to be around   d. all of the above

11. New restaurants have begun to *burgeon* all over town.
    a. to pop up   b. disappear   c. go out of business   d. none of the above

12. *Capricious* means
    a. nasty   b. unfriendly   c. likely to change one's mind   d. fair

13. To categorically deny something means
    a. without stipulations   b. completely   c. strongly   d. all of the above

14. To *castigate* someone means to
    a. support   b. harshly reprimand   c. encourage   d. reward

15. Judicial standards state that laws must be applied in a non-arbitrary or *capricious* manner.
    a. evenly and fairly   b. without reason   c. without consideration   d. all of the above

circumvent (sir-kum-vent) v. to get around; to avoid. The businessman circumvented the tax code by keeping money in offshore bank accounts that were in other countries.

cogent (ko-jent) adj. influential; able to persuade or convince. The salesman gave a cogent speech for buying the car today.

cognizant (kog-ni-zent) adj. to be aware; related to mental knowledge observed or perceived. The teacher was cognizant of the student's reading problem.

commensurate (ko-men-sher-it) adj. fair; in the proper amount; equal to. The punishment must be commensurate with the crime.

conjecture n. v. / n. an assumption; a guess or conclusion made by guessing. The scientist's theory was only conjecture and not based on facts. / v. to make an assumption or conclusion by guessing.

consanguinity (kon-san-gwin-i-tee) n. a relationship by blood or from the same ancestors. Royalty and consanguinity often go hand in hand.

conspicuous (kon-spi-kyu-us) adj. 1. obvious; easy to see. 2. attracting attention. The thief looked very conspicuous with the ski mask on his head on the summer day.

contentious (kon-ten-sheeous) adj. willing to argue or hotly contested. The discussion became so contentious at times it seemed like the disagreement might end their friendship.

corollary n. a likely or natural result. Good grades should be a corollary of studying hard.

corrugated (kor-ru-gate-ed) adj. created with thick folds or ridges. Many types of drain tile pipes are now made out of corrugated materials.

credulous (kre-ju-lus) adj. naïve; gullible; ready to believe anything. The young girl was credulous in that she always believed her friend's lies.

culpable (kul-pol-bul) adj. to be guilty or responsible for something. The concert venue was culpable for all the injuries people suffered because they did not have enough security to control the crowd.

cutaneous (kyu-tay-nee-us) adj. on or related to the skin. The wound was only a cutaneous cut.

deference n. 1. act of showing respect. Out of deference for the senior citizen, the boy offered his seat to the older man. 2. act of respectfully submitting to another's opinion.

deleterious adj. (de-le-teer-ee-ous) harmful or damaging. The politician made deleterious comments.

delineate (de-lin-nee-ate) v. to clearly show or explain something using drawings or words. The vacation route was delineated on the map.

demure (de-myur) adj. acting reserved, shy, or modest. The girl was quite demure.

denigrate v. to harm the reputation of someone. The scandal denigrated the man.

Multiple Choice Quiz # 2

1. His *deleterious* actions affected the entire family.
   a. harmful   b. dangerous   c. drastic   d. irresponsible

2. Teachers must be *cognizant* of students' academic and emotional needs.
   a. not care about   b. be aware of   c. avoid   d. report

3. The map clearly *delineated* the correct route back to camp.
   a. to outline   b. hide   c. clearly show   d. emphasize

4. The drunk driver was *culpable* for the injuries caused in the accident.
   a. responsible   b. cleared   c. innocent   d. victimized

5. The disagreement between the two became so *contentious* everyone else left the room.
   a. friendly   b. funny   c. heated   d. popular

6. *Conspicuous* means
   a. noticeable   b. attracting attention   c. obvious   d. all of the above

7. The salary must be *commensurate* with the duties of the job.
   a. fair   b. equal to   c. in the proper amount   d. all of the above

8. Out of *deference* for the woman with a cane, the boy gave up his seat for her.
   a. loyalty to   b. respect for   c. avoidance of   d. none of the above

9. The young doctor *deferred* to the experienced doctor's opinion.
   a. ignored   b. disagreed with   c. submitted to   d. argued with

10. It was just *conjecture* that the manager quit to take a better job.
    a. an assumption   b. a lie   c. a fact   d. something unknown

11. Persuasive or convincing
    a. lucid   b. cogent   c. illuminating   d. credulous

12. Naïve or gullible
    a. lucid   b. cogent   c. illuminating   d. credulous

13. Having many folds or ridges
    a. demure   b. cogent   c. rigid   d. corrugated

14. Acting modest or reserved
    a. circumspect   b. cogent   c. cognizant   d. demure

15. To put down or harm the reputation of someone
    a. denigrate   b. delineate   c. beguile   d. abrogate

238

derivation (der-i-vay-shun) n. 1. act of deriving. 2. the origin of something. The derivation of many English words come from Greek and Latin.

diatribe (die-oe-tribe) n. a long verbal attack in which someone expressed a strong opinion. At the forum a voter went into a diatribe against the mayor and her policies.

didactic adj. something that teaches, especially that has a moral lesson. The didactic manner of his supervision won him the respect of his workers. / **didactics** n. the art of teaching or improvement.

differentiate (dif-er-en-shee-ate) v. to understand the difference between things. They could not differentiate between the two scientific theories.

discern (di-sern) v. to understand something difficult or hidden; to see clearly. The boy's father discerned the truth about his son's trouble.

discretionary adj. something that is left to one's own decision; freedom to deicide for oneself. Schools should have more discretionary money the principal can spend in a variety of ways.

disparate (dis-pair-ret) adj. opposite or unequal; incompatible. The friendship faded away because the children's interests and personalities became so disparate over time.

dogma n. accepted values or belief system; Much of today's educational dogma states that all children can achieve at the same level. / **dogmatic** adj.

effervescent (e-fer-ve-sent) adj. 1. cheerful, spirited, very outgoing. 2. literally to produce bubbles of gas. The effervescent attitude of the fellow made him very popular. / **effervescence** n.

egalitarian (e-gal-li-tair-ee-an) adj. n. / adj. belief that all people are or should be equal. His egalitarian side came out when he offered a job to the homeless person. / n. a person who thinks everyone is or should be equal.

elucidate (e-loo-si-date) v. to explain or make more clear. The scientist elucidated on the theory.

empirical adj. based on firsthand knowledge, experience, or observation. She favors empirical evidence not scientific theory that nobody can see.

equivocal (ee-kwi-vi-col) adj. 1. something that has two or more meanings; unclear or uncertain. 2. something that is not clearly stated or decided. Stacy's thoughts were equivocal; they were contradictory and subject to examination.

ephemeral (ee-fe-mer-ral) adj. not lasting, having a short life span, fleeting or temporary. Human life seems so ephemeral compared to the trees, oceans, and mountains.

epistemology (e-pi-stoe-mo-loe-gee) n. branch of philosophy that studies the nature of human knowledge along with the origins and limits of knowledge and reality.

erudite (air-yoo-dite) adj. educated; knowledgeable from studying. The teacher seemed quite erudite to her students.

Multiple Choice Quiz # 3

1. The origin of something is known as its
    a. dogma   b. diatribe   c. derivation   d. definition

2. To *differentiate* between things means to
    a. show similarities   b. show differences   c. emphasize   d. highlight

3. To further explain or make more clear
    a. discern   b. differentiate   c. denigrate   d. elucidate

4. If something is left to one's own decision it is
    a. disparate   b. discretionary   c. opinion   d. didactic

5. Things that are so different they become incompatible
    a. disparate   b. egalitarian   c. didactic   d. ephemeral

6. To understand or see something that is unclear or difficult to see
    a. derive   b. discern   c. denigrate   d. disparate

7. Based on firsthand knowledge or observation
    a. epistemology   b. ephemeral   c. emphasize   d. empirical

8. People are often more concerned with *ephemeral* pleasures.
    a. long lasting   b. short-sighted   c. important   d. temporary

9. The politician's answer was *equivocal* and open for interpretation.
    a. unclear   b. confusing   c. not clearly stated   d. all of the above

10. Dealing with the limits and origins human knowledge
    a. ontology   b. philosophy   c. etymology   d. epistemology

11. Writing a book stressing the importance of vocabulary could be considered
    a. didactic   b. disparate   c. discerning   d. ephemeral

12. Adhering to staunch educational *dogma* does not work in all situations
    a. rules   b. laws   c. accepted beliefs   d. guidelines

13. The conversation became quite *erudite*.
    a. scholarly   b. sophisticated   c. well-informed   d. all of the above

14. The teacher went off on a *diatribe* about the importance of doing homework.
    a. opinionated speech   b. verbal attack   c. angry & critical rant   d. all of the above

15. The belief that all people are or should be equal
    a. ephemeral   b. egalitarian   c. didactic   d. equivocal

240

eschew (es-choo) v. to avoid or stay away from; shun. Reasonable people eschew drinking and driving.

esoteric adj. something that only a few people would understand; meant for select people to know; technical or complicated information. His esoteric answer was confusing and probably only understood by the professor.

etymology (et-i-mo-loe-jee) n. the study of the origin, meaning, and history of a word. Etymology and linguistics are closely related.

euphemism (yu-fe-miz-um) n. a polite or delicate way of stating something. Frugal is a euphemism for cheap.

exacerbate (eg-zas-er-bate) v. to make worse. The fall exacerbated her previous injury.

expatriate (ex-pae-tree-et) 1. n. someone who has moved away from their native country. Many expatriates from Cuba came to the united states. 2. v. (ex-pae-tree-ate) to remove one's self from their native country to another or to be forced into exile to another country. The rebels were expatriated.

extrapolate v. to infer or conclude possibilities from what is already known; to extend a method or trend to a logical conclusion. Good detectives can extrapolate knowledge from a little information.

facetious (fuh-see-shus) adj. displaying inappropriate humor. His facetious remarks annoy people.

fiduciary (fi-doo-shee-air-ee) adj. something that is held in trust. A lawyer has a fiduciary responsibility to his clients.

fledgling (flej-ling) adj. struggling to succeed or new at something. The fledging business just started to make a profit. / **fledgling** n. literally a bird just learning to fly.

forbearance (for-bair-ens) n. the act of restraining oneself or keeping from doing something through self-control. The assertive employee held his tongue in an unusual case of forbearance.

forensic adj. the application of science, scientific test, and medical knowledge to investigate crimes and used in courts of law. A forensic medical expert explained the evidence to the judge.

fortuitous (for-tu-i-tus) adj. occurring by luck or chance; not planned. It was fortuitous to run into an old friend at the store.

galvanize v. 1. to energize or spur to action. The tragedy galvanized the community to a new level of commitment. 2. literally to charge with electricity.

gilded adj. 1. something appearing better on the surface than it is. 2. something shinny and nice. 3. covered with a precious metal such as gold. The gilded cup was really only lead with gold plating.

gradient (gray-dee-ent) n. the angle by which a slope, such as a road, goes up or down (often expressed as a percent); the grade. Trucks must be careful of steep gradients, especially in bad weather. The road has a two percent gradient.

Multiple Choice Quiz # 4

1. Many religions *eschew* eating meat on Fridays during lent.
   a. avoid   b. emphasize   c. look down upon   d. none of the above

2. The professor's answer was too *esoteric* for most of the students to understand.
   a. complicated   b. technical   c. understood by the few   d. all of the above

3. A polite way of saying something
   a. esoteric   b. euphemism   c. facetious   d. fortuitous

4. To make things worse
   a. extrapolate   b. fortuitous   c. galvanize   d. exacerbate

5. To extend a set of circumstances to a logical conclusion
   a. exacerbate   b. extrapolate   c. eschew   d. galvanize

6. The accountant has a *fiduciary* responsibility to her clients.
   a. respectful   b. honest   c. held in trust   d. legal

7. The *fledging* business barely survived during the COVID lockdowns.
   a. struggling to succeed   b. profitable   c. not profitable   d. none of the above

8. Applying medical knowledge in a court of law
   a. extrapolate   b. expatriate   c. fiduciary   d. forensic

9. Lucky
   a. fortuitous   b. gilded   c. facetious   d. none of the above

10. The incident at the school *galvanized* parents.
    a. angered   b. spurred to action   c. humiliated   d. offended

11. The act of restraining oneself
    a. exacerbate   b. eschew   c. forbearance   d. elucidate

12. Something that is covered in a shiny metal
    a. erudite   b. fledging   c. ephemeral   d. gilded

13. The study of the origin of a word
    a. forensics   b. etymology   c. epistemology   d. none of the above

14. Displaying inappropriate humor
    a. esoteric   b. euphemism   c. facetious   d. fortuitous

15. To appear better than something really is
    a. euphemism   b. gilded   c. fortuitous   d. fledging

gregarious (gre-gair-ee-us) adj. outgoing; happy to be around others. The movie star was quite gregarious.

hyperbole (hy-per-boe-lee) n. exaggeration; a statement containing exaggeration. Writers use a lot of hyperbole to create the desired effect.

ideology n. a belief system; a set of beliefs; a philosophy. The Republican ideology regarding economics is now quite different than the Democrats' ideology.

idiosyncrasy (i-dee-oe-sing-kra-see) n. a strange habit or character trait. Among her many idiosyncrasies was washing her hands every ten minutes.

impertinent adj. not showing respect; rude. The student's impertinent reply angered the teacher.

impetus n. something that leads to or causes something. Money is a good impetus for work.

implacable (im-plak-ble) adj. not capable of calming down, being appeased, or made less angry. Once he got mad he became completely implacable, and it was just better to leave him alone for a while.

incontrovertible adj. not able to be proved false or denied; very clear and certain. The evidence against the man was incontrovertible.

incredulous (in-kre-ju-lus) adj. not believing; skeptical. The man was quite incredulous regarding flying saucers.

incremental adj. in increments; a little bit at a time. The man made incremental improvements.

indemnify (in-dem-ni-fy) v. to compensate for loss. The insurance company indemnified him for the house fire. 2. to protect from loss. Home insurance is a good way to indemnify one's property.

indifference n. lack of care or concern about something. His indifference over his grades is disappointing. /**indifferent** adj.

indignant (in-dig-nant) adj. being very upset with something that is not right or fair. The people were indignant over the harsh treatment of the animals.

ingratiate (in-gray-shee-ate) v. to make people pleased with oneself. He ingratiated himself with the woman with flattery and expensive gifts.

innocuous (i-nok-yu-us) adj. harmless. The remark turned out to be innocuous.

impugn (im-pyoon) v. to challenge the credibility or truth of something. The attorney impugned the evidence against the defendant.

Multiple Choice Quiz # 5

1. The *gregarious* neighbor was always out and about.
    a. nervous   b. outgoing   c. sad   d. reserved

2. The politician used a lot of *hyperbole* in his speeches.
    a. exaggeration   b. indifference   c. hypocrisy   d. drama

3. The facts of the case were *incontrovertible*.
    a. biased   b. subject to interpretation   c. clear   d. not able to be proved false

4. People have insurance policies to *indemnify* themselves.
    a. protect from loss   b. prove in court   c. protect from wrongdoing   d. eliminate debt

5. It was obvious the guest was trying to *ingratiate* herself with everyone else as the party.
    a. compete with   b. show off   c. get others to like her   d. avoid

6. Something that leads to something else.
    a. impugn   b. idiosyncrasy   c. hyperbole   d. impetus

7. The manager was so *implacable* at the bad call he was kicked out of the game.
    a. disappointed   b. not able to calm down   c. shocked   d. none of the above

8. What is an *idiosyncrasy*?
    a. strange habit   b. character flaw   c. strange name   d. unusual appearance

9. The patient made *incremental* improvements.
    a. all at once   b. not much   c. little at a time   d. none at all

10. The politician showed his *indifference* when asked about the effects of the new law.
    a. lack of concern   b. concern   c. calm attitude   d. aggressive attitude

11. The remark turned out to be *harmless*.
    a. implacable   b. indifferent   c. incredulous   d. innocuous

12. To challenge the credibility of something.
    a. implacable   b. impugn   c. indemnify   d. none of the above

13. To be very upset over some type of unfair treatment.
    a. implacable   b. impugn   c. indifferent   d. indignant

14. System of beliefs.
    a. idiosyncrasy   b. hyperbole   c. ideology   d. impetus

15. Refusing to believe something.
    a. implacable   b. incredulous   c. incontrovertible   d. indifferent

Advanced Vocabulary Part II

impunity (im-pyoo-ni-tee) n. freedom or protection from punishment. Children often have a certain degree of impunity that adults do not.

inscrutable (in-scroo-tah-bul) adj. something that cannot be understood because not much is known about it. The inscrutable circumstances left everyone bewildered.

intangible (in-tan-ji-bul) adj. 1. hard to understand. The idea seemed too intangible to many people. 2. not capable of being touched.

integral adj. an important part of; essential; necessary part of. Good people skills are an integral part of being a manager.

intractable (in-trak-ta-bol) adj. disobedient or stubborn. The intractable youth had to learn many lessons the hard way.

intransigent (in-trans-si-jent) v. being very rigid and unwilling to compromise. If both sides remain intransigent and don't give up their extreme views an agreement will never be reached.

isometric adj. having equal measurements or sides. The walls are isometric.

judicious (jew-dish-us) adj. having or exercising good judgment. The policeman was most judicious about the whole incident.

jurisprudence (jur-is-pru-dens) n. the study of law or its application. Jurisprudence dictates the way the judge could interpret the law.

juxtapose (jux-tah-pose) v. to put close together or side-by-side so a comparison can be made. You must juxtapose the two pieces of evidence. /**juxtaposition** n.

lionize (lie-oe-nize) v. to admire greatly or assign a great deal of importance to a person. Great military generals and political leaders are often lionized by the public.

logistics (lo-ji-stiks) n. 1. the actual planning or carrying out of tasks. 2. the science or art of careful planning and carrying out of duties. Good logistics requires much forethought and anticipation of potential problems. /**logistical** adj. Feeding a thousand people will take a logistical miracle.

loquacious (lo-kway-shus) adj. talking a lot. She is a loquacious youth.

lucid (loo-sid) adj. thinking clearly; coherent; making sense. The man was lucid even after the blow to his head. /**lucidity** n.

magnanimous (mag-na-ni-mus) adj. of great or noble spirit (intentions); unselfish and forgiving. Helping those who have hurt you in the past is quite magnanimous. / **magnanimity** n.

magnate (mag-not) n. a very successful or wealthy business person. Aristotle Onassis was a famous shipping magnate.

Multiple Choice Quiz # 6

1. The study of the law and its application is known as
   a. legal precedent   b. jurisprudence   c. judicious   d. impunity

2. *Inscrutable* means
   a. able to understand   b. concise   c. clear   d. not able to understand

3. The concept was too *intangible* for the kids to grasp.
   a. concrete   b. clear   c. confusing   d. hard to understand

4. *Isometric* means
   a. having equal sides   b. having unequal sides

5. The boy was sent away to military school because of his *intractable* behavior.
   a. disobedient   b. civilized   c. criminal   d. inscrutable

6. Children often have a greater degree of *impunity* than adults.
   a. freedom from judgement   b. freedom from punishment   c. flexibility   d. punishment

7. Computer chips are now an *integral* part of a car's operational capabilities.
   a. optional   b. unnecessary   c. expensive   d. essential

8. The policeman was incredibly *judicious* regarding the incident.
   a. displaying good judgement   b. displaying poor judgement   c. unfair   d. unreasonable

9. The manager was very *intransigent* with his expectations for the employees.
   a. flexible   b. willing to compromise   c. kind   d. unwilling to compromise

10. Running a business or a military operation both require solid *logistics*.
    a. planning and forethought   b. hard work and practice   c. price controls   d. luck and pluck

11. The woman was still *lucid* after the car accident.
    a. thinking clearly   b. making sense   c. coherent   d. all of the above

12. The girl is quite *loquacious* in school.
    a. quiet   b. shy   c. talkative   d. loud

13. Having a great or noble spirit.
    a. loquacious   b. judicious   c. intractable   d. magnanimous

14. To *juxtapose* for comparison means
    a. put side-by-side   b. put on top of each other   c. to separate   d. none of the above

15. *A magnate* is
    a. something magnetic   b. successful business person   c. wealthy person   d. poor person

246

maladroit adj. not good at something; clumsy or awkward. The maladroit painter got paint all over the place.

malaise (muh-laze) n. a sickened, disturbed, or uncomfortable condition. A malaise overcame the room when the layoffs were about to be announced.

malcontent adj. n. / adj. unhappy, unpleased, or unsatisfied. The malcontent employees were even more upset after the bad news. / n. All the malcontents gathered to protest the new policy. / **malcontented** adj.

malediction n. the act of speaking bad or evil things about someone. The old woman was quite skilled in malediction directed toward her family.

malfeasance (mal-fee-zens) n. wrongdoing by an official or other person held in public trust. The mayor was guilty of gross malfeasance when he misused public money.

mandamus n. a law or order handed down from a higher authority to a lower authority requiring that a certain act be done. The Supreme Court handed down a mandamus to the school board to change its admissions policy.

matriculate (ma-tri-kyu-late) v. to advance to the next level or to be admitted to school. Students must meet certain requirements before they matriculate to the next grade. / **matriculation** n.

mendacious (men-day-shus) adj. untruthful; lying. The mendacious students came up with a story to protect themselves from punishment.

mercurial (mer-kyer-ree-uhl) adj. 1. liable to change easily. His mercurial temperament finally got him in trouble. 2. quick; always moving. The mercurial youth was always first in line.

milieu (mil-yu) n. environment; surroundings. Arizona's dry climate is just the milieu the man needed for his allergies.

misanthrope (mis-san-thope) n. person who hates or mistrusts people.

momentous (moe-men-tus) n. of great importance; memorable. College graduation is a momentous occasion.

nebulous (ne-byu-lus) adj. 1. literally not having a solid form; gas or cloud-like. 2. confusing; not clear or certain; vague; obscure. His thoughts on inflation are nebulous at best.

nihilism n. 1. the negative view that life is useless and only full of suffering and death with no objective sense of right and wrong. 2. the negative view or rejection of established beliefs of a society such as government or religion. 3. the belief that violence and terror are acceptable means of achieving a goal. Nihilism found a voice in many philosophers like Nietzsche. /**nihilistic** adj.

nocuous (nah-kyu-us) adj. harmful; poisonous. The nocuous fumes chased everyone out of the room.

Multiple Choice Quiz # 7

1. A sick or uncomfortable condition.
    a. milieu   b. momentous   c. nocuous   d. malaise

2. A wrongdoing by a public official.
    a. mandamus   b. malediction   c. malfeasance   d. malaise

3. To advance to the next level.
    a. matriculate   b. momentous   c. mandamus   d. malign

4. One's environment or surroundings.
    a. nocuous   b. mendacious   c. mercurial   d. milieu

5. Something of great importance.
    a. nocuous   b. momentous   c. nebulous   d. mendacious

6. Confusing or not certain.
    a. nocuous   b. nebulous   c. mercurial   d. mendacious

7. The view that life is pointless, full of suffering, and with no right or wrong.
    a. nihilistic   b. mercurial   c. malcontent   d. nocuous

8. A *nocuous* gas is
    a. harmful   b. not harmful   c. invisible   d. visible

9. Liable to change easily.
    a. mendacious   b. nebulous   c. mercurial   d. malcontent

10. *Maladroit* means
    a. good at something   b. not good at something   c. lazy   d. not smart

11. The act of speaking badly about someone.
    a. malfeasance   b. matriculate   c. nihilism   d. malediction

12. The bully was a *malcontent*.
    a. tough   b. never happy   c. strong   d. selfish

13. Someone who dislikes or mistrusts people.
    a. malcontent   b. maladroit   c. mercurial   d. misanthrope

14. An order handed down from a higher authority to a lower authority.
    a. mandamus   d. matriculation   c. malediction   d. malfeasance

15. The *mendacious* student always had an excuse for not doing his homework.
    a. exaggerating   b. lying   c. serious   d. mercurial

obligatory (o-blig-ah-tor-ee) adj. something required by obligation. His appearance in court was made obligatory by the summons.

obsequious (ob-see-kwee-us) adj. eagerness to please; politeness out of duty or hope of future reward or fear of punishment. The secretary's obsequious manner did not sit well with her boss.

obtrusive adj. overstepping one's bounds; interfering when not asked. The obtrusive employee invited himself to the party.

ontological (on-to-loj-i-kal) adj. related to the philosophy concerned with the study of reality. Descartes' ontological pursuits made him a legend among philosophers. / **ontology** n.

oscillate (os-si-late) v. to move or swing back and forth or to vary between two points. The desk fan provided a cool breeze as it oscillated on the desk. Electrical waves oscillated on the screen of the oscilloscope.

ostentatious (os-ten-tay-shus) adj. done for show. His interrupting the speech with obscure facts about the subject was quite ostentatious.

panacea (pan-uh-see-ah) n. a cure for many problems or diseases. New genetic discoveries could lead to a panacea in medicine.

parenthetical adj. something that further explains something else, as if it were in parentheses. / **parenthetically** adv. Tom doesn't go to movies a lot, unless, parenthetically, it's a Star Wars movie.

parsimonious (par-si-moe-nee-us) adj. not wanting to spend money; cheap; <u>frugal</u>. The General Assembly had no choice but to approve the parsimonious budget.

partisan adj. support for a particular person or group, often based on tradition or allegiance. Partisan politics between the Democrats and Republicans have slowed the political process. /**partisanship** n.

pathos (pa-thos) n. feeling sorrow, sympathy, or pity. Seeing children in the hospital or elderly people eating alone always invokes pathos in me.

pedantic (pe-dan-tik) adj. showing off one's knowledge. The professor likes to be pedantic when she has an audience.

penance (pe-nance) noun. Voluntary self-punishment or action to make up for a wrongdoing or sin.

pejorative adj. likely to make matters worse; showing contempt. His pejorative manner combined with his questionable judgment does not make him a good candidate for the job.

penitence n. sorrow for a sin or wrongdoing. The man showed no penitence for his crime. /**penitent** adj. showing sorrow for a wrong.

Multiple Choice Quiz # 8

1. *Obligatory* means
   a. not required   b. required   c. polite   d. abrasive

2. The celebrity's *ostentatious* behavior was obvious.
   a. done to show off   b. reserved   c. polite   d. awkward

3. The fan *oscillated* on the desk.
   a. moved up and down b. moved in a circle c. moved back and forth d. remained still

4. A cure for many diseases or problems.
   a. pathos   b. obsequious   c. panacea   d. pedantic

5. To further explain something
   a. obsequious   b. pejorative   c. obtrusive   d. parenthetically

6. Overstepping one's bounds
   a. obtrusive   b. pathos   c. pejorative   d. obligatory

7. Another word for being cheap or not wanting to spend money.
   a. pedantic   b. ostentatious   c. obsequious   d. parsimonious

8. A feeling of pity or sorrow
   a. ostentatious   b. pathos   c. obligatory   d. pejorative

9. Showing off one's knowledge
   a. ostentatious   b. obsequious   c. parsimonious   d. pedantic

10. Showing contempt or disapproval
    a. partisan   b. pejorative   c. parsimonious   d. pathos

11. Sorrow for a sin or other wrongdoing
    a. penitence   b. pathos   c. obsequious   d. obligatory

12. Showing support to only one group based on loyalty or tradition
    a. pathos   b. obligatory   c. partisan   d. pedantic

13. Act of making up for a wrongdoing or sin
    a. penance   b. pathos   c. partisan   d. none of the above

14. Eagerness to please.
    a. ostentatious   b. obsequious   c. pathos   d. parsimonious

15. "The girl loves school, but, *additionally* speaking, history is her favor subject."
    a. parenthetically   b. ontologically   c. pejoratively   d. obtrusively

perfidy n. betrayal or treachery. The king's perfidy against his subjects did not go unnoticed. /**perfidious** adj.

peripatetic (per-i-pa-te-tic) adj. always traveling or wondering around. Gypsies were known to be a peripatetic group.

peripheral adj. associated with; connected with. 1. The computer's peripheral equipment, such as the printer, was outdated. 2. On the side as in peripheral vision.

periphery (per-ri-fer-ee) n. on the sides or outside of something. The team stood at the periphery of the field.

pernicious (per-ni-shus) adj. causing much damage or harm. The pernicious drinking habits of some people have destroyed many families.

plenary adj. 1. complete, absolute. The plenary resources of the military were used in the attack. 2. with everyone present. A new marketing plan was revealed at the monthly plenary meeting of the board of directors.

pontificate (pon-ti-fi-kate) v. to speak or express opinions in a pompous, know-it-all, ideological, or conceited manner. The professor often pontificated his views to the class.

parochial (pa-roe-kee-eal) adj. 1. related to a church or religion. Catholic schools are parochial schools. 2. Limited in scope or outlook. Thinking there is only one way to solve the problem is a very parochial view.

posthumously (poe-st-hu-mus-lee) adv. after death. The scientist was awarded credit for her discovery posthumously.

pragmatism (prag-ma-ti-sm) n. school of thought based on finding solutions to problems that are practical given the situation. Favoring a practical approach to issues or problems rather than solutions based on ideals or theories that might not work in the real world. Sometimes a pragmatic approach is the best approach. / **pragmatic** adj./ **pragmatist** n. Teddy Roosevelt was a pragmatist.

precocious (pre-koe-shus) adj. occurring or developing sooner than normal. A precocious interest in reading led the child to the head of her class in reading scores.

predicate (pre-di-kate) v. to base a statement or thought on something. The notion that dinosaurs came before man is predicated by early fossil records.

preponderance n. a greater quantity; a quantity that is greater than another. Only a preponderance of the evidence was needed to find the defendant guilty in the civil case.

prodigal (pro-di-kal) adj. needlessly wasteful or extravagant. In the Bible Jesus explains the parable of the Prodigal Son, a man who squandered his inheritance and was forced to move back home.

proliferate v. 1. to increase in number; to multiply. 2. to spread or filter into other areas. The rumor proliferated throughout the office. /**proliferation** n.

Multiple Choice Quiz # 9

1. What group would be considered *peripatetic*?
   a. colonists   b. invaders   c. Gypsies   d. settlers

2. The spectators stood on the *periphery* of the field.
   a. in front   b. behind   c. on the sides   d. in the middle

3. The teacher would often *pontificate* to the class.
   a. debate   b. express opinions   c. argue   d. discuss

4. Which is an example of a *parochial* school?
   a. public school   b. charter school   c. Catholic school   d. private school

5. Which would be an example of a *pernicious* habit?
   a. drinking   b. gambling   c. smoking   d. all of the above

6. The Archdiocese held a *plenary* meeting of priests?
   a. all-present   b. important   c. immediate   d. serious

7. The scientist was awarded the Nobel Peace Prize, *posthumously*.
   a. after the fact   b. after death   c. by mistake   d. none of the above

8. *Precocious* means
   a. later than normal   b. too late   c. too soon   d. sooner than normal

9. To base a statement on something.
   a. predicate   b. proliferate   c. pragmatic   d. perfidy

10. Favoring a practical approach to solving problems.
    a. prodigal   b. plenary   c. parochial   d. pragmatic

11. A guilty verdict in civil court simply requires a *greater quantity* of the evidence.
    a. peripheral   b. pragmatic   c. prodigal   d. preponderance

12. Wasteful or extravagant
    a. precocious   b. pernicious   c. prodigal   d. plenary

13. To increase in number or spread
    a. proliferate   b. pontificate   c. posthumously   d. periphery

14. Thomas Jefferson accused the King of England of *perfidy* toward the colonists.
    a. taxation   b. betrayal   c. punishing   d. killing

15. On the side or connected to
    a. plenary   b. peripatetic   c. pernicious   d. peripheral

252

promulgate (pro-mul-gate) v. to spread or make widely known. The media promulgated the false story because they did not have all their facts first.

propensity n. a natural tendency toward something. The boy has a propensity for fixing things.

propitious (proe-pi-shus) adj. favorable; likeable. Chicago was a propitious location for a city due to its proximity to the lake and rivers.

qualitative (kwol-li-tay-tiv) adj. related to the quality of something. Teachers should be more concerned with qualitative assignments rather than how many assignments they give.

quantitative (kwan-ti-tay-tiv) adj. related to quantity or numbers. Students should not be as concerned with quantitative facts as they should with the quality of their information.

query (kweer-ee) v. n. /v. to inquire about something; to ask about. The organization queried people with a survey. /n. an inquiry; the act of asking or looking into something. A query was made into the rise in crime.

quintessence (kwin-te-sens) n. the very nature of something; the purest form of something; the best example of something. A Ferrari is the quintessence of a sports car. /**quintessential** adj.

rapacious (ruh-pay-shus) adj. taking something by force. The theft was a rapacious act.

rapprochement (ruh-proech-ment) n. the creating of a good relationship with someone; establishing a good rapport. The belligerent nations finally reached a stage of rapprochement.

recalcitrant (ri-kal-si-trent) adj. unruly; refusing to obey; hard to control. The recalcitrant student was always in the Dean's office.

recidivism (ri-si-di-viz-um) n. tendency to repeat an act (especially an act of crime) or to relapse into a past behavior. If his past recidivism is any indication of future behavior, he will probably be arrested again.

remuneration (re-myu-ner-ay-shun) n. monetary compensation. The girl received a twenty-dollar remuneration for her dog-walking services.

repository (ree-po-si-tor-ee) n. a place where things are kept, real things or ideas and information. The boy's closet became a repository for dirty laundry. The database was a repository of people's personal information. The men's locker room was a repository of bad language.

reproach v. to express disapproval or disappointment. The boss reproached his employee for not giving him all the necessary information. / n. Their kind actions were beyond reproach.

reticent (ree-ty-sent) adj. quiet; not speaking much. The girl was reticent as a child, but now she is the public spokesperson for the company.

reverence n. a high regard or respect for someone or something. The man was held in reverence within the community for his philanthropy.

Multiple Choice Quiz # 10

1. The media *promulgated* the story.
   a. made up   b. recanted   c. spread   d. edited

2. A *query* was made into the rising cost of gasoline.
   a. an investigation   b. a crime   c. a statement   d. none of the above

3. There were many *propitious* locations for the proposed athletic center.
   a. problematic   b. favorable   c. reasonable   d. nice

4. The *recalcitrant* student was sent to the principal's office.
   a. friendly   b. dangerous   c. outspoken   d. refusing to obey

5. Tendency to relapse into prior behavior or repeat an act, especially a crime.
   a. rapacious   b. reticent   c. recidivism   d. recalcitrant

6. A natural tendency toward something.
   a. propensity   b. propitious   c. reverence   d. quintessence

7. Related to numbers or the amount of something.
   a. qualitative   b. quantitative   c. query   d. propensity

8. Related to the quality or deeper knowledge about something.
   a. qualitative   b. quantitative   c. query   d. propensity

9. The purest form or best example of something.
   a. rapacious   b. quintessence   c. reverence   d. quantitative

10. Carjacking is a *rapacious* act.
    a. taking something by force   b. subtle   c. obvious   d. scary

11. A place where things are stored.
    a. query   b. promulgation   c. repository   d. rapprochement

12. Quiet, not speaking much.
    a. rapprochement   b. reverence   c. rapacious   d. reticent

13. Payment or monetary compensation for something.
    a. rapprochement   b. reverence   c. remuneration   d. propensity

14. To express disapproval
    a. reproach   b. reticent   c. query   d. rapprochement

15. A high regard or respect for something.
    a. reticent   b. reverence   c. rapprochement   d. none of the above

254

sagacious (su-gay-shus) adj. perceptive, shrewd or keen; able to see or discern things. The detective was very sagacious.

sanctimonious (sayn-kti-moe-nee-ous) adj. acting morally superior in an effort to show off. His acceptance speech was quite sanctimonious and not very humble.

sanction (sank-shon) v. 1. to officially approve of something. The tournament was sanctioned by the tennis association. 2. penalty imposed on one nation by another nation.

sanguine (san- gwu-ine) adj. happy, confident, or optimistic, especially in a bad situation. The girl was quite sanguine despite the fact her plans got cancelled.

sapience (say-pee-ens) n. wisdom. The sapience of her idea was not appreciated until much later. /**sapient** adj.

sardonic adj. showing much disapproval or contempt. The sardonic look on the mother's face explained everything.

semblance n. the appearance of something. The house had a semblance of <u>Victorian</u> charm.

serendipitous (se-ren-di-pi-tus) adj. by chance or luck. The entrance to the secret cave was a serendipitous discovery. / **serendipity** n.

sophist (soe-fist) n. a person who engages in clever but deceptive reasoning. The word "sophist" is derived from the Sophists, who were highly skilled teachers of philosophy in ancient Greece.

stoic (stoe-ik) adj. not showing emotion, especially pain or pleasure; always calm. The woman always had a stoic look on her face.

supposition n. the act of supposing or basing something on a possibility or uncertainty. The jury's initial supposition of innocence was based upon the defendant's proof that he was out of town when the crime occurred.

surreptitious (ser-ep-ti-shus) adj. acting with secrecy or without permission. A surreptitious attempt was made to obtain more money for the project.

syllogism (sil-oe-jiz-um) n. form of reasoning that draws conclusion based on two premises or truths; reason based on <u>deduction</u>. "Joe goes out for lunch every Friday. Joe went out for lunch today. Therefore, today must be Friday." Shakespeare was known for his syllogisms in his writing.

symbiotic (sim-by-o-tik) adj. serving a mutually beneficial purpose. Many life forms on earth have a symbiotic relationship. / **symbiosis** n. / **symbiont** n. one who is in a symbiotic relationship.

synergy (sin-er-jee) n. energy, power, or effort working together to achieve a greater outcome. The construction project was the result of political, financial, and architectural synergy.

systemic (sis-te-mik) adj. related to or affecting the whole system. The problems in the accounting office were systemic because they resulted in budget mistakes for the entire company.

Multiple Choice Quiz # 11

1. Shrewd, perceptive, or discerning.
   a. sanctimonious   b. sagacious   c. serendipitous   d. surreptitious

2. A happy or optimistic nature.
   a. sanguine   b. sardonic   c. serendipitous   d. stoic

3. Showing disapproval or contempt.
   a. stoic   b. sardonic   c. sanguine   d. surreptitious

4. The *sapience* of her suggestions earned her a lot of respect among her colleagues.
   a. wisdom   b. flexibility   c. restraint   d. assertiveness

5. The man's outburst was devoid of even a *semblance* of proper decorum.
   a. appearance of   b. opposite of   c. related to   d. none of the above

6. Winning the lottery was an act of *serendipity*.
   a. hard work   b. effort   c. luck   d. all of the above

7. Belief based on an uncertainty or possibility.
   a. surreptitious   b. sanguine   c. syllogism   d. supposition

8. There are *systemic* problems in the school.
   a. affecting the entire system   b. broad   c. specific   d. serious

9. Serving a mutually beneficial purpose.
   a. synergy   b. symbiotic   c. surreptitious   d. serendipitous

10. The speaker gave a *sanctimonious* speech about morality.
    a. divisive   b. humble   c. morally superior   d. hypocritical

11. The student was *surreptitiously* looking around the teacher's desk.
    a. blatantly   b. openly   c. quietly   d. secretly

12. Joe goes out for lunch every Friday. Joe went out for lunch today. Therefore, today must be Friday." This line of reasoning is an example of a:
    a. sophist   b. synergy   c. supposition   d. syllogism

13. To officially approve of something
    a. sanctimonious   b. sanction   c. serendipitously   d. symbiosis

14. Combination of different factors and forces working together to achieve a greater result.
    a. symbiosis   b. syllogism   c. synergy   d. supposition

15. A person who engages in clever but deceptive reasoning.
    a. sophist   b. symbiont   c. cynic   d. sanguine

256

tangential (tan-jen-tial) adj. in addition to but deviating from the main idea at hand./ **tangentially** adv. Trees use photosynthesis to make food and give off oxygen; tangentially, Bill likes oak trees.

tantamount adj. the same as, equal to. Not paying your bills is tantamount to being irresponsible.

tenable adj. something that can be protected. The fort's tenable location gave it an advantage.

tenuous (ten-yu-us) adj. not firm or serious; weak. The girl had a tenuous excuse for being late.

trepidation n. fear; uneasiness about something. The job interview caused a lot of trepidation.

ubiquitous (yu-bik-kwi-tus) adj. existing or present in all places at all times. Death and taxes are ubiquitous aspects of life.

unadulterated adj. pure; not changed, affected, or contaminated by anything. Listening to the music was unadulterated enjoyment.

unequivocal (un-ee-kwi-vo-kuhl) adj. clear and without doubt or exception. Her final position on the subject was the unequivocal support of the plan.

vacillate (vas-i-late) v. to hesitate or change one's mind often because one is unsure about something. The boss vacillated for weeks over the new program.

venerable (ven-er-uh-bul) adj. respected, important; deserving merit because of quality, age, or accomplishment. The venerable artist was rarely seen in public anymore.

veracity (ve-ras-i-tee) n. the correctness or truthfulness of something. The scientist's veracity was questioned when the experiment failed.

vicarious (vy-kair-ee-us) adj. experiencing something through another; indirect. Watching his son play baseball is a vicarious way for the man to enjoy sports again. / **vicariously** adv. He is living vicariously through his son.

vicissitude (vi-sis-i-tude) n. a change in the condition or situation of something. The vicissitudes of politics can easily turn an unpopular candidate into the most popular candidate.

virtuosity (ver-chu-os-i-tee) adj. having a special skill or interested in some aspect of the fine arts or high culture, such as music or art. The woman's virtuosity impressed everybody.

visceral (vis-er-al) adj. figurative for emotional or affecting feelings rather rational thought. The lovely music had a visceral effect on the audience.

vituperative (vie-too-per-a-tive) adj. nasty; mean; abusive. The challenger launched vituperative attacks against the current mayor during the campaign hoping to score political points.

vociferous (voe-si-fer-us) adj. characterized by quick, emotional, or loud outbursts. The parents became more vociferous at the school board meeting because they were getting so upset over the new policies.

Multiple Choice Quiz # 12

1. The Chicago bungalow is *ubiquitous* throughout the city.
   a. existing all over   b. non-existent   c. expensive   d. important

2. Experiencing something indirectly through another.
   a. virtuosity   b. visceral   c. vociferous   d. vicariously

3. The *vituperative* nature of the speech caught everyone off guard.
   a. gentle   b. polite   c. abusive   d. dangerous

4. Truthfulness or correctness of something.
   a. visceral   b. virtuosity   c. veracity   d. venerable

5. His emotional response was a clear sign that something was wrong.
   a. visceral   b. veracity   c. venerability   d. virtuosity

6. The *venerable* actor was never seen in public anymore.
   a. respected   b. reclusive   c. famous   d. outspoken

7. The *vociferous* parents became more outspoken at the school board meeting.
   a. angry   b. displaying loud outbursts   c. confused   d. none of the above

8. Clear and without exception
   a. unadulterated   b. tenuous   c. unequivocal   d. visceral

9. Pure and not changed or contaminated
   a. unadulterated   b. tenuous   c. unequivocal   d. visceral

10. The girl's *trepidation* was clear to all her friends.
    a. anger   b. calmness   c. resistance   d. fear

11. The principal was in a *tenuous* position over all the problems in the school.
    a. strong   b. serious   c. weak   d. dangerous

12. The same as or equal to
    a. tantamount   b. tenable   c. tangential   d. tenuous

13. "Bill had a baseball game today; _____, Bill likes Star Wars."
    a. tantamount   b. unequivocally   c. ubiquitously   d. tangentially

14. The fort held a *tenable* position at the mouth of the river.
    a. weak   b. dangerous   c. defendable   d. high

15. To change one's mind often
    a. vicissitude   b. vacillate   c. visceral   d. virtuosity

Common Useful Conversions of Measure

1 mile = 5,280 feet

1 mile=1.6 kilometers

1 acre = 43,560 square feet (208.7 ft. by 208.7 ft.)

1 meter = 39.37 inches

1 centimeter = .3937 inches

1 millimeter = .03937 inches

1 inch= 2.54 centimeters

1 yard = 3 feet

1 fathom = 6 feet

1 knot = 6,076 feet

1 league = 18,228 feet (3.44 miles or 3 knots)

1 furlong = 660 feet

16 ounces = 1 pound

1 kilogram = 2.2 pounds

1 ton = 2,000 pounds

1 gram = .035 ounces

1 gram = 1,000 kilograms

1 liter = 1.057 quarts

1 liter = 1,000 milliliters

1 gallon (4 quarts) = 3.785 liters

2 pints = 1 quart

1 pint = ½ quart

4 quarts = 1 gallon

31 ½ gallons = 1 barrel

12 units = 1 dozen

12 dozen = 1 gross

3 teaspoons = 1 tablespoon

States and Postal Abbreviations and Capitals

Alabama (AL)	Montgomery
Alaska (AK)	Juneau
Arizona (AZ)	Phoenix
Arkansas (AR)	Little Rock
California (CA)	Sacramento
Colorado (CO)	Denver
Connecticut (CT)	Hartford
Delaware (DE)	Dover
Florida (FL)	Tallahassee
Georgia (GA)	Atlanta
Hawaii (HI)	Honolulu
Idaho (ID)	Boise
Illinois (IL)	Springfield
Indiana (IN)	Indianapolis
Iowa (IA)	Des Moines
Kansas (KS)	Topeka
Kentucky (KY)	Frankfort
Louisiana (LA)	Baton Rouge
Maine (ME)	Augusta
Maryland (MD)	Annapolis
Massachusetts (MA)	Boston
Michigan (MI)	Lansing
Minnesota (MN)	St. Paul
Mississippi (MS)	Jackson
Missouri (MO)	Jefferson City
Montana (MT)	Helena
Nebraska (NE)	Lincoln
Nevada (NV)	Carson City
New Hampshire (NH)	Concord
New Jersey (NJ)	Trenton
New Mexico (NM)	Santa Fe
New York (NY)	Albany
North Carolina (NC)	Raleigh
North Dakota (ND)	Bismarck
Ohio (OH)	Columbus
Oklahoma (OK)	Oklahoma City
Oregon (OR)	Salem
Pennsylvania (PA)	Harrisburg
Rhode Island (RI)	Providence
South Carolina (SC)	Columbia
South Dakota (SD)	Pierre
Tennessee (TN)	Nashville
Texas (TX)	Austin
Utah (UT)	Salt Lake City
Vermont (VT)	Montpelier
Virginia (VA)	Richmond
Washington (WA)	Olympia
West Virginia (WV)	Charleston
Wisconsin (WI)	Madison
Wyoming (WY)	Cheyenne

Answers to Fill-in-the-Blank Quizzes

Quiz # 1
1. acceleration
2. amphibian
3. carcinogen
4. catalyst
5. centrifugal
6. centripetal
7. chronic
8. density
9. dilute
10. fossil fuel
11. forensics
12. germination
13. greenhouse
14. anthropology
15. friction

Quiz # 2
1. hemispheres
2. heredity
3. indigenous
4. inherit
5. luminous
6. metamorphosis
7. mutation
8. opaque
9. permeable
10. permutation

Quiz # 3
1. propagation
2. qualitative
3. quantitative
4. quantum
5. seismic
6. sphere
7. spectrum
8. subterranean
9. symbiotic
10. synthesis

Quiz # 4
1. terrestrial
2. vertebrate
3. velocity
4. volume
5. translucent
6. trait

Quiz # 5
1. allegory
2. allusion
3. anachronism
4. antagonist
5. anthropomorphism
6. colloquialism
7. connotation
8. denouement
9. dramatic irony
10. genres
11. climax
12. fate

Quiz # 6
1. hyperbole
2. irony
3. juxtaposition
4. metaphor
5. onomatopoeia
6. oxymoron
7. paradox
8. personification
9. protagonist
10. resolution
11. rising action
12. hubris

Quiz # 7
1. simile
2. soliloquy
3. irony
4. tone
5. tragedies
6. vernacular

Quiz # 8
1. acute
2. algorithm
3. adjacent angle
4. array
5. absolute value
6. bell curve
7. binomial
8. area

Quiz # 9
1. circumference
2. coefficient
3. complementary
4. congruent
5. constant
6. bisect
7. Cartesian coordinates
8. denominator
9. calculus
10. common denominator

Quiz # 10
1. inequality
2. hypotenuse
3. function
4. exponentially
5. exponent
6. diameter
7. improper fraction
8. integer
9. interval
10. derivative

Quiz # 11
1. obtuse
2. Isosceles
3. mean
4. linear
5. numerator
6. ordered pair
7. mode
8. median
9. multiples
10. irrational number

Fill-in-the-Blank Quiz Answers

Quiz # 12
1. parallel
2. perpendicular
3. probability theory
4. plane
5. polygon
6. polynomial
7. product
8. quotient
9. prime number
10. Pythagorean theorem
11. radius
12. range
13. quadratic equation
14. outlier
15. parabola

Quiz # 13
1. vertex
2. supplementary
3. ratio
4. proportion
5. right angle
6. symmetrical
7. vector
8. variable
9. volume
10. reciprocal
11. scalene

Quiz # 14
1. appraisal
2. appreciation
3. accrue
4. amortized
5. balloon payment
6. assets
7. balance
8. annual percentage rate
9. adjustable rate mortgage
10. aggregate
11. annuity

Quiz # 15
1. bonds
2. cosigner
3. commodity
4. commerce
5. capital
6. collateral
7. credit score
8. cooperative
9. commercial
10. certificate of deposit

Quiz # 16
1. currency
2. disclosure
3. equity
4. economies of scale
5. default
6. depreciation
7. deficit
8. dividend
9. compound interest
10. debit
11. exchange rate
12. economy
13. exports

Quiz # 17
1. fixed rate
2. funds
3. graduated payment
4. federal funds rate
5. finance
6. finance charge
7. Federal Deposit Insurance Corporation
8. Federal Reserve
9. fiscal policy
10. futures market

Quiz # 18
1. gross
2. imports
3. inflation
4. gross domestic product
5. Home Equity Line of Credit
6. mature
7. market
8. levy
9. individual retirement account
10. interest payment
11. margin

Quiz # 19
1. recession
2. prorated
3. principal
4. reserves
5. points
6. net
7. pension
8. mortgage
9. profit margin
10. mutual fund

Fill-in-the Blank Quiz Answers

Quiz # 20
1. speculator
2. shareholder
3. revolving credit
4. stock
5. trust
6. yield
7. variable rate
8. demand
9. supply
10. tariff
11. tendered
12. securities
13. trade deficit
14. time value of money
15. capitalism
16. socialism

Quiz # 21
1. brokered
2. articulate
3. allocate
4. adapt
5. advocate
6. acumen
7. accountable
8. accomplishments
9. address
10. analysis

Quiz # 22
1. collaborate
2. communication
3. compile
4. conceptualize
5. data-driven
6. cultivate
7. coordinate
8. consensus
9. consolidate
10. conserve

Quiz # 23
1. delegate
2. devise
3. delineate
4. efficient
5. diagnose
6. expedite
7. execute
8. evaluate
9. demonstrate
10. develop

Quiz # 24
1. expertise
2. initiate or institute
3. galvanize
4. facilitate
5. increase
6. institute or initiate
7. innovative
8. generate
9. fidelity
10. integration
11. inspire
12. foster

Quiz # 25
1. integrity
2. launched
3. mediate
4. logistics
5. outpaced
6. procure
7. project management
8. organizational
9. promote
10. proposal
11. prospects
12. prospects

Quiz # 26
1. secure
2. revitalize
3. results-oriented
4. revise
5. resolve
6. restructure
7. self-starter
8. reduce
9. pursue
10. shared-decision making

Quiz # 27
1. value
2. skills set
3. transformed
4. sustain
5. specialize
6. validate
7. yield
8. transparency
9. stakeholders
10. utilize
11. timely
12. solution

Answers to Matching Quizzes

Quiz # 1: 1c 2d 3i 4b 5g 6h 7j 8a 9f 10e

Quiz # 2: 1e 2h 3f 4b 5g 6i 7c 8j 9a 10d 11k

Quiz # 3: 1i 2h 3o 4j 5l 6n 7m 8k 9d 10e 11b 12c 13f 14a 15g

Quiz # 4: 1l 2h 3o 4i 5n 6j 7k 8m 9c 10e 11b 12f 13g 14a 15d

Quiz # 5: 1f 2n 3a 4c 5m 6b 7d 8l 9o 10j 11h 12k 13g 14e 15i

Quiz # 6: 1f 2b 3l 4n 5m 6j 7c 8d 9e 10o 11h 12g 13i 14a 15k

Quiz # 7: 1o 2d 3m 4j 5b 6l 7k 8n 9e 10g 11a 12c 13f 14h 15i

Quiz # 8: 1l 2n 3a 4m 5k 6h 7d 8i 9e 10g 11o 12f 13j 14c 15b

Quiz # 9: 1h 2o 3k 4n 5m 6l 7b 8g 9c 10i 11f 12j 13a 14d 15e

Quiz # 10: 1h 2m 3o 4b 5c 6i 7d 8e 9f 10g 11j 12n 13k 14l 15a

Quiz # 11: 1m 2j 3k 4l 5n 6o 7d 8c 9a 10e 11f 12g 13h 14b 15i

Quiz # 12: 1j 2l 3n 4k 5i 6d 7e 8c 9f 10g 11h 12o 13b 14a 15m

Quiz # 13: 1o 2l 3k 4n 5b 6c 7d 8e 9g 10f 11m 12h 13i 14j 15a

Quiz # 14: 1n 2e 3c 4m 5j 6f 7d 8b 9h 10l 11i 12g 13o 14a 15k

Quiz # 15: 1f 2j 3m 4o 5k 6g 7c 8d 9b 10e 11l 12h 13i 14n 15a

Quiz # 16. 1n 2l 3a 4i 5b 6m 7c 8d 9e 10o 11f 12g 13h 14k 15j

Quiz # 17: 1e 2i 3l 4o 5k 6j 7f 8a 9b 10n 11c 12d 13g 14h 15m

Quiz # 18: 1k 2n 3o 4j 5c 6l 7f 8d 9e 10g 11h 12m 13i 14a 15b

Quiz # 19: 1n 2f 3m 4i 5l 6o 7h 8g 9c 10b 11a 12 d 13j 14e 15k

Quiz # 20: 1j 2k 3f 4b 5n 6i 7g 8o 9l 10m 11h 12d 13e 14c 15a

Quiz # 21: 1i 2g 3k 4j 5h 6d 7c 8e 9f 10n 11m 12o 13b 14a 15l

Quiz # 22: 1f 2g 3n 4l 5b 6m 7d 8c 9e 10o 11h 12i 13j 14k 15a

Quiz # 23: 1h 2i 3m 4o 5g 6n 7l 8e 9b 10f 11j 12k 13d 14a 15c

264

Quiz # 24: 1n 2k 3i 4g 5l 6h 7b 8c 9d 10m 11o 12j 13f 14e 15a

Quiz # 25: 1j 2k 3m 4o 5a 6b 7c 8n 9i 10d 11e 12f 13g 14h 15l

Quiz # 26: 1e 2n 3f 4o 5b 6c 7i 8j 9m 10a 11l 12d 13k 14g 15h

Quiz # 27: 1i 2n 3o 4j 5l 6c 7k 8b 9d 10e 11f 12g 13a 14h 15m

Quiz # 28: 1g 2k 3l 4i 5m 6h 7a 8b 9c 10d 11f 12e 13j 14o 15n

Quiz # 29: 1l 2j 3a 4m 5b 6n 7c 8o 9d 10e 11f 12g 13h 14i 15k

Quiz # 30: 1h 2e 3k 4n 5l 6o 7j 8m 9i 10c 11d 12f 13g 14b 15a

Quiz # 31: 1f 2l 3k 4n 5b 6m 7g 8c 9a 10d 11h 12i 13e 14j 15o

Quiz # 32: 1o 2k 3j 4n 5l 6e 7m 8c 9d 10f 11a 12g 13h 14i 15b

Quiz # 33: 1e 2g 3j 4i 5k 6h 7a 8f 9b 10d 11n 12c 13l 14m 15o

Quiz # 34: 1g 2i 3k 4j 5a 6c 7b 8o 9h 10f 11d 12e 13l 14n 15m

Quiz # 35: 1g 2j 3a 4i 5l 6o 7n 8m 9b 10d 11f 12e 13h 14k 15c

Quiz # 36: 1h 2m 3j 4i 5a 6c 7b 8f 9k 10d 11e 12g 13n 14l 15o

Answers to Multiple Choice Questions

Quiz # 1:   1d 2a 3a 4c 5b 6c 7d 8a 9b 10b 11a 12c 13d 14b 15a

Quiz # 2:   1a 2b 3c 4a 5c 6d 7d 8b 9c 10a 11b 12d 13d 14d 15a

Quiz # 3:   1c 2b 3d 4b 5a 6b 7d 8d 9d 10d 11a 12c 13d 14a 15b

Quiz # 4:   1c 2d 3b 4d 5b 6c 7a 8d 9a 10b 11c 12d 13b 14c 15b

Quiz # 5:   1b 2a 3d 4a 5c 6d 7b 8a 9c 10a 11d 12b 13d 14c 15b

Quiz # 6:   1b 2d 3d 4a 5a 6b 7d 8a 9d 10a 11d 12c 13d 14a 15b

Quiz # 7:   1d 2c 3a 4d 5b 6b 7a 8a 9c 10b 11d 12b 13d 14a 15b

Quiz # 8:   1b 2a 3c 4c 5d 6a 7d 8b 9d 10b 11a 12c 13a 14b 15a

Quiz # 9:   1c 2c 3b 4c 5d 6a 7b 8d 9a 10d 11d 12c 13a 14b 15d

Quiz # 10: 1c 2a 3b 4d 5c 6a 7b 8a 9b 10a 11c 12d 13c 14a 15b

Quiz # 11: 1b 2a 3b 4a 5a 6c 7d 8a 9b 10c 11d 12d 13b 14c 15a

Quiz # 12: 1a 2d 3c 4c 5a 6a 7b 8c 9a 10d 11c 12a 13d 14c 15b

Answers to Crossword Puzzles
History and Social Science Crossword Puzzle

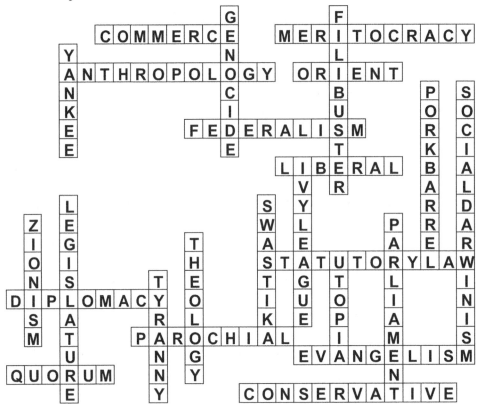

ACROSS	DOWN
3 the buying and selling of goods	1 the killing of an entire group or race
4 system that values people with the highest skills	2 long speech that delays an action
6 the study of man	5 person from the northern/northeastern part of the United States
7 the East as in China or other parts of Asia	8 laws or deals that benefit a specific area or group
10 system of government where power is divided between states and the federal government	9 idea that society progresses through a natural competition among people
11 having an open mind or favoring more government intervention	12 group of old and prominent universities
18 laws made by a law-making body	13 law-making body of government
21 communicating carefully between people or countries	14 symbol of the Nazi Party
22 associated with a church	15 movement for a Jewish homeland in Palestine
23 the spreading of religion	16 law-making body of government in many European countries
24 the smallest number of people needed to conduct business	17 the study of God and religion
25 resisting change or favoring little government intervention	19 a perfect place
	20 harsh or unfair use of power

Puzzle made at puzzle-maker.com

Religion Vocabulary Crossword

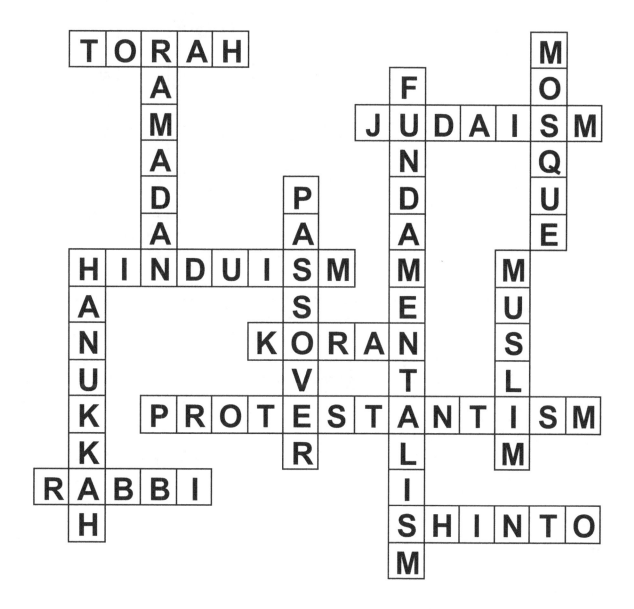

ACROSS	DOWN
1 the Hebrew name for the Old Testament	2 Muslim religious holiday
5 religion of the Hebrews	3 Muslim church
7 religion of many people in India	4 interpreting the Bible word-for-word
9 the holy book of Islam	6 Jewish religious holiday celebrating
10 Christian religion that split with the	deliverance from captivity
Catholic Church in the 1500s	7 Jewish holiday lasting eight days
11 teacher of Jewish religion	8 believer in Islam
12 the oldest Japanese religion	

Puzzle made at puzzle-maker.com

AA Crossword Puzzle AA

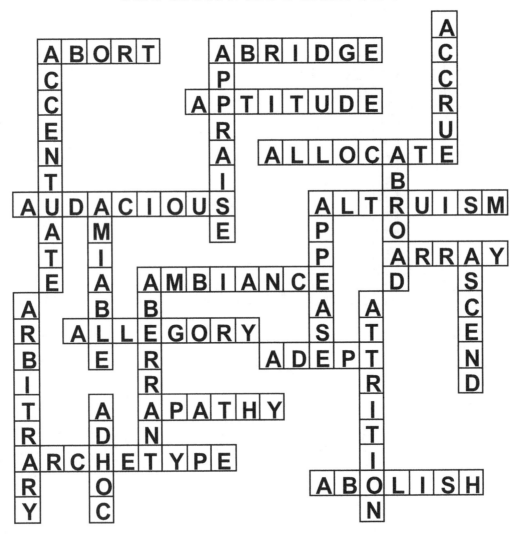

ACROSS	DOWN
2 to stop	1 to increase over time
3 to shorten	2 to emphasize or point out
4 skill or competence in something	3 to estimate value
5 to divide up and distribute	6 in another country
7 bold, courageous	8 likeable, friendly
9 unselfish concern for others	9 to give in to someone
10 a wide range of something	11 to move up or climb
12 atmosphere in a room	12 odd, irregular, not normal
15 story that symbolizes something else	13 going with one's personal feelings, not well thought out
16 good at something	14 process of decreasing in number of time
18 lack of feeling for something	17 on a case-by-case basis
19 original form of something	
20 to end or do away with something	

Puzzle made at puzzle-maker.com

BB Crossword Puzzle BB

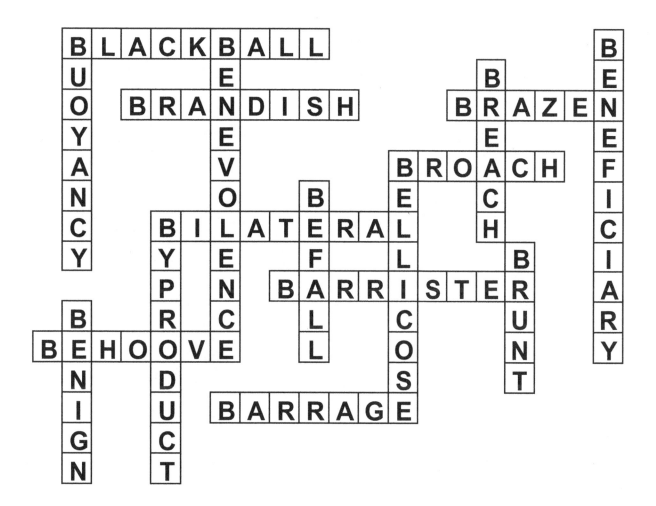

ACROSS	DOWN
1 to work to exclude someone from something	1 the ability to float
5 to take out and show in a hostile way	2 kindness or good will
6 bold and sassy	3 person who benefits from something
7 to bring up a subject	4 to force an opening or break n something
9 having two sides or two opinions	7 quarrelsome or argumentative
11 a lawyer in an upper court in England	8 to affect or happen to
13 to be in one's best interest	9 the effect or result of something
14 an attack with weapons at once	10 the full force of something
	12 not harmful or life-threatening

Puzzle made at puzzle-maker.com

CC Crossword Puzzle CC

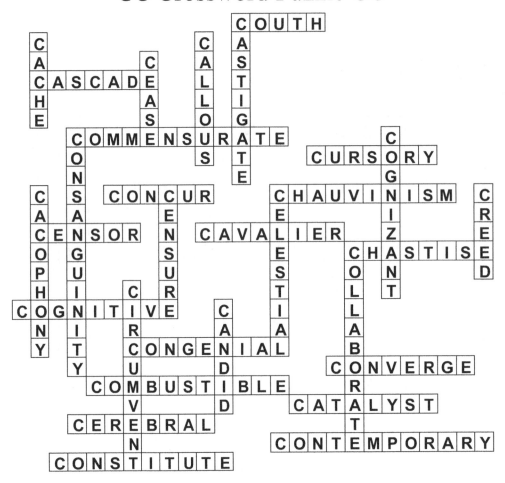

ACROSS	DOWN
1 sophisticated, cultured, or refined	1 to criticize harshly
5 to flow downward	2 place where similar things are stored
6 in the proper amount, appropriate	3 hard or rough, showing now emotion
8 not thorough or complete	4 to stop doing something
10 to agree with	6 related by blood or ancestry
12 belief that one gender is better than the other	7 to be aware of
14 to cut out something considered unacceptable	9 loud, harsh, or annoying sounds
15 a lazy or uninterested manner	11 to blame or rebuke a person
16 to punish or criticize for improvement	12 related to the stars, space, or the sky
18 related to thinking or thinking process	13 statement of belief
20 pleasant or friendly	16 to work together
21 to meet or come together at a point	17 to get around or avoid something
22 capable of burning	19 to be honest, frank, or open
23 something that causes a reaction or change	
24 related to the brain, using reason over emotion	
25 of the current or same time period	
26 to form or make	

Puzzle made at puzzle-maker.com

DD Crossword Puzzle DD

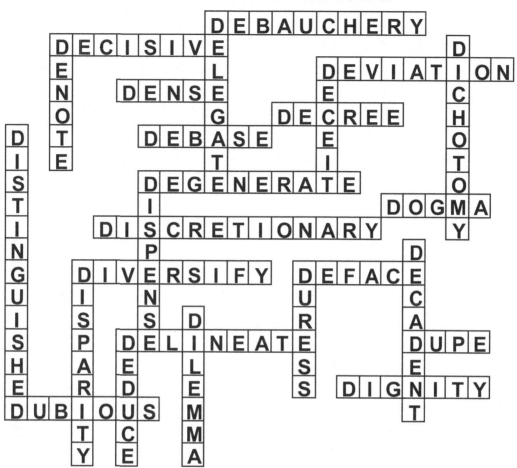

ACROSS	DOWN
2 not sincere or genuine, not clear or certain	1 accepted values or belief system
4 to state firmly	3 to grow worse
9 an imbalance of some type	5 situation requiring a choice between two bad options
14 to ruin the appearance of something	6 left to one's own decision
15 standing noticeably apart from others	7 something not honest or true
17 person easily tricked or fooled	8 to lower the value or importance, to diminish
18 process of moving away from something	10 to give out
21 to assign a duty someone else	11 lacking good taste, ethics, or morality
22 clear, unchallenged	12 using force to achieve cooperation
23 to indicate	13 lifestyle of sinful pleasure
	15 self-respect
	16 having differing or opposing ideas
	17 to create a variety
	18 to clearly show or explain
	19 to figure out using logic and reason
	20 thick or closely arranged

Puzzle made at puzzle-maker.com

EE Crossword Puzzle EE

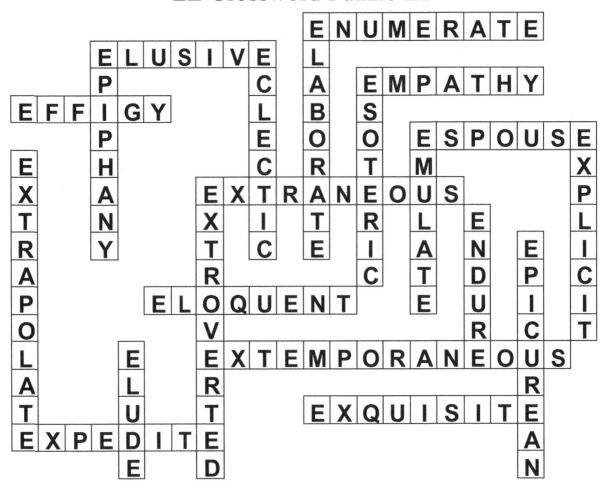

ACROSS	DOWN
1 to list one-by-one	1 complicated, well thought out
2 hard to find or catch	2 sudden exposure to knowledge, an idea, or religious experience
4 an understanding of another's thoughts and feelings	3 using a variety of ideas, methods, or materials
5 a likeness or image of something	4 something that only a few people would understand
6 to adopt or make use of something	6 to copy or to the same thing
9 unrelated or not part of the topic at hand	7 very detailed or clear
12 sophisticated in speech or writing	8 to draw conclusions from what is already known
14 without planning or preparation, spontaneous	9 likes to be around people, very outgoing
15 wonderful or brilliant	10 to put up with or suffer through
16 to speed up a process	11 having expensive tastes or enjoying luxurious items
	13 to avoid

Puzzle made at puzzle-maker.com

FF Crossword Puzzle FF

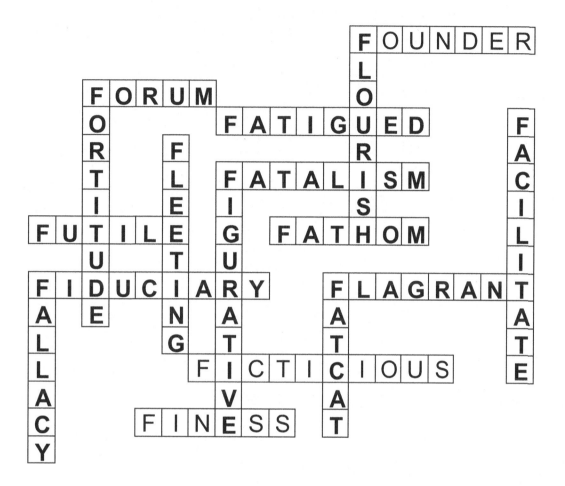

ACROSS	DOWN
1 to struggle in a clumsy manner	1 to grow and do quite well
2 opportunity for public discussion	2 ability to deal with pain, hardship, or
3 worn out from hard work	challenges
6 belief that people have no control over	4 to lead, help, or oversee something
things	5 temporary, passing, not lasting
7 pointless, without hope of achievement	6 non-literal meaning of something
8 to understand	9 something that is not true
9 something that is held in trust	10 figurative for an importance person with many
10 something obviously done on purpose	privileges
or without regard	
11 imaginary, not real, made up	
12 skill at handling a delicate or tough	
situation	

Puzzle made at puzzle-maker.com

GG Crossword Puzzle GG

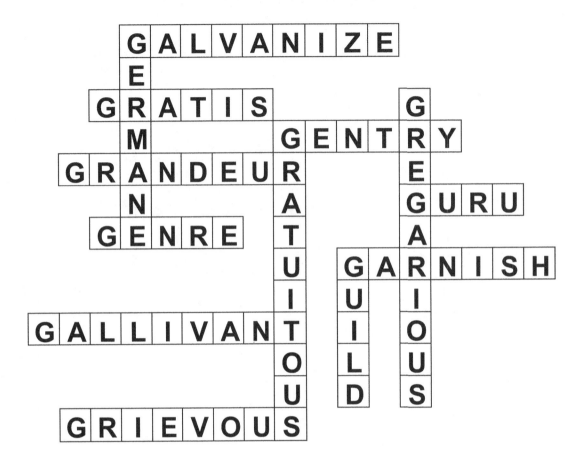

ACROSS	DOWN
1 to energize or spur into action	1 of importance or related to the topic
2 free	3 happy to be around others, outgoing
4 the noble, wealthy, or sophisticated class	4 given for no apparent reason or free of charge
5 importance, greatness	8 group of similar people or workers organized together for a common benefit
6 spiritual or influential teacher in something	
7 type of category or classification	
8 to withhold money as payment for a debt	
9 roam around looking for excitement	
10 serious in a bad or upsetting way	

Puzzle made at puzzle-maker.com

HH Crossword Puzzle HH

ACROSS	DOWN
1 concerned with the well-being or good treatment of people	1 person who does not do as he tells others to do
5 tendency to remain balanced, stable, or neutral	2 up to this point
6 looking worn out or tired	3 eager for more information or to learn for themselves
7 careless, not thorough	4 ordering of things according to importance

Puzzle made at puzzle-maker.com

LL Crossword Puzzle LL

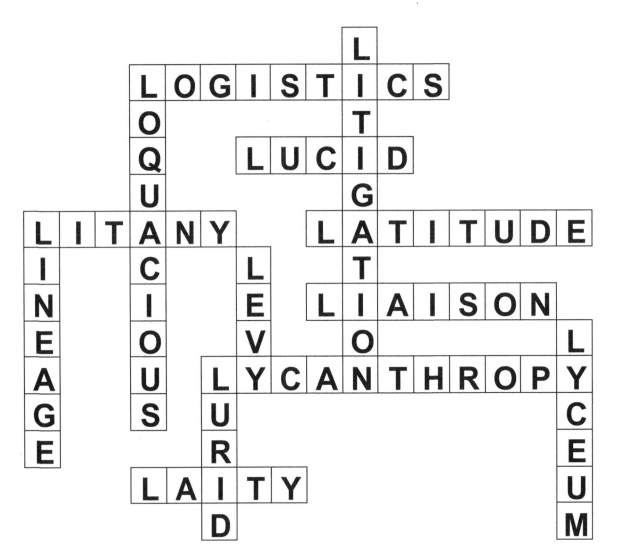

ACROSS	DOWN
2 the planning and carrying out of tasks	1 legal proceedings, process of legal action
3 aware, coherent, making sense	
4 large number of things	2 talking a lot
5 freedom to act or think	4 line of descent from one's ancestors
7 secret meeting between people	6 to require that something be paid
9 mental disorder in which a person thinks he is a wolf	8 place where lectures and other educational gatherings take place
10 people associated with a church but not part of the priesthood	9 unpleasantly vivid, shocking, explicit

Puzzle made at puzzle-maker.com

MM Crossword Puzzle MM

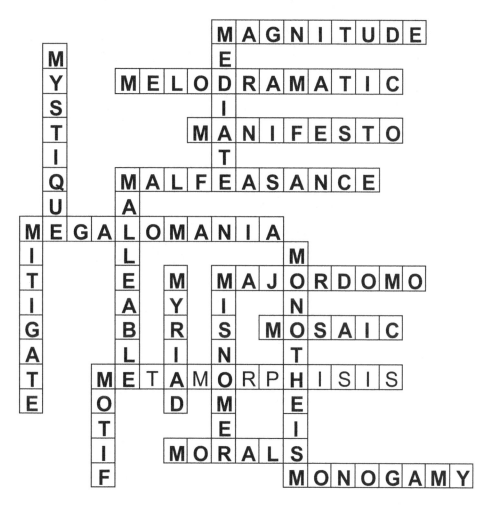

ACROSS	DOWN
1 importance, size, or degree of something	1 to help solve a disagreement between people
3 showing exaggerated emotions for effect	2 having a quality of mystery or intrigue
4 public statement, often written, of one's beliefs	5 able to be shaped or influenced, adaptable
5 wrongdoing doing by elected officials or those held in public trust	6 to lesson or make less severe
6 obsession associated with one's own power or greatness	7 belief in one god
9 paid, live-in person in charge of a large household or estate	8 a large number or variety of something
10 artwork made from arranging colorful tiles	9 wrong way of describing something
11 change in structure or appearance	11 the theme or main idea in an artistic work
12 standards of right and wrong and good and bad	
13 being married to or having sexual relations with only one person	

Puzzle made at puzzle-maker.com

NN Crossword Puzzle NN

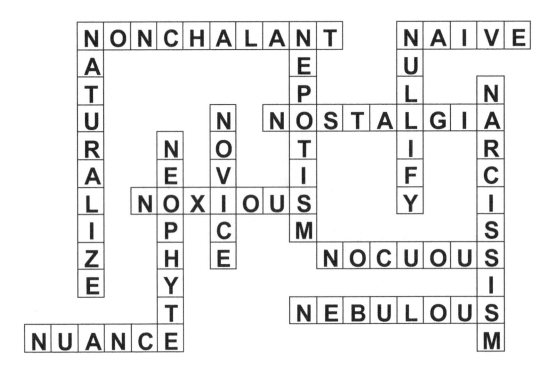

	ACROSS	DOWN
1	in a calm and casual manner	1 to make an immigrant an official citizen of the country
3	not experienced in the ways of the world, too trusting	2 showing favoritism to one's relatives
6	fond feelings for the past	3 to render something useless or invalid
8	poisonous or harmful	4 great love of oneself
9	noxious, harmful, poisonous	5 a beginner, someone not good at something because they are new to it
10	unclear or uncertain, vague	7 a beginner
11	slight difference in the way something looks, acts, or functions	

Puzzle made at puzzle-maker.com

OO Crossword Puzzle OO

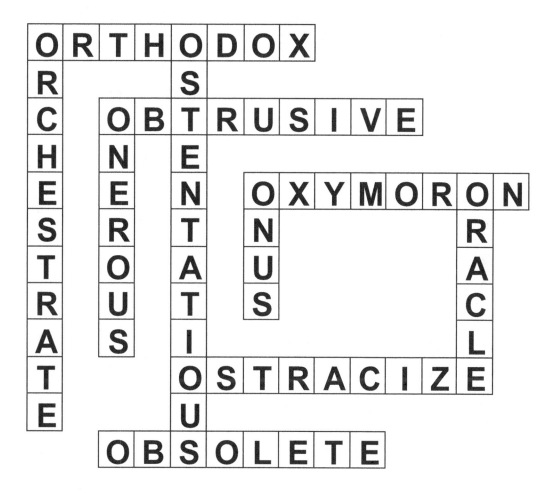

ACROSS	DOWN
1 traditional, commonly accepted	1 to manage or arrange things
3 interfering when not asked	2 done for show
4 statement that contains a contradiction	3 hard to handle
6 to make unwanted or push out	4 responsibility
7 outdated, no longer useful	5 mystic person who reveals truths

Puzzle made at puzzle-maker.com

PP Crossword Puzzle PP

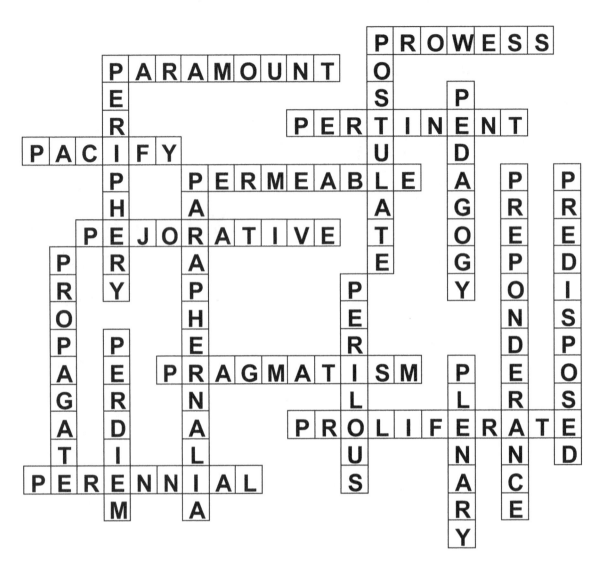

ACROSS	DOWN
1 great skill at something	1 assume something is true without real proof
2 of great importance	2 on the sides
4 related to the matter at hand	3 teaching practices or methods
5 to satisfy or make a person calm	6 personal belongings, especially needed for a specific activity
6 allowing something to pass through	7 of greater quantity
9 likely to make matters worse	8 having a general tendency or attitude toward something
13 favoring a practical approach to problems	10 to increase in number, to spread or promote
15 to spread into other areas	11 dangerous
16 occurring often or over a long period of time	12 per day
	14 complete, with everyone present

Puzzle made at puzzle-maker.com

RR Crossword Puzzle RR

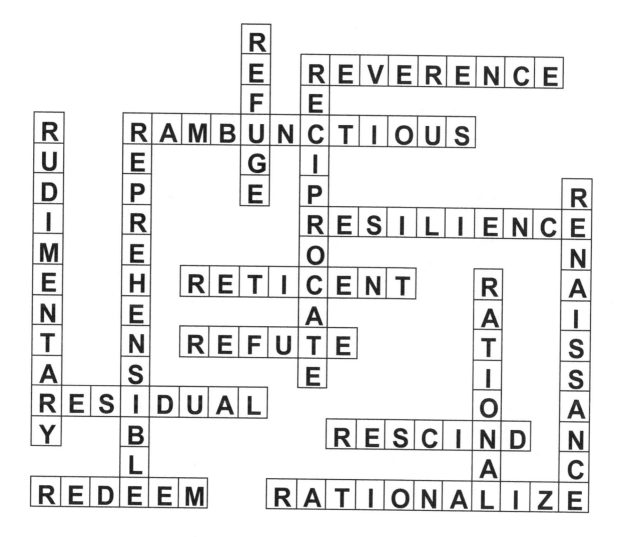

ACROSS	DOWN
2 high regard or respect for someone or something	1 place of safety or protection
4 playful and noisy	2 to do or give in return for something else
6 ability to recover from a setback	3 basic, the basics of something
7 quiet, not willing to speak much	4 deserving of blame
9 to prove something is wrong or false	5 rebirth or a new beginning
10 referring to what is left over	8 something that makes sense, reasonable
11 to take back or cancel	
12 to take or get back	
13 to justify one's thoughts or actions	

Puzzle made at puzzle-maker.com

2282

SS Crossword Puzzle SS

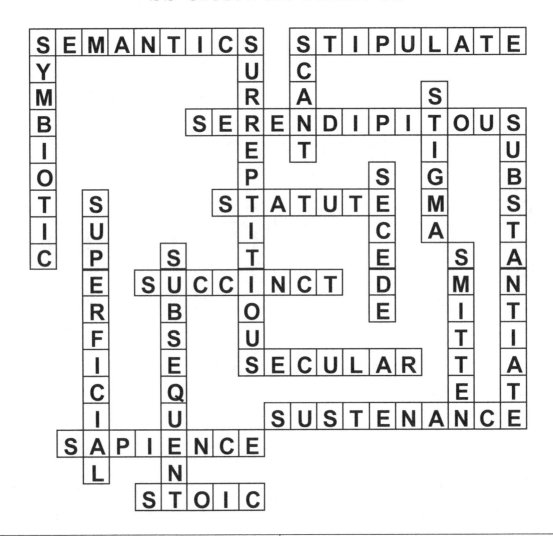

ACROSS	DOWN
1 the study and use of meanings of words	1 serving a mutually beneficial purpose
3 to demand something as part of an agreement	2 acting with secrecy or without permission
5 by luck or by chance	3 a small amount
9 a formal rule or law written by a law-making body	4 something that denotes something negative
12 short and to the point	6 to prove, support, or verify
13 related to worldly matters and not related to religion	7 to withdraw from a group or association
14 means of staying alive or sustaining something such as food or water	8 pertaining only to what appears on the surface
15 wisdom	10 coming after or next in order of occurrence
16 showing no emotions or feelings	11 having strong feelings of affection or attraction

Puzzle made at puzzle-maker.com

TT Crossword Puzzle TT

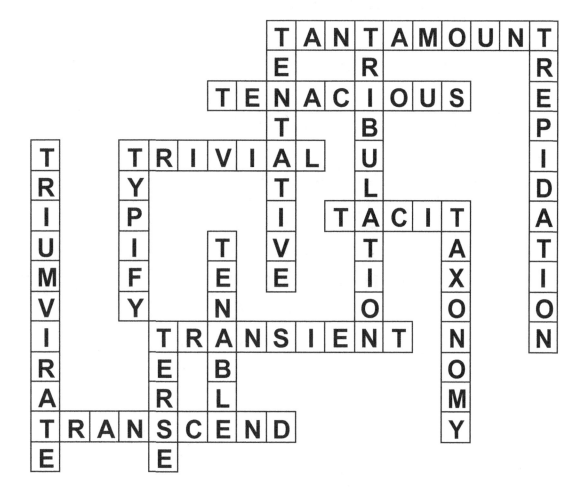

ACROSS	DOWN
1 means the same as	1 no finalized or official yet
4 not giving up	2 great problem or obstacle
6 not that important	3 fear or uneasiness about something
7 assumed or implied without being directly stated	5 government or organization run by three people
10 not lasting or permanent, passing	6 to be an example
11 to go beyond or to surpass	8 the act of classifying things
	9 able to be defended, maintained, or protected
	10 not using many words, brief and unfriendly

Puzzle made at puzzle-maker.com

UU Crossword Puzzle UU

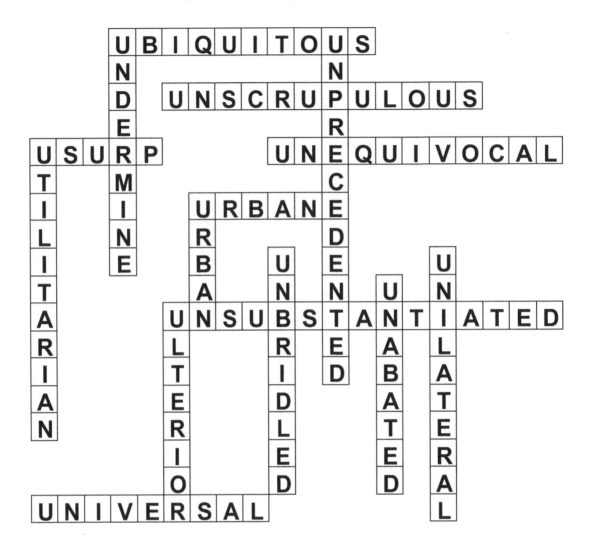

ACROSS	DOWN
1 existing in all places at all times, very common	1 to weaken one's authority by going around them
3 showing a lack of concern for others	2 never happening before, very unusual
4 taking power away from someone without permission	4 serving a purpose or being useful
5 clear and without a doubt or exception	6 related to a city
6 having a sophistication associated with a city	7 uncontrolled or not restrained
10 without any proof or evidence	8 one-sided
11 widely accepted or known, existing all over	9 not weakened or diminished
	10 having another purpose, sometimes a hidden purpose

Puzzle made at puzzle-maker.com

VV Crossword Puzzle VV

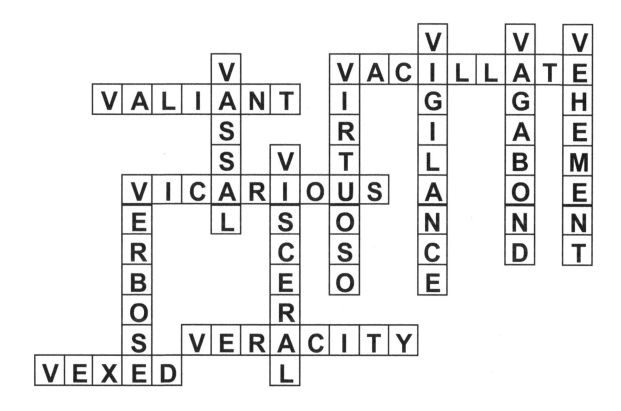

ACROSS	DOWN
5 to hesitate or waver, to change one's mind often or to be indecisive	1 state of caution or alertness
6 brave, showing much effort or courage	2 person who wanders around with no permanent home
8 experienced through the actions or feelings of another	3 firm, forceful, not backing down
9 the correctness or truthfulness of something	4 person who is controlled by another in some way
10 annoyed, agitated, frustrated	5 person highly skilled in something specific, such as music or others arts
	7 affecting feelings rather than rational thought
	8 using too many words

Puzzle made at puzzle-maker.com

Answers to Word Search Puzzles
History and Social Science Word Search

```
D  R  Q  X  W  R  B  P  R  L  M  W  R  Y  B  L  B  J  M
X  Y  F  M  C  B  Q  U  A  C  N  S  G  M  A  W  J  Y  H
F  B  Z  H  W  Y  M  D  R  R  L  O  I  V  T  X  M  T  T
K  H  H  D  T  N  F  L  Z  E  L  F  E  L  C  H  Z  F  R
L  L  P  Z  V  T  F  T  G  O  A  I  R  R  A  W  B  W  R
D  M  A  L  T  E  R  F  E  S  D  U  A  T  N  I  M  Y  C
N  T  R  Y  Y  B  D  H  C  E  R  J  C  M  K  V  C  W  O
T  Y  O  G  J  C  C  I  M  E  Y  L  R  R  E  M  X  O  N
M  G  C  O  K  R  S  Q  C  N  L  N  X  K  A  N  K  Z  S
S  O  H  L  A  M  T  E  N  O  N  K  K  T  V  C  T  D  T
I  L  I  O  D  H  S  A  D  R  N  Q  N  W  W  Y  Y  M  I
L  I  A  I  N  S  R  D  K  G  F  E  M  R  X  C  X  K  T
A  P  L  C  I  Y  M  N  C  Y  K  N  G  Y  C  F  M  F  U
I  O  P  O  T  T  G  A  R  I  S  T  O  C  R  A  C  Y  E
R  R  N  S  T  T  O  T  A  L  I  T  A  R  I  A  N  X  N
E  R  N  S  M  S  I  L  A  R  E  D  E  F  L  W  K  H  R  M  C
P  T  X  R  J  L  P  R  O  P  A  G  A  N  D  A  T  L  Y
M  N  K  E  C  N  A  S  S  I  A  N  E  R  K  R  R  Z  F
I  A  I  N  D  U  S  T  R  I  A  L  I  Z  A  T  I  O  N
```

ANTHROPOLOGY	GENOCIDE	RECESSION
ARCHEOLOGY	IMPERIALISM	RENAISSANCE
ARISTOCRACY	INDUSTRIALIZATION	SOCIALISM
BUREAUCRACY	MEDIEVAL	SOCIOLOGY
CONSTITUENCY	PARLIAMENT	TOTALITARIAN
FASCISM	PAROCHIAL	TYRANNY
FEDERALISM	PROPAGANDA	

Puzzle made at puzzle-maker.com

AA Word Search Puzzle AA

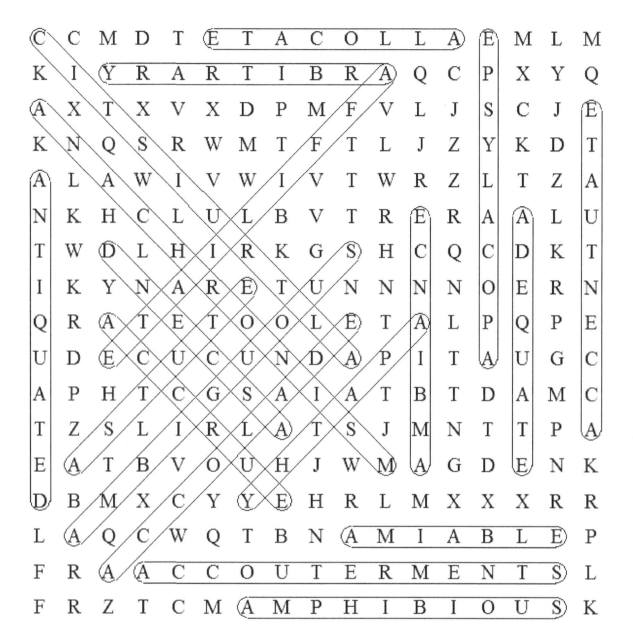

ACCENTUATE	ALTRUISTIC	ANTIQUATED
ACCOLADE	AMBIANCE	APATHY
ACCOUTERMENTS	AMBIGUOUS	APOCALYSPE
ACCRUE	AMIABLE	ARBITRARY
ADEQUATE	AMPHIBIOUS	ASCEND
AFFILIATE	ANACHRONISM	ASTUTE
ALLOCATE		

Puzzle made at puzzle-maker.com

BB Word Search Puzzle BB

```
B  B  E  N  E  V  O  L  E  N  C  E  B  C  R  S
M  U  X  L  L  X  T  Z  R  L  K  K  L  K  U  L
X  R  O  N  F  K  M  V  H  L  K  N  X  O  K  E
K  L  W  Y  F  P  C  L  R  F  D  M  R  K  G  T
T  P  D  R  A  H  F  J  C  B  Y  E  C  A  D  B
N  V  C  F  B  N  M  X  E  H  T  M  R  Y  B  E
B  N  M  N  L  Q  C  N  P  S  K  R  R  N  E  L
J  E  J  J  L  V  C  Y  I  V  A  D  J  L  N  L
N  Q  H  L  T  H  R  O  L  B  C  L  X  A  E  I
D  E  L  O  M  C  B  N  J  Z  Z  H  P  U  F  G
N  K  G  A  O  B  E  G  R  U  D  G  E  G  I  E
Z  C  R  E  C  V  R  V  V  N  G  W  M  N  C  R
R  K  L  Q  I  M  E  T  B  J  M  P  C  I  I  E
K  B  K  P  V  S  T  K  T  W  C  T  B  L  A  N
R  O  T  C  A  F  E  N  E  B  B  K  R  I  R  T
Z  B  T  H  B  Z  W  B  Q  M  K  Q  C  B  Y  C
```

BAFFLE	BENEFICIARY
BARRAGE	BENEVOLENCE
BEGRUDGE	BESIEGE
BEHOOVE	BILINGUAL
BELLIGERENT	BOISTEROUS
BENCHMARK	BUOYANCY
BENEFACTOR	

Puzzle made at puzzle-maker.com

CC Word Search Puzzle CC

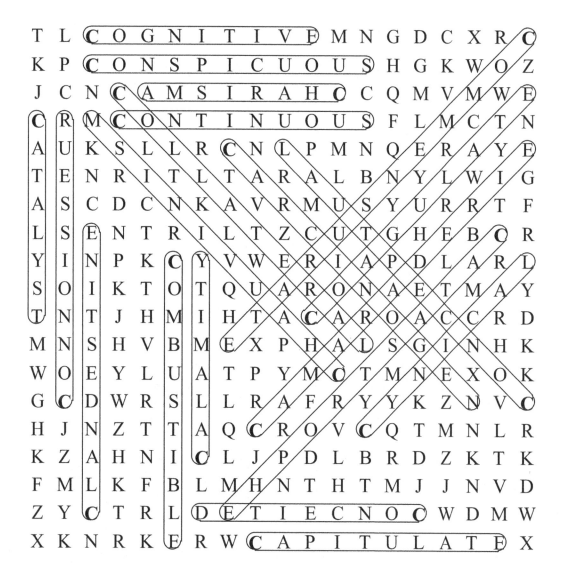

CALAMITY	CHAUVINISM	CONCEITED
CAMARADERIE	CLANDESTINE	CONCEPTUAL
CAPITULATE	COAGULATE	CONNOISSEUR
CARCINOGEN	COGNITIVE	CONSPICUOUS
CATALYST	COLLATERAL	CONTINUOUS
CATASTROPHE	COMBUSTIBLE	CYNICAL
CHARISMA	COMMENSURATE	

Puzzle made at puzzle-maker.com

DD Word Search Puzzle DD

```
N C T N J R L R R R Q W B K H R R F
Y J D C O H S I U G N I T S I D R P
L K I R Q I A E T A I C E R P E D Z
K N S G Z N T Y M Z D C R K T E B G
M L C T O W H A R N Q H M W L R N D
D M R B K B D R I J D Z R I N D X N
I R E Y W E F H G V K E B Q I L N R
S D P M X L D H D M E E C S C E J Y
C G A O Q C E E V I R D P I C V D F
R W N T X A F N G A S E Z N M R T I
E K C O K B I K T R N C E X S A T S
T G Y H Z E A E N S E G E U P L T R
I D P C T D N Z E T I V O R R Q L E
O N Z I J K C T K L F I I M N P R V
N B G D L L E M I N B R L D J K C I
A N H H L R V D H U E S R E P S I D
R D E C E I V E D G N X D V M H V M
Y L T M L P J M D I S B U R S E W J
```

DEBACLE	DEVIATION	DISPENSE
DEBONAIR	DICHOTOMY	DISPERSE
DECEIVE	DILIGENCE	DISTINGUISH
DECIMATE	DISBURSE	DIVERGE
DEFIANCE	DISCERN	DIVERSIFY
DELIBERATE	DISCREPANCY	DUBIOUS
DEPRECIATE	DISCRETIONARY	

Puzzle made at puzzle-maker.com

EE Word Search Puzzle EE

```
N  M  E  F  J  K  M  W  Z  L  E  T  P  K  E  L  E  H
F  S  X  X  E  M  E  P  J  P  V  R  T  T  Q  N  N  W
K  U  P  W  F  N  K  X  I  L  P  L  A  Q  R  R  L  N
K  O  E  L  X  N  D  C  O  R  Q  B  Y  T  E  L  I  A
K  E  D  D  T  N  U  E  X  N  R  K  M  H  T  M  G  I
B  N  I  R  L  R  M  K  A  E  E  M  T  B  I  K  H  R
Z  A  T  F  E  C  M  T  C  V  J  R  D  F  D  F  T  A
N  R  E  A  V  N  Y  A  N  F  O  H  A  P  U  M  E  T
Q  O  N  F  L  N  X  X  Y  E  E  R  E  T  R  Z  N  I
V  P  M  L  J  E  C  D  Q  X  L  T  D  B  E  Q  R  L
E  M  A  N  C  I  P  A  T  E  A  A  W  D  K  T  L  A
V  E  V  R  Y  D  M  R  F  R  T  G  V  H  H  Y  H  G
L  T  N  H  K  Z  A  Q  O  C  T  T  J  I  T  D  V  E
M  X  D  Q  M  N  M  B  G  M  D  X  M  F  U  R  W  M
K  E  L  K  E  R  A  H  E  L  B  A  T  I  U  Q  E  M
Z  N  R  O  F  L  W  K  T  K  J  D  P  K  F  X  E  V
H  T  U  N  E  Q  Y  M  M  E  X  C  A  V  A  T  E  B
T  S  Y  M  D  V  N  O  I  S  R  U  C  X  E  R  K  N
```

EGALITARIAN	ERUDITE
ELABORATE	EXACERBATE
EMANCIPATE	EXCAVATE
ENDEAVOR	EXCURSION
ENLIGHTEN	EXONERATE
EPICUREAN	EXPEDITE
EQUITABLE	EXTEMPORANEOUS
EQUIVALENT	EXTRANEOUS

Puzzle made at puzzle-maker.com

292

FF Word Search Puzzle FF

```
H T N A R G A L F R C F X F H L
Y W N M W F K W F R O N T I E R
F M R N Z R F R V P T X M N L H
P I V Q N K C R T M S L I B K N
R M C W K L P R U U M M G V F Z
K K G T M R H C O G A R E R I D
H B M N I T T H F A M T F G E L
R S L F A T I G U E D L A U L B
N T I M C U I C K N B L C R A A
G K Q R T L N O Q L W F I M A D
I M L R U F P H U M L T R A T I
E G O B I O G N X S N H B T I I
R F C N G D L R K Q R R A I V M
O F I P F F T F N T L H F V E R
F T L N K C H R J Q G L B E R O
E K F U N D A M E N T A L M P F
```

FABRICATE	FINITE	FORMIDABLE
FAMINE	FLAGRANT	FORTUITOUS
FATIGUED	FLOURISH	FRONTIER
FICTITIOUS	FOREIGN	FRUGAL
FIGURATIVE	FORMATIVE	FUNDAMENTAL

Puzzle made at puzzle-maker.com

GG Word Search Puzzle GG

```
M  F  X  L  L  N  R  Y  E  K  P  K
C  R  E  D  U  T  I  T  A  R  G  G
R  N  B  Z  G  K  A  I  N  K  R  R
G  Y  G  U  Q  T  R  L  Q  H  A  A
M  R  I  R  I  K  L  A  P  G  T  N
H  L  I  V  A  E  G  R  R  N  U  D
D  U  A  E  E  N  D  E  L  I  I  I
F  R  R  T  V  V  D  N  N  L  T  O
G  H  N  U  N  A  Y  E  J  E  O  S
M  E  H  Y  G  W  N  G  U  U  U  E
G  B  L  L  N  D  L  C  R  R  S  T
N  M  G  E  S  T  U  R  E  G  L  L
```

GENERALITY	GRATUITOUS
GENTEEL	GRAVITATE
GESTURE	GRIEVANCE
GRANDEUR	GRUELING
GRANDIOSE	GUILD
GRATITUDE	GURU

Puzzle made at puzzle-maker.com

294

HH Word Search Puzzle HH

```
S W T S U A C O L O H F F N H
I N R C J G L E K N B R X Y H
S P S I X X J L M L P T L E E
A H I T L W Y G D H X V T T K
T O S S Q J Y G K I U E I L W
S M E I N R B A T Y R R K Z L
O O H L R T M H T O C B B B R
E G T O R K T I G O N K Y I C
M E O H N T D E P R H F B H S
O N P M R E N Y C R Z J F C B
H E Y N R E H T B N Z D Y B G
G O H E O P C H E R I T A G E
K U H U G X N L K B P R T N J
M S S H U M A N I T A R I A N
M Y H C R A R E I H W H L Q P
```

HAGGLE	HOLISTIC	HURBIS
HEREDITY	HOLOCAUST	HYBRID
HERITAGE	HOMEOSTASIS	HYPOCRITE
HETEROGENEOUS	HOMOGENEOUS	HYPOTHESIS
HIERARCHY	HUMANITARIAN	

Puzzle made at puzzle-maker.com

II Word Search Puzzle II

```
X L N V I N F A L L I B L E
B N E L B I G I R R O C N I
Y Y T I L E D I F N I T R Z
P K I N A L I E N A B L E E
R E L I Q T V F D E N O T C
N T J R W J F L S O I A T R
Y A Q O G H T I I S R H F T
T R T N Y W V T N O L Q R K
I G N I Z O I I P V B N V V
N E M C R U R R C M O M Z X
U T D P T T O Y H Z R K R V
M N M N N C K F T N F W E Z
M I I I N Q U I S I T I V E
I Y T I R G E T N I L Y K L
```

IMMUNITY	INFALLIBLE	INTRINSIC
IMPROVISE	INFIDELITY	INTUITION
INALIENABLE	INQUISITIVE	INVOKE
INCORPORATE	INTEGRATE	IRONIC
INCORRIGIBLE	INTEGRITY	

Puzzle made at puzzle-maker.com

MM Word Search Puzzle MM

```
M E L A N C H O L Y  P F T C M
M L C H H M E T H O D I C A L
X A C J Y T M D M P M M H Q M
M L T L X E A M K E R O S L A
N T W E C I Y X T R D R U M T
W P R I R S C I X B R A O L R
N N L Y T I C M J A T L T R I
B A M I X U A K F C L E N Y C
M P Q L L R J L F A D B E F U
K U B O U N H K I M T W M Y L
E D U C J G W N T Z R D O L A
R S K L W Y O P F Q E J M M T
L K F N L T V M R T P Y R P E
T Y F K J S C I N O M E N M K
N Z G M A L I G N A N T T M L
```

MACABRE	MELANCHOLY	MOMENTOUS
MALICE	METHODICAL	MORALE
MALIGNANT	METICULOUS	MYRIAD
MATERIALIZE	MNEMONICS	MYSTIQUE
MATRICULATE	MOGUL	

Puzzle made at puzzle-maker.com

RR Word Search Puzzle RR

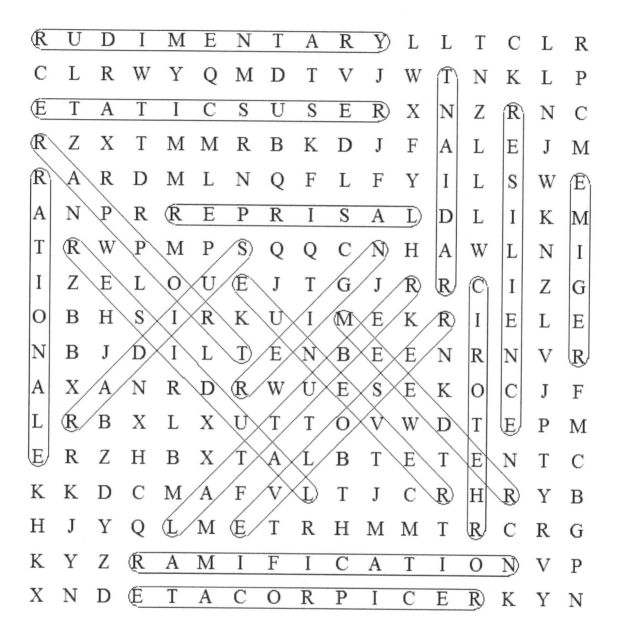

RADIANT	RECIPROCATE	RESILIENCE
RADIUS	REDEEM	RESOLVE
RAMIFICATION	REGIME	RESUSCITATE
RAPPORT	REIGN	REVENUE
RATIONALE	REPRISAL	RHETORIC
REBUTTAL	RESIDUAL	RUDIMENTARY

Puzzle made at puzzle-maker.com

SS Word Search Puzzle SS

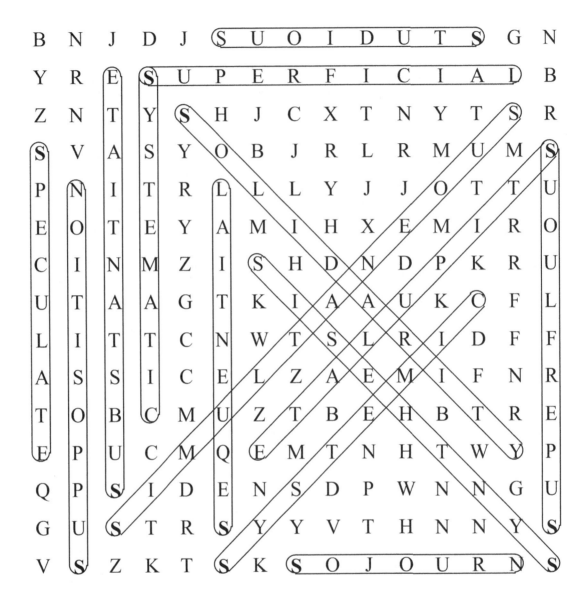

SEQUENTIAL	STIPULATE	SUPPOSITION
SIMULTANEOUS	STUDIOUS	SYNTHESIS
SOJOURN	SUBSTANTIATE	SYSTEMATIC
SOLIDARITY	SUPERFICIAL	SYSTEMIC
SPECULATE	SUPERFLUOUS	

Puzzle made at puzzle-maker.com

Made in the USA
Middletown, DE
26 May 2023

31505870R00166